DIGGING OUT

Global Crisis and the Search for a New Social Contract

Charles Clark

Steve Clark

iUniverse, Inc.
Bloomington

Digging Out
Global Crisis and the Search for a New Social Contract

iUniverse books may be ordered through booksellers or by contacting:

iUniverse
1663 Liberty Drive
Bloomington, IN 47403
www.iuniverse.com
1-800-Authors (1-800-288-4677)

ISBN: 978-1-4620-1987-8 (sc)
ISBN: 978-1-4620-1986-1 (hc)
ISBN: 978-1-4620-1985-4 (e)

Cover Design: Arianna M. Hodges.

Library of Congress Control Number: 2011908392

Printed in the United States of America

iUniverse rev. date: 07/20/2011

To our father, who was patient and selfless with a scientific orientation, and our mother—a critical thinker, skeptic, and daydreamer with a political bent.

Table of Contents

Introduction

Obituary for an Old Hat. xi

    Crisis and Accountability in Our Time xi

    We Brothers. xii

    Political Manifesto. xiv

    The Simultaneity Principle. xv

    Rising Tide xviii

    Commercial Transaction Fee xix

    Financial Sector Accountability xx

    Digging Out. xxi

Chapter 1

If the Ancients Could Do It, So Can We!. 1

    Change the World! 3

    The Science of Social Collapse. 4

    Collaboration: Foundation of Human Nature 9

    The Neolithic Socioecological Crisis and Its Agricul-
    tural Rescue. 15

    The Agricultural Social Contract and Its Systemic
    Social Dysfunction 19

Chapter 1 Response

Am I Alone Out There?—A Skeptic's Last Hope 25

    A Model of Cultural Materialism 25

    My Undivided Skepticism 27

Chapter 2

Jumpstarting Tomorrow—Turning the Steel Stone. 35

    Skipping Class in Social Science 35

    Civilization Rises, then Falters 39

Flipping the Production Switch—Industrial Divergence 42

Necessity Intervenes for a New Social Contract 45

Sunset for the Industrial Age 48

Vetting about Leftist Roots 49

Chapter 2 Response

What We Choose to Do Matters 52

Chapter 3

Conjuring Up Ghosts—Some Things Must Be Believed to Be Seen 58

Contradictions Push a Social Transformation Forward 58

The Service Class 67

Adding a Cautionary Voice 74

Chapter 3 Response

Servers of the World, Unite! 79

Service Age Social Security 82

One Class or More? 89

Chapter 4

Population Paradox—Improve Human Welfare, and Fewer Will Come 96

The Global Curse of Maternal Mortality 96

From Infanticide to Unrestrained Population Growth 100

Women's Liberation and a New Vision of Population
Management 102

Retro Reaction to Population Control 105

Gaining Control of Our Numbers 108

Chapter 4 Response

More Headaches for the Skeptic in All of Us 111

Chapter 5

Social Contracts Are Really Generational Things 118

The Temporality and Tipping Points of Social Contracts 119

Mass Psychology in Social Development 121

Mood Swings in the Post-War Era 125

The Fourth Turning Has Begun................130

Chapter 5 Response

Avoiding Visions of Armageddon 135

 The Specter of Practical Skepticism Is Seen Again 135

 A Rosier Glimpse of Things to Come 139

Chapter 6

Opening the Door for Future Diversity 143

 Bottom-line Socioecological Theory for the Service Age 145

 Personal Notes on Alternatives................153

Chapter 6 Response

The Middle Class—Love 'Em or Leave 'Em? 164

Chapter 7

Why Do We Keep Following the Pied Piper When We Already Know the Story? 172

 Inside the Workings of Civil Society................174

 The Transformation of Relations of Production in Service-led Production 177

 A Changed Social Structure Emerges with a Global Culture...181

 A Personal Account of Globalism................184

Chapter 7 Response

Global Problem-Solving Just Isn't Business as Usual 193

 Non-Profit History in America................193

 Corporate "Giving" and Cause Marketing................195

 A Service Economy Finances Social Problem-Solving 197

Chapter 8

A Social Bulimic's Dream—Disgorging the State 200

 Revisioning the Current Crisis................200

 The Real Crisis Is the Underinvestment Crisis 204

 Service, Economic Contraction, and the State................207

Chapter 8 Response

Visions of a Global Social Contract 219

  Next Contract Will Set the Stage for Generations to Come. . . . 220

  Politics in the Global Era 222

  Global Problem-Solving 224

  Commercial Enterprise. 228

  Banking as a Public Utility 230

Chapter 9

Share the Burden, Change the World. 233

Sources 237

Introduction

Obituary for an Old Hat

Charles and Steve:

Crisis and Accountability in Our Time

Across America and around the world, "change" is in vogue. Rightly so.

The world has entered a period of global crisis, and only a concerted, sustained, worldwide effort can halt the cataclysmic slide toward ecological and social chaos. A new *dark age* looms. The signs of a threatened global order are everywhere—six major international financial failures in the last twenty years; spreading poverty, social polarization, and violent conflict; environmental stress, habitat destruction, species extinction, and climate change. As we will demonstrate, these are not accidental occurrences but result instead from a failing industrial mode of production and a decrepit world order.

So, yes, we need change, and it's great that so many people now clamor for it. But still, we must answer, what kind of change and how?

Change for the better, of course, but that doesn't tell us much. If you're a thoughtful person, you know there is no "change agenda" today that is substantially different than doing more of the best of what has already been done. Bigger bailouts, more stimulus, cleaner energy, more democracy, faster trade, greater entrepreneurial efforts. Take the good examples from what seemed to work in the past and—with whatever money we can squeeze out by raising taxes, borrowing, printing money, extending bank credits, cutting waste, or correcting priorities—incrementally expand investments in them.

We two brothers don't think that's good enough, not for the global crisis in which we are all now awash. Pointedly, we offer a different answer to *what kind of change is needed* and *how it can be implemented*. We believe we know a way to *actually* change the world.

The purpose of this book is to explain that answer. But we know you're probably already thinking some variation of "I've heard this before" or "Who the hell do they think they are?" We know you have good reason to be skeptical—talk of change is cheap, and we've all heard a lot of it. So, we're going to get to the point and say it right now in this Introduction. Then, we will elaborate in the chapters that follow.

Most fundamentally, our world needs to embrace a new mode of production, the service-led mode of production, and the values that come with it.

What is the service-led mode of production? Just like the Industrial Age followed the Agriculture Age as a way of sustaining human life, now industrialism is being succeeded by the Service Age. Today, people, organizations, and businesses survive by providing service to others. In contrast to the hegemonic, hoarding, me-first, do-or-die competition of humanity's last few centuries, our future now depends on how well we serve each other.

Today, the service sector dominates most social relationships and the world's economy, but it is undercapitalized and lacks authoritative power. Filled with ethical contradictions that need to be resolved, the service economy remains compromised by Industrial Age values. In this book, we clarify why change is imminent and provide a cogent theory of the service-led mode of production to empower social mobilization against entrenched industrial capital.

The good news is that we don't have to create this new mode of production. It has already appeared amidst decaying industrial relations. We need only unleash and mobilize its full potential. But that requires a cultural revolution with a new standard of social values.

We Brothers

We brothers—Charles and Steve—are two Boomer Generation Americans who were first aroused to action and investigation by the movements of the Sixties. We were activists and advocates as well as academics and analysts.

As it happens, following largely separate paths, we each embarked on a life of social struggle, investigation, and experimentation that proved deeply educational and personally rewarding. We want to share those lessons here.

We learned that our individual experiences were hardly unique, that the Sixties marked a general, worldwide awakening to the problems of population, polarization, oppression, war, and the environment. Yet, when you are young and coming of age, you question and criticize but are not in a position to change the world very much. All you can do is carry your insights into the activity of your life. Much later—if past experience is a guide—an aging and lucky few find themselves in a position to make more of a difference.

As we will see, however, the beauty of the service-led mode of production is that, now, we *all* are the lucky ones, old and young, each empowered with an opportunity like never before to embrace change and impact the future. The Service Age is upon us, and we each can make a difference in our world. Today, in these times when truly fresh perspectives are required, we brothers wish to offer both new theory and a pragmatic course of alternative, global action.

You may wonder who we are. You'll learn as you read, for this book, as it expounds our theory of social change, employs personal narratives and a dialogue of chapter counterpoints to express our common understanding as well as our differences in opinion.

For now, think of Charles as a tree, rooted in place yet reaching for the sky. He's practiced to a fault, rural, skilled in all forms of manual labor from carpentry to mechanics, a man of the West. Yet, he has a Ph.D. in environmental sociology and Latin American studies, and he once served as a Fulbright and National Science Foundation scholar studying deforestation in the Central American tropics. He spent another dozen years working in the forests of the American Northwest. He taught at several universities and now directs a program that provides rural renewable energy assistance for farms and small businesses.

Steve is much the opposite—urban, an economist by training, a former community organizer, then a high school teacher, and now a communications and marketing professional. Always an issues guy and social activist, he is focused on the big picture. Yet, he worked for decades at the grass roots in local unions, non-governmental organizations (NGOs), and diverse communities. He's an Easterner and lives inside the Beltway. Until Obama, he never voted for a winning president and was proud of his record.

We think our dichotomy is useful. After all, real solutions must embrace diversity, or they won't be solutions at all.

Political Manifesto

This book is a political manifesto for truly revolutionary change—change we can count on to alter social relations for the better, to empower the powerless, to redistribute wealth away from speculators and moneylenders toward real investment. Humanity has big, transnational problems to solve, and this manifesto demonstrates the real ways that they can be attacked and resolved.

Our proposal funds global problem-solving to the tune of a trillion dollars annually through a transaction fee on speculation and global commerce. Under our proposal, the revenue stream of this fee, collected by the global banking system, will promote civil society expansion and ecological restoration while reestablishing stability in human affairs by reversing social polarization worldwide. That's a huge and vital step in the right direction.

However, we'll be blunt about this: The creation of a Global Consciousness Movement to compel banking industry collaboration in global problem-solving *is* a *revolutionary* agenda. Not revolutionary in the old sense of overthrowing governments by force, but, rather, revolutionary in the only meaningful way now imaginable—the creation of a popularly-directed Global Problem-Solving Authority (GPSA) that *operates above and beyond the domains of states, with its own independence and initiative.* This worldwide, civic collaboration will run on the moral authority of its positive programs rather than any military might of its own. While it desires and, in some ways requires, the cooperation of states, the GPSA will not be subordinate to them. The Global Problem-Solving Authority's only allegiance will be to the people as a whole, that is, to social and environmental justice for communities, the earth, and our common future together.

We know most people have been trained to fear revolution, but, still, most of us know there are times when it is truly liberating. To cite U.S. history, the American Revolution in 1776 cleared away colonial rule and empowered a nation to create a government founded on the rights of its citizens. Some of the imperfections of that uprising were later addressed in another revolutionary upheaval, the Civil War.

Virtually all nations have their own revolutionary histories. It is always precisely at those junctures when society is trapped by outdated but entrenched economic and social relations that revolutionary theory and social innovation provide the way out. In such times, revolution is liberating.

Today, we are at precisely such a time, though the scale has enlarged from a national to a global one. The economic and social relations of industrial corporations and big, imperial states now interfere with strident efforts to break through and address our vital, common concerns as people of this world. A revolution, global in its scope and practicality, has begun. It is time to get clear on its path—that is, on the way it will unfold and change our world—so that we can both make the most of its potential and avoid getting in its way. How will we manage this embroiling global crisis that will take generations to resolve? How do we know what to do? How will we keep on course?

The Simultaneity Principle

The answer, we say, is to put science to work. Not the technical science that has for decades filled our lives with gadgets and detailed information, yet failed to question the wisdom of wasting resources that will be needed by future generations. Not the growth science of capitalist production that assumes that more of everything is the answer to everything. Rather, we mean to use science that has critical initiative, the type that comes when connected citizens and communities, with access to the world's vast insight and experience, assess their own problems and seek their own solutions. Technology, then, can be put to practice with a purpose other than maximizing profit for the few. Adopting a scientific perspective, the world can assess possibilities, engage in social experimentation, critique failures, and advance rapidly along the paths of success.

What science has this perspective? We are talking about socioecology, the advocacy science that combines analysis of the interdependence of human society and the environment *with* social action. This is the science that looks at the boundary between nature and society, but it also demands effort at real change through practice, experimentation, collaboration, and reevaluation. Socioecology measures success on both the local and global levels, what we call the local-global nexus. It will bring meaningful change to societies that need change, to ecosystems that need change, to all of us who need change. In this book, we draw together the thus-far disconnected threads of leading social and natural scientists, demonstrating the history and nature of our present crisis and, more importantly, clarifying the path of its successful management.

Yes, we decidedly reject the phony skepticism of politicians like those who populated the Bush Administration—the ones who profess to accept science but then always point out that science has yet to prove anything. "We can't act until we know the truth," they say. They miss the point. Science *is* subject to interpretation. Its nature is of a negotiated social contract, worked out by the people who face problems with those who have the knowledge and ability to help solve them.

Therefore, we propose the Simultaneity Principle to guide and test scientific assertions: *Will proposed actions simultaneously reduce global social inequality and restore our broken environment?* Let's debate what that entails! No more equivocation. Let's choose a course of action based only on what actually advances this dual cause.

Of course, it's not a simple determination when you consider that the whole world's six and a half billion people could, potentially, be involved in the debate and decision-making. Ultimately, even with the interjection of science, the decisions about how to attack problems will be political ones, decided by the people who take up the cause of the Global Consciousness Movement and local-global problem-solving. Ways must be found and developed for popular, global participation. Yet, does anyone doubt that the communications technology exists (or can be developed) to enable effective global dialogue and decision-making? The stumbling way we now conduct social discourse—that is, largely through fickle national media and reliance on nation-states to represent the peoples' interests in world affairs—can and must be brought into the Service Age.

Already, through civil society organizations, millions of people around the globe collaborate for a better tomorrow. But these efforts are impossibly constrained by limited funding and the lack of mainstream support. Civil society and the global grassroots organizers can't imagine an alternative to the trickle of funding from industrial capitalism and its imperiled philanthropic benevolence, and they can't find a way to unite in global political action. Together, we must clarify an alternative social contract and come together to fight to make it a reality.

We brothers know we're talking about groundbreaking efforts, but we also know we're not drifting into fantasy land. Global discourse is possible, and once forged, a global problem-solving authority is equally practical. We're excited about these possibilities, but we're also confident because, as socioecologists, we study and understand the way social and ecological forces are already driving change in our world, independent of human will. Though much of the world's turmoil is obviously bad, worsening, and highly problematic, we know that underlying forces are struggling to open vast, new, liberating horizons. But liberation demands replacing traditional culture and politics with new visions. It demands that we choose to embrace new ideas and relationships, indeed, a new social contract among us.

The problem is that most of us can't see the potential and the possibilities for real change because we don't understand the actual forces at work. It's something like trying to heal wounds back in the days before we knew about germs. If we're going to solve the problems of our world—the problems of society and the environment—we must be scientific. We must look inside the processes around us and learn of the forces at work in our lives.

Chief among these is the contradiction between rising population and finite natural resources. Nine billion humans by mid-century, demographers say. During the Industrial Age, with mass consumption key to a successful economy, population growth was an imperative, encouraged under the more-is-better syndrome. Long ago, that system overshot the limits of its own sustainability. Now, we vastly over-consume the earth's resources, fouling our water and air in the process and brutally diminishing biodiversity. Population growth must be reversed. We need a contracting global economy, one that rebuilds community stability and cuts the pilfering of resources that later generations will need.

Another critical factor is the world's sharply increasing economic and social polarization which is the root cause of humanity's expanding resort to terrorism and war. Real stability requires finding ways for *all* the world's people to have clean water, sanitation, health care, literacy, electricity, access to the global economy with its scientific and technological knowledge, a line of credit to take advantage of opportunity, and old age security. If "change" can't meaningfully promise to provide *all* these things to *everyone*, it is not worthy for our time, and it will not stop our slide into social disarray.

Rising Tide

Yet, in an already depleted world, how is it possible to restore a sense of confidence among so many desperate people on the edge of survival? Fortunately, as socioecology shows, throughout history when our numbers exceeded available resources, transformations began in our basic mode of production which, once embraced by human culture, brought changes for the better to the human condition. Agriculture and industrialism were once solutions to the chaotic, life-threatening, socioecological conditions of earlier times. But while these remedies have been well-studied, the solutions now offered by the emergent, service-led mode of production are but poorly understood.

In particular, we persist in failing to recognize that the new mode of production is creating a new array of interests that need elaboration and support. As these forces are advanced, progress will accelerate:

- *Class:* The rising service class earns its living by providing service to others, whether through private commercial enterprise, government operations, or public-spirited, non-governmental organizations.
- *Gender:* The women of the world possess innate, service-oriented talents that are vital to Service Age problem-solving.
- *Nations:* Developing nations and minority populations that are stymied by the entrenched power of multinational corporations and militarized states offer culturally based alternatives.

- *Generations:* The cohorts born since the advent of global mass communications sense intuitively that the people of the earth can and must master global collaboration.
- *Individuals:* Citizens of all nations and the members of all ethnic groups and religions—despite narrow, standardized, often oppressive social constraints—see themselves first as human beings, unique and with unlimited potential.

If a way can be found to express their common interests, these forces can be united in a powerful movement that expresses service values and demands the change necessary for a different and better tomorrow.

These forces of change can be rallied by a sound, grounded-in-reality, forward-looking political agenda. But science is the key. It is the means by which we can overcome the narrowness of our individual existences and personal perspectives to find common cause with others for a sustainable, equitable future. Based on socioecological science, we propose to unite these forces in a movement to compel the banking industry's compliance with the people's problem-solving agenda.

Commercial Transaction Fee

We support the coalescence of a popular, transnational political movement whose purpose is to pressure the global banking system to automatically and routinely collect a small—say, 0.1 percent—fee on *every* commercial transaction that runs through the system's electronic processing mechanisms. This fee would operate as your VISA card does during the holiday season when it donates one percent of your charges to a charity you have selected. In this case, however, a fee will be imposed on *every* transaction, everything from credit cards to corporate payouts to bank transfers to currency speculation—every electronic commercial transaction. Each participant in the global economy pays directly in proportion to the extent of his, her, or its participation in global commerce.

The revenue of this fee will not be retained or dispersed by the banks that collect it. Rather, the revenue stream will be channeled to the account of a Global Problem-Solving Authority, popularly controlled and directed by the world's people. The authority will invest to catalyze flexible, evolving, NGO-corporate-community partnerships designed to address our world's great necessities—environmental restoration, population reduction, social equity, economic opportunity, and peaceful conflict resolution. These programs will run not through national governments and their client international federations (the UN, IMF, World Bank , or WTO) but, instead, through and along the local-global nexus of civil society and the global grassroots, with the purpose of strengthening human collaboration as we move through the crisis-management epoch before us.

Because everyone who participates in global exchange—people, NGOs, commercial enterprises, and states—will contribute exactly in proportion to their activity in global commerce, the fee will play no favorites and will not distort markets. Yet, a per transaction fee will curtail fast-paced, speculative transactions while creating and deploying a catalytic fund adequate to attack all our great needs.

While our concept of the commercial transaction fee (CTF) differs in application from his proposal, James Tobin—1981 Nobel laureate, Yale University economist, and a member of the Board of Governors of the Federal Reserve—was the first to identify this means of imposing accountability on financial speculation. After a brief ascendancy in progressive circles during the 1990s, the "Tobin Tax" was seemingly lost to history during the go-go, free-market excess of the last decade. Since the 2008 financial crisis, however, it has resurfaced in some intellectual and political circles, not as a systemic means to address the global crisis, but as a deficit reduction mechanism for financially strapped G-8 states. Drawing a sharp distinction with efforts to co-opt the CTF for this purpose, our plan insists on a new social contract to channel these vital funds to global problem-solving.

Financial Sector Accountability

Nation-states can support this plan or not, but the real struggle is not between us—the people—and our governments. Rather, it is between us and the financial services industry (hopefully, our governments will be among our allies). Even while corporately run, banking must be converted to a public utility. We demand accountability from the industry. We demand responsibility. We insist on curbing speculation. We insist on the financial industry's contribution to the cause of global problem-solving and on its assistance in collecting the resources necessary for success in that endeavor. Indeed, what can be more in the interest of a truly responsible global banking industry than the future prosperity of the world's people, our exchange, and our environment? Can there be a sustained global marketplace without these things?

Digging Out

Managing a fund for global crisis management requires science, both social science and environmental science. Relying on the Simultaneity Principle—to relieve social polarization *and* restore the environment—we can assess how to invest public funds to address the needs of the world's underprivileged people and its degraded ecosystems. Piece by piece, we can rebuild ourselves out of the moral, political, and economic morass of four hundred years of industrialism.

The world is in crisis, but we can dig ourselves out. To do so, however, we must know the present forces of change and determine the program that will bind them in a new social contract for the crisis era ahead. We brothers think socioecological science shows the way.

Now, let us explain…

Chapter 1

If the Ancients Could Do It, So Can We!

Steve:

The world has serious problems, I'm sure you agree. In fact, as we will now explain, it faces a *socioecological* crisis. A socioecological crisis is one along the conjunction of human society and its natural environment. Such crises occur periodically in human history, always resulting in stagnate periods of decline known as *dark ages* that last for centuries. What is unique about the crisis we face at this stage in history is its universality, that is, its global scope. But the good news is that social organization is also global, so opportunity for change abounds if only we can find a way to face the reality of our situation.

Overpopulation, climate change, species extinction, fossil fuel depletion, pandemic illness, food shortages, terrorism, weapons of mass destruction, human migrations—these problems transcend national borders and the power of individual states to address them. In these matters, even the world's remaining superpower, the United States, cannot impose its will. But such disintegration has happened before. We can learn from history.

History shows, however, that, humanity has not yet demonstrated the capacity to manage a socioecological crisis, much less reverse its trajectory. In the past, when faced by such crisis, civilization always succumbed to the forces of dissolution.

Now, a global *dark age* threatens. Since the very nature of the present crisis is global, not national, we must rightfully question whether the world's collection of nation-states can gather themselves and mount a comprehensive, collaborative, generations-long program to restore global vitality.

I very much doubt that possibility, not because people don't want to survive the crisis or are incapable of acting conscientiously toward long-term goals, but because states are institutions of the Industrial Age and its epic, competitive conflicts. Fitted for domination and defense, they were not established and are not suited to lead the solution of transnational or global problems. Neither, unfortunately, is their international federation, the United Nations (UN), or their self-interested sub-alliances such as the World Bank, the IMF, the World Trade Organization, the European Union, NAFTA, OPEC, or NATO. These institutions exist to serve narrow national interests or, at best, the transient convergence of nations' interests in particular geopolitical situations.

Of course, nations, their states, and their alliances—being very real entities—will be significant players in any eventual solution to our socioecological crisis, but the Industrial Age, itself, and its uneven, conquest-driven competition for markets and resources is unsustainable in today's highly integrated world society. Inevitably, in the passing of any age, new forces, new values, and new institutions emerge and eventually assume social leadership. If we are going to get through this crisis, we must identify and unleash the nascent potentials of the emergent Service Age.

History does not set tasks for which it offers no means of success, but history also shows that people and their leaders sometimes fail to grasp these means. In the course of the last 10,000 years, we have endured at least five *dark ages*, epochs of immense crisis and social failure which required generations of suffering and conflict before we discovered the means of success.

Yet, human understanding is cumulative; we can and do learn from the past. Our insight—our science—does advance and become more instructive. Today, socioecological science is highly developed, though not very broadly disseminated. Despite its relatively small circle of devotees, the science is rooted in the broad experience of people worldwide and is benefitting from the rapid expansion of our capacity for scientific investigation and exchange. Despite the severe crisis at hand, this science explains the root causes of our problems. It illuminates the rising forces and values that can be organized and projected so that humanity—in all our diverse localities and concentrations—can unite in a sustained, collaborative, global project. We can sidestep this *dark age* and save ourselves through the creation of new institutions of self-management and a new, post-industrial, post-national way of life.

This isn't a fantastic dream. It is a practical necessity. Science is our guide. Let's start at the beginning. What does it take to change the world!

Change the World!

Change the world! This once-inspiring Boomer mantra is widely ridiculed today. No one even speaks anymore about the possibility for truly revolutionary, global change. Yet with this book, my brother and I, who never abandoned hope, are taking another shot at it.

I concede that I usually overestimate the potential of various situations and their social dynamics. Speaking of my political activism, someone once actually called me "the little engine that could." I suspect that it is my optimism that leads me to politics—because it makes no sense that politics could have made me optimistic—but I think it is the fact that I am so scientifically oriented that prevents me from drifting into despair. No matter how bad the crisis gets, no matter how befuddled and devastating is the American government's response, I can't help but search for a way to fix the problem and get society back on track.

Why am I like this?

I don't really know, but I have a theory.

When I was turning ten and first realizing that the society beyond our family had its own powerful dynamics which I didn't fully understand, our father was a U.S. Air Force pilot in the Strategic Air Command (SAC), stationed at Plattsburg AFB in the far north of New York, as near to the North Pole as practical. His job, should the Cold War suddenly turn hot, was to fly a B-47 across the Pole, drop his A-bombs on Soviet targets and glide to a landing at some distant air field, hopefully still intact, in Turkey. What bothered me was how he was going to get back to us in all the chaos and devastation of nuclear war. From those earliest days of social awareness, I knew I had a problem to solve.

Perhaps it was because I was the oldest child, the first son, in a white American middle class family that I didn't latch on to any more intermediate or close-to-home injustice. I started out concerned about the *whole* mess.

It's been fifty years. Long ago, the Cold War was squeezed to the side by history, replaced by other pressing concerns. Yet, trained by Cold War contingencies, I've always carried around and lived by the reality that the world, with its big problems to solve, *is* fully integrated and very much maxed out. I've always known that this is a crowded earth, that there are no more unexploited spaces or resources with which to mitigate conflict, that mounting conflict is inevitable, and that problems ignored or shoved aside always come back to bite. I've sensed since I was a kid that humanity has reached some kind of *global limit,* and we must become masters of problem-solving collaboration or civilization, itself, is in trouble.

The Science of Social Collapse

To fulfill my self-imposed responsibility to help humanity master this awesome collaboration, I've studied extensively in economics, politics, law, education, communications, marketing, and sociology, but I've gained the most from anthropology. Anthropology is the investigation of the origins, nature, and trajectory of the human species. From its study, we can learn about the *basic nature* of humans, that is, about *the way we are,* independent of the widely diverse times, places, or cultures in which we live or have lived. Knowing our nature, we can discern the common character that must form the foundation blocks of global collaboration.

Like any field of thought, anthropology has various trends. I adhere firmly to the trend of cultural materialism, meaning I accept that the way we live develops from and within the necessities of our survival in the evolving natural world. In this, despite the unique skills of our species, we are like all other animals—we collectively adapt to changing conditions or we face extinction.

Our species, *Homo sapiens*, has lived on earth for roughly 200,000 years. It evolved through a succession of earlier human—and still earlier proto-human—species over the course of eight million years. The trait that first distinguished and then sustained this succession of life is the *capacity for cooperation and exchange.* Early on, our cooperation was direct and overt. For instance, we cooperated in the hunt and shared the proceeds not only with our hunting partners but also with our companions back at the base camp. Today, however, the things we need to survive are manufactured all over the world and transported to local stores where we go buy what we want, and the vastness of modern exchange masks the complexity of the cooperation necessary to achieve it. Although competition, survival of the fittest, and "Numero Uno" often appear to dominate modern relations, in fact, working together and exchanging the fruits of our labor remains the foundation of human nature and the basis of our existence and survival as a species.

As noted, the character of our exchange varies with time and place in history. And, according to both the premise of cultural materialism and the facts of history, as the character of our exchange has changed, so, too, has our culture. Understanding why and how these changes occur is a key question if, indeed, we are on the brink of a major socioecological crisis in civilization which now requires a profound cultural transformation.

In 1980, Alvin and Heidi Toffler published *The Third Wave* (Toffler 1980) and made the world aware that human culture had entered a historic transformation. In this seminal work, the Tofflers—who did not write as academics or self-proclaimed social scientists but, instead, as contemporary social observers—alluded to the earlier transformations from hunter-gatherer to agricultural culture (in their schema, the *first wave*) and from agricultural to industrial culture (the *second wave*), but they concentrated their main attention on two things: the character of industrial era culture and a vision of the post-industrial culture of the future (the *third wave*). More intuitive than scientific, the Tofflers made little effort to explain why these cultural transformations occur.

In contrast to the Tofflers, the renowned American anthropologist Marvin Harris (1927-2001) spent the bulk of his career investigating precisely this question. From his own studies and those of the world's foremost social scientists, he developed a theory (Harris 1977) which ties the evidence together in a coherent and revealing explanation of each of the earlier cultural transformations. Unfortunately, he made no effort to apply his theory to the present transformation, in part, no doubt, due to his yeoman effort to defend cultural materialism against insistent intrusions of post-modern trends in anthropology during the last decade of his life. I only encountered Harris in his last years but feel fortunate to have secured from him, via private email, encouragement for the assessment which follows.

First, however, I want to acknowledge the contribution to this book's assessment advanced by Humboldt State University professor Sing Chew. If the perspectives of the Tofflers and Harris are one's only guide, it would be easy to presume that, whatever the obstacles to social transformations, they are steadily overcome as we humans encounter the problems and move on. Chew's research and analysis of recurrent *dark ages* in human history (Chew 2007) blows a big and very important hole in that perspective.

By analyzing pollen counts from various times and places in history, Chew showed that all past socioecological crises were associated with periods of extreme deforestation in regions of civilization. Reviewing and correlating historical accounts of the rise and fall of civilizations, Chew demonstrated that all the great collapses of history—which he calls *dark ages*—lasted at least 500 years, were associated with forced, chaotic, desperate, and devastating population contractions—that is, massive die-offs caused by starvation, disease, and warfare—and were not overcome until a new critical mass of people developed in different, as yet still-forested-regions, and embarked on the slow path of rebuilding civilization.

The lesson for us is that our future may not be a straight line to a new, successful way of life. Instead, a long socioecological collapse is likely, but, this time, there is no remaining forested region to which to move and start again. If "forests" are, in fact, a proxy for an array of environmental conditions that are fundamental to civilization, to know the duration of our emerging crisis, we should ask ourselves how long it will take for the Earth's forests to restore themselves. The coming *dark age* could easily exceed 1,000 years. That's not a future to which we should aspire.

With Chew's cautionary analysis firmly in mind, let's return to the description of the general process of human development as offered by Harris.

Let's begin by stripping away the complexity of human existence and take a look at its essence. We are an animal species and, like all species of life, have two basic necessities: production and reproduction.

Production is all the activities required to provide the sustenance of life (most basically, food). Reproduction is all the activities required to produce offspring and successors. We are genetically programmed to achieve these two necessities. Our senses, instincts, emotions, and thinking are our main tools; all are bio-chemical and electro-magnetic processes in our bodies. Essentially, they provide us with the capacity for cooperation and exchange with other humans.

The production of sustenance is another way to say we consume natural resources. We succeed in environments which have the resources we need and can learn to use; we cannot live where adequate resources do not exist. Harris' theory elucidates the relationships among human production, reproduction, and the natural environment. It goes like this.

In a given environment, humans exist through the consumption of resources supplied by nature. Reproduction comes easily, and our numbers tend to grow. In order to sustain the standard of living to which we are accustomed, we try to control our numbers, but that is not easy. Thus, we also pursue the other option, the intensification of production.

One way to intensify production and, thereby, sustain the established standard of living as population grows is to bring more skill, knowledge, and collaborative energy to the effort. Creativity—technological as well as social—has always played a major role in enhanced production. Technological inventions are obviously important; less well appreciated are developments in social organization and the cultural norms that support these more complex—in most cases, hierarchical and, often, coercive—structures. Also important is the willingness to work longer and harder. As you may know, our early ancestors were hunters and gatherers. Instead of hunting three hours a day, they might have extended to six. Another way to intensify production is to bring more resources into use. Instead of hunting over just the traditional range, our ancestors tried hunting also on the other side of the mountain.

In reality, as our early ancestors sought to sustain their survival, all forms of intensification were employed. They devised new tools, employed more complex and collaborative hunting strategies, worked harder, and consumed more of the available resources, but as their numbers grew, some moved on to new hunting grounds previously unoccupied by any human life. In fact, this is why and how *Homo sapiens,* which first evolved in sub-Saharan Africa, eventually came to occupy every inhabitable corner of the earth.

Generally, when our production intensifications prove successful, we sustain our standard of living at the price of more natural resource consumption. Steadily, however, in particular regions, the series of intensifications leads to the depletion of the key resources, and, eventually, a socioecological crisis—a *dark age*—ensues. The crisis endures—typically for hundreds of years—killing off humans through starvation, disease, warfare, and other desperate human acts while a new mode of production is discovered, one which no longer depends on the depleted resources but, instead, on other natural resources. As the new mode of production develops, it forges new classes and relations in production which, on the rise relative to traditional powers, begin to contest for social legitimacy and influence. With their own, different way of sustaining life, the new forces need to be freed from the constraints of the old social order, but the old ways are institutionalized and buttressed by entrenched cultural norms that are resistant to change. As the underlying crisis in production deepens, the cultural clash intensifies. Survival necessities drive more and more people to accept the new mode and its budding culture. Eventually, the rising forces accumulate enough practical power and influence to subvert or overthrow the old order and broadly unleash their new way of life. At long last, a cultural transformation occurs, and society begins reconstructing its culture in harmony with the new mode of production.

Social Transformation Cycle

- Population Growth
- Production Intensification
- Resource Depletion
- Socioecological Crisis
- Enduring *Dark Age*
- New Mode of Production
- Cultural Transformation

This cycle of population growth, production intensification, resource depletion, socioecological crisis, an enduring *dark age*, advance of a new mode of production, and cultural transformation has occurred twice in our history, and we are now in the midst of a third. In three other *dark ages,* no new mode of production was discovered, and, after the decimation of life and civilization, the re-establishment of the old mode in a new place merely set conditions for another, relatively rapid socioecological collapse. All these historic outcomes unfolded spontaneously, that is, without much human awareness of or conscious intervention in the process. The big question this time around is whether human consciousness and social organization has developed enough for us to systemically engage the process and, thereby, minimize the social collapse and broad human suffering—the *dark age*—that has characterized previous socioecological crises.

To maximize chances of the best possible outcome in the crisis era ahead, we begin by investigating the first socioecological crisis, that of the Neolithic Age, the transition from hunting and gathering to agriculture. The nature of human life, itself, is our first consideration.

Collaboration: Foundation of Human Nature

First, take note of the fact that about 3.2 million years ago (relatively recent in the earth's 4.6 *billion* year history), for reasons which are still not fully understood, the earth entered a period of cyclical ice ages which continue to this day. This period has been characterized by swings in average global temperatures (as much as 5.4 degrees F) over roughly 100,000 year intervals. Temperatures fall quickly and stay very cold for about 60,000 years, then rise slowly, plateau and stay warm for about 12,000 years. For the purposes of our discussion, two things about the ice age should be noted.

First, with regard to the Sahara desert which blankets northern Africa, ice age fluctuations have the effect of opening and closing passage between the region to the south—sub-Saharan Africa—and the Middle East to the north. During the long cold periods, snowfall at the poles and in mountainous regions fails to melt, instead piling up year after year and turning into huge sheets of glacial ice which spread wherever cold temperatures allow. As moisture is preserved in ice, sea levels drop (500 feet is typical) and more land is exposed. The general lack of moisture causes extreme desertification in some areas and causes climatic and ecological change everywhere. During the relatively short warmer periods, however, the general climate becomes more moist and deserts become less harsh. In particular, the Sahara softens, allowing animals a few routes of escape from conditions to the south.

Second, for a variety of reasons, some ice age fluctuations are more extreme than others, and research shows that these extreme fluctuations are associated with the evolution of new species (Fagan 1990). In two extreme fluctuations—approximately 2.5 million and 1.8 million years ago—Homo habilis and Homo erectus, respectively, evolved, each time in sub-Saharan Africa. Arguably, habilis was the first and erectus the most enduring of twenty-some human species that preceded our own (Sawyer 2007). The last extreme fluctuation, about 200,000 years ago, brought our species—Homo sapiens—into existence. Why and how did this happen?

Our species began its life on earth in the Rift Valley region of sub-Saharan Africa when a mutant child of Homo erectus parents was born. The child had a deformed voice box.

A new human life is launched when, through impregnation, a split pair of genes from a male (in the sperm) combine with a split pair from a female (in the egg) to provide a full pair for a successor. Sometimes, these combinations are less than perfect, resulting in a mutant gene of some sort. The vast majority of mutations prove irrelevant to life. Most which are relevant are harmful, usually acting to prevent their on-going reproduction by killing the mutant before it is able to mature and reproduce. Occasionally, in the context of a changing natural environment, a particular mutation is conducive to survival. In that case, the possessor actually has a better chance to survive and reproduce than the species from which it evolved. The mutant trait is passed along successfully, and slowly, an entire new species of life emerges and forges a niche for itself, using its superior mutant trait to compete for survival, often against the very species from which it descended.

Such was the case of our mutant great-great-...-great-grandmother, who lived about 10,000 generations ago. Unique in her time, she possessed the natural ability to speak—not just the crude sounds of her parents and their erectus peers, but also an array of sounds never before heard from a human voice. Her talents may have ostracized her or made her powerful among her people or she may have been only "the girl with the odd sounds," but when she passed that mutant gene on to her children, she unknowingly changed the direction of life on earth. The mutant's children and their offspring had the ability to speak as we know it today. That is, they had the ability to make a language.

Language is a system of sound refinement and tonal nuance that can distinctly express virtually any notion that an individual conceives. Apparently, despite other species' intelligence and desire to communicate, humans are the only one with the capacity for language. Consider the plight of our common dog or cat pets. My cat can make a number of different sounds, but must rely on repetition—meow, meow, meow, meow—to convey the simple concept that he obviously understands: Give me some of that leftover chicken I just saw you take out of the refrigerator. Moving beyond such limitations, our mutant great-great-...-great-grandmother and her descendants could communicate with each other on a level then unknown on earth. It was this communication that gradually made us the planet's dominant species.

When our mutant great-great-...-great-grandmother was born, the humans of that time—*Homo erectus*—had long since out-competed their predecessors and occupied all areas of the sub-Saharan continent that were conducive to their survival. During earlier interglaciation intervals—when global temperatures warmed, rainfall increased, and the Sahara softened a bit—some *erectus* people had followed the game north, across the desert and into the Middle East. The discovery of *Homo erectus* fossils—old but not as old as the oldest found in Africa—in the Middle East, southern Europe, south Asia, southeast Asia and China confirms the theory that *erectus* evolved in Africa, then spread out into other regions of the world. Nevertheless, despite the escape of some during ice age warmings, the humans left south of the Sahara were reconfined each time cold and desertification returned. As scavengers and plant gatherers, their overall number was limited by the ebb and flow of flora and fauna necessary for their survival. Two hundred thousand years ago, however, conditions worsened as an extreme ice age fluctuation decimated life forms of all sorts. Competition for survival intensified; no doubt, disease, starvation, and intra-human warfare began to wreak havoc among *erectus* groups. It was into this kind of distressed situation that our mutant great, great-...-great-grandmother was born.

The ability to speak allowed her kind—*Homo sapiens*—to win a long battle for survival with our *erectus* ancestors because *it enabled a new and unprecedented level of cooperation* for the new species. A couple examples will illustrate the point.

On the one hand, speech enabled larger cooperative societies. Other animals that are close relatives of humans but which do not speak—such as chimpanzees—spend a considerable portion of each day grooming one another. Grooming not only improves sanitation, it also expresses concern on behalf of the groomer for the well-being of the groomee. This expression helps cement relationships in the band and, thereby, enables more effective conflict resolution. Undoubtedly, *erectus* bands groomed each other and relied on the practice to sustain cohesion and cooperation. However, as success in production and reproduction enlarged human groups, they had to spend more and more time grooming to ensure confidence that all could be counted on to appropriately prioritize the interests of the group. Then, when the ice age imposed environmental constrictions and *erectus* was forced to devote more time to hunting and gathering, social cohesion broke down due to the lack of groom time. The splintering of groups further reduced hunting and foraging efficiency and worsened survival. In these conditions, *Homo sapiens'* ability to speak helped solve the crisis by providing another way to ensure social cohesion.

> What language seems to do, says [anthropologist Robin] Dunbar, is to allow you to overcome that barrier and use what time you have in a much more efficient way. You can talk to several different people at the same time. You can talk while you eat, talk while you walk, or talk while you work. This allows you to expand the network of individuals whom you have a relationship with (Caird and Foley 1994:97).

Speech also increased the capacity to hunt. *Erectus* had been restricted to scavenging and hunting small game. With speech *Homo sapiens* could share knowledge about the habits of game, share lessons in the construction of weapons, and coordinate intricate actions in the actual hunt. Now, humans could go after the real prizes, the truly big game. Successful predation of big game greatly enhanced the productivity of hunting (calories and proteins per hunt hour), sharply raising the people's standard of living. Steadily, the new *Homo sapiens* expanded their territorial range to include every area in southern Africa in which big game were plentiful. That success spelled doom for *Homo erectus*, and they were driven to extinction south of the Sahara.

Beyond more complex cooperation, speech also allowed humans to draw upon lessons from near and far, from the present as well as the past. Harris refers to this event as the "linguistic takeoff" (1989:66) and equates it with the "cultural takeoff" which is generally marked by the advent of civilization. Today's human culture is the direct outgrowth of our ability to summarize, store, and share our experience over the last 200,000 years.

The culture of big game hunting societies is known as Neolithic (Stone Age) and was shaped (see below) more by our relations in reproduction than in production. Nevertheless, the totality of that culture is what is *natural* for our species—natural in that it is the way we lived before we acquired a dominant relationship to the rest of nature and were able, thereby, to have a culture more of our own making. Neolithic culture is the kind enjoyed, for instance, by Native Americans before the coming of European settlers in the 1500s.

To fully appreciate natural, Neolithic culture, we must take a brief look at the way our species cooperated in reproduction and childrearing. In this, begin by noting that the lives of hunter-gatherers were migratory, following the annual migrations of game. Living in pair-bonded families with children (as we do today), a group of related families (the clan) followed game from their traditional, higher terrain, rainy season hunting grounds to low-land lake regions as the summer dry season developed. At the height of the dry season, all the animals and clans in the region would be assembled in the low-lands.

Now, consider that in the warm climate of sub-Saharan, equatorial Africa, our adult ancestors lived and slept out in the open, only lightly clothed, and in full view of their children. As the child play of even today's hunter-gatherer clans often shows, children grew up well aware of the sex act (Fisher 1992; Wolf 1997).

However, due to the low-fat diets of hunter-gatherers, women did not become fertile until age 18 or so, this despite the fact that, like young women today, their sexual interest would surge when they reached the age of menarche. As Fisher and other sociobiologists demonstrate, young women (and men) are seldom sexually attracted to the siblings or cousins with whom they grow up; thus, it was during the annual assemblage in the lake country low-lands that young women first experimented with sexual engagements with young men from other clans. Yet, despite this early experimentation, women could not become pregnant for another four or five years. They had plenty of time to learn about men and to learn how to choose a mate who could be a reliable provider, a successful father, and an able collaborator with the elder men of her clan.

In learning how to make this assessment, young women had full-bodied support and encouragement from their female elders. In fact, accounts from early Christian explorers and their accompanying priests reveal the horror with which they observed how Native American clans exalted reproduction in elaborate sexual rituals, anxiously awaiting and announcing the time when young women would join in sex and, one day, contribute to the succession of life in the clan.

Though they might have experimented sexually with several different males during the course of their adolescence, when they were ready to have their first child, young women were well-prepared to make a wise choice. When they chose a particular young man and became pregnant, he left his clan and went with his mate and her clan into its highland, wet season hunting grounds. He joined the men of her clan—all of whom, including, of course, the elder men, had come originally from other clans—in hunting and the other male responsibilities of clan life. When the child was born, the young mother had her mother, sisters, aunts, grandmothers, and their well-established childrearing systems from which to draw guidance and support. Boys and girls grew up in this kind of culture and were trained to accept these gender protocols and roles as they came of age.

While women shared and ensured childrearing duties, they also contributed to the clan's productive endeavors through their gathering of fruit, vegetables, grains, and firewood. Indeed, data show that women's activities in today's remaining hunter-gatherer societies contribute about 70 percent of the clan's caloric intake. While men made spears and spear points, women made pottery, baskets, clothing, and other implements.

Given these realities, *natural human culture was decidedly more female-based and female-oriented than is typical, modern culture.* Nevertheless, it was this culture that enabled the survival of our species for the bulk of its time on earth.

The Neolithic Socioecological Crisis and Its Agricultural Rescue

Today, obviously, our natural, Neolithic lifestyle is mostly gone from the earth. Despite differences in particularity, the reason and means of that disappearance are the same ones driving today's global crisis and the threatening *dark age*. The driving trends of socioecological collapse are always the same—population growth, resource depletion, growing systemic poverty, a break-down of social cohesion, and inter-group competition leading to militarization. A look at the first cultural transformation that saved humanity at the end of the Neolithic Age will help us understand the dimensions and possibilities of our current way out.

The evolution of *Homo sapiens* in sub-Saharan Africa about 200,000 years ago pitted its survival against that of its remaining *Homo erectus* ancestors. Though *sapiens* focused on big game and *erectus* relied on scavenging, the two species competed over hunting grounds, firewood, small game, and caves for shelter. Steadily, *sapiens* won out, driving *erectus* to extinction south of the Sahara.

After driving *erectus* to extinction some 200,000 years ago, *sapiens*, with its numbers continually growing, had no choice but to keep intensifying production. Artifacts demonstrate that once *Homo sapiens* came on the scene, improvements in weapons technology developed in steady succession. No doubt, our ancestors also hunted for longer periods of each day and each week. We do not know how difficult survival became for the first of our kind in sub-Saharan Africa, yet, we know from the fossil record that after the next interglaciation briefly opened, then closed the Sahara (about 120,000 years ago), *Homo sapiens* was living, for the first time, outside Africa in the Middle East (Fagan 1990). Apparently, some had felt the need to leave and did so. Most likely, it was resource depletion that drove them.

Then, after the return of ice age cold, *Homo sapiens* found itself—like *Homo erectus* before—in two pockets, each isolated from the other by the Sahara desert: one in sub-Saharan Africa, the other in the Middle East. In the south, the respite created by the escape to the north was temporary, and difficult times quickly returned. In the north, however, the situation was much improved. At that time, the Middle East had abundant forests with large game—an excellent homeland for the former Africans. Also there were the *erectus* descendants (later known as Neanderthals) of people who had left Africa during earlier breaks in ice age glaciation. In the Middle East and Europe, their numbers never exceeded 10,000. Competing for the same resources, *sapiens* slowly drove them to extinction over the next 40,000 years.

Meanwhile, population growth in the Middle East increased pressure on our ancestors, and some bands moved on to regions where big game remained plentiful. Gradually, our kind spread out from the Middle East and occupied every region on earth, eliminating *erectus* in the process. As good as the life of the big game hunters was, it is no wonder that we went "to the ends of the earth" to sustain it.

However, even as those of us on the *frontier* of human occupation pursued the good life of big game hunting, most of us—back in the *interior* of human occupation, in sub-Saharan Africa and in the Middle East—dealt with the age-old reality of declining standards of living in the face of rising population. In both regions, we intensified production activities, improving social organization so that more and better attention could be devoted to survival. We organized more systematic cooperation in child care so that women could devote more time to gathering fire wood, fruits, vegetables, and—in the Middle East, but not in sub-Saharan Africa where no native strains existed—grains. We invented new weapons technology and hunted for longer hours each day. In the Middle East, big game herds were decimated, and we returned primarily to hunting smaller animals. To keep ourselves warm and to cook our food, we cut the forests until they were gone. The destruction of the forest habitat drove much of the larger game out of the region. Women began the first experiments in planting seeds and growing food.

The steady intensification of our production endeavors, however, hit a real crisis 12,000 year ago as the last ice age cold cycle came to an end. "It is safe to say that people [then] living on earth…confronted global warming on a scale which we have not even remotely begun to experience in our own times" (Fagan 1990:214).

The interglacial warming restored moisture to the Saharan region. Again, the desert opened a few northern passage ways, and the stressed hunter-gatherers of the Middle East were suddenly (relatively speaking) inundated by an influx of immigrants from the south. In combination with the vanishing forests and diminished game, the rapid rise in human population created an unprecedented socioecological crisis in the region as the hunter-gatherer mode of production breached an ecological limit. Warring over depleted hunting grounds intensified, along with malnutrition and disease. Facing devastation, our ancestors had no way to survive—unless they could find a new way to exploit nature, one that did not depend on forests or game. They found the answer in agriculture.

"[F]ood production was a logical survival strategy for people faced with the age-old need to feed growing populations" (Fagan 1990:225). And it saved our lives.

Ice Age Impacts on Human Evolution and Migration		
Ice Age Event	Years Before Present	Outcome
Extreme glaciation	2.5 million	*Homo habilis* evolves in sub-Saharan Africa.
Periodic, less extreme glaciations	2.5 million to 900,000	*Homo habilis* never crosses the Sahara.
Extreme glaciation	1.9 million	*Homo erectus evolves* in sub-Saharan Africa.
Periodic, less extreme glaciations	1.8 million to 200,000	At roughly 100,000-year intervals, *erectus* bands cross the Sahara and subsequently spread across warmer regions of southern Europe and Asia.
Extreme glaciation	200,000	Evolution of *Homo sapiens* in sub-Saharan Africa.
Less extreme glaciation	120,000	First *Homo sapiens* escape sub-Saharan Africa and subsequently spread to all regions of Europe, Asia, Australia and the Americas.
Less extreme glaciation	12,000	Influx of sub-Saharan *Homo sapiens* causes socioecological crisis in the Middle East.

Agriculture's impact was so dramatic for one important reason: surplus.

Despite the fact that meat could be salted and fruits and vegetables dried, the surplus of hunting and gathering had always been meager and fleeting. In contrast, agriculture created significant surplus in two new, enduring, and accumulating ways: stored grains and animal herds. In dry climates, grains could be stored indefinitely, and, so long as grain supplies endured, animal herds could be sustained. Thus, by storing grain and building herds, we could accumulate surplus for protection against possible future disaster.

Necessity drove us to adopt agriculture, and its discovery as our means of survival was inadvertent. Unable to sustain the Middle East region's population in the face of forest and big game depletion, we first tried intensified gathering. Fortunately, in what is present-day Turkey, huge natural fields of wheat and other grains were so productive that a family, in three weeks' time, could harvest enough grain to last an entire year. The problem was storage. A year's supply of grain could not be carried around; yet, if left alone, it would be eaten by other animals or destroyed by wind and weather. We solved this problem by building our first permanent shelters, not to house ourselves, but to store the grain while we continued our migratory lifestyle in pursuit of the remaining small game.

Of course, many animals previously depended on the grain for their own survival, and our consumption of it was a factor in their own dispersion and depletion. We soon noticed, however, that certain animals—chickens, goats and sheep, especially—thrived on the stubble remaining after our harvest. We realized we could use a portion of our harvest to feed these animals, encouraging them to stick around after the stubble was gone. In short order, we domesticated these animals and established small flocks and herds under our nourishment and control. The animals provided a steady supply of eggs, milk, and meat.

The migratory, hunter-gatherer lifestyle was ingrained through hundreds of thousands of years of human experience, and for awhile we continued it, using the grain and our dogs to move our animals with us as we went. However, it soon proved wiser to abandon the nomadic life altogether and concentrate on building larger, stable herds in the grain-growing regions. But bigger herds meant sharing a larger portion of the grain with the animals so, necessarily, we began systematic planting, expanding nature's fields and greatly enlarging our annual crop.

By roughly 10,000 years ago, we were farming along the Tigris and Euphrates rivers in the Middle East and the Nile river valley in Africa; by 8,000 years ago in southeast Asia, the Indus river valley, and the Hwang Ho in today's China; after 7,000 years ago in Central America; and by 6,000 years ago in Europe (Fagan, 1990). With agriculture, instead of disaster, our ancestors faced a bountiful payoff from the cultivation of land and renewed population growth was possible. "Beginning with 100,000 people in 8,000 B.C., the population of the Middle East probably reached 3.2 million shortly before 4,000 B.C.—a forty-fold increase in 4,000 years" (Harris 1977:43).

I stress *necessity* in all this to emphasize that farming was not some creative new idea, conceived suddenly by an exhausted hunter while sitting around the campfire one evening with tribal relatives. Rather, we had known for thousands of years that plants could be grown by placing seeds in the ground. Yet, so long as hunting and gathering were productive, we had little use for this knowledge. For hunting, mobility was critical; for planting, settlement was necessary. The two were mostly incompatible, and until the socioecological crisis struck, hunting was easier and far more productive than nurturing plants.

Knowledge is like that. It often exceeds its usefulness. But when necessity compels its application, it takes off in previously unimaginable directions and with often stupefying results. Once people abandoned hunting and gathering in favor of agriculture, our understanding hurtled onward to forge a wholly unanticipated, new social contract.

The Agricultural Social Contract and Its Systemic Social Dysfunction

A social contract is the broadly-accepted way that the most powerful and influential forces in a society manage social relations in support of a given mode of production. Most fundamentally, it is built around control of the key resources in production and the relationships among people required for effective production and exchange. Today, we are in need of a new social contract, one consistent with our emerging new mode of service production.

Ten-thousand years ago in the Middle East, a new social contract, based in agriculture's necessities, was vital to human survival.

To illustrate, in hunter-gatherer societies, no one "owned" or controlled the key resource, big game, but the hunting grounds of a clan were protected from intrusion by other clans. The only things owned were the particular implements created by individual hunters or gatherers. In actual production—that is, in hunting or in gathering—people worked in teams. For instance, a group of hunters might surround a herd, and then noisily approach in a way that drove the herd off toward a cliff. Inevitably, some animals would be injured in the fall and could be readily killed by hunting companions positioned below. Similarly, women tended to each other's children so that groups could forage together.

Less intrinsic to production but still critical to its overall success was having a process to manage conflict—minor and serious—within the clan. Most fundamentally, because clans were matrilineal and all the women were related, women exercised the primary authority. When conflict had to be resolved, it was generally the women who decided. If necessary, the men were called upon to enforce their decision. Consider the situation of a young male who forced himself sexually on a woman. Rape was intolerable, and the women might banish him. Then, the men would no longer tolerate his presence in the hunt or on the hunting grounds.

Though hunter-gatherer cultures worldwide differed (and differ) in countless ways due to local climate and resource particularities—we say, bioregional conditions—it is safe to say that all of them shared (and share, though the penetration of more recent modes of production have diluted their original character) values and social systems that enhanced their collaboration and prospects in hunting and gathering.

It is equally safe to say that the adoption of agriculture, with its sedentary foundation and its surplus production, was bound to require a different kind of social contract. It did indeed. What is seldom analyzed and appreciated, however, is the strategic impact of this transformation on humanity itself. In the space of what was probably less than a few hundred years, the culture that had nurtured our survival for 200,000 years was overthrown. Though absolutely vital to the survival of our species, the culture that resulted was nevertheless *flawed* and *counter* to our natural social relations. As we shall see, we have struggled with this ever since. Let me briefly elaborate.

The key natural resource in agriculture is land, not big game. Good land is land with access to water and sunshine. Gradually, we learned that good land eventually turns bad, and as it did, we cleared new land and moved on, a process known as swidden agriculture. As experience led to accumulated insight, we discovered ways to restore some of the land's vitality through burning and letting it lay fallow. We also developed more sophisticated social organization as "big men" assumed leadership within our clans, organizing us to cooperate in the clearing of land, the construction of irrigation systems, and the concentrated efforts of the harvest season. To facilitate storage, we constructed centralized facilities and entrusted our leaders to manage them in our common behalf.

Inevitably, as we cleared land and raised herds, families needed to occupy and develop specific land parcels. Thus, whereas previously a clan's hunting grounds were held in common, now, as land was occupied for farming, a new cultural norm necessarily affirmed its use by specific families in perpetuity. As Frederick Engels (1972) first noted, however, a problem developed around the disposition of this right to occupancy upon the death of the family elder.

In traditional clan culture, there was never any wealth to pass upon death, but now land and its accumulated surplus (grain and animals) were very vital assets to be passed to the next generation. Moreover, in natural culture, women had chosen their mates, and the young men moved into the women's clans. In agriculture, however, where the physical strength of men (and their lack of "disability" due to pregnancy) was critical for clearing land and plowing fields (this turned out to be less the case in Southeast Asia where the main cereal crop, rice, is planted in paddies, a task suitable even for pregnant women), the ultimate survival of the clan might be jeopardized when sons, coming of age, left the clan for marriage, replaced by young men from a distant clan. Should the incoming young man's clan face some sort of natural or social crisis, would he be loyal to his new family or would he attempt to use his new land and surplus to help his old relatives? No doubt, actual situations played out in different ways, but the reality of divided loyalties revealed a problem in matrilineal culture.

Some clans solved the problem by converting from female to male mate selection so that young men could remain in their own clan where their knowledge, labor power, and loyalty would always accrue to the clan's long-range benefit. Overall, clans that adopted this new cultural norm proved more stable, and the pattern predominated. In the space of no more than a few generations, women lost the right to choose their mates and, instead, were forced to leave their homes and maternal support for the relative isolation of life in a patriarchal clan.

The full implications of this shift will be explored in Chapter 4, but we will say at this juncture that systemic *social dysfunction* was thus introduced into the gender relations and culture of human society.

The development of social stratification—classes and political power based on uneven control of key economic resources—was another major consequence of the adoption of agriculture, also first explained by Engels. As time passed and agricultural clans greatly expanded in numbers and geographic dispersion, uneven development of land and accumulation of surplus was inevitable. Through a combination of luck, hard work, successful family planning, and, in some cases, deceit, manipulation, or theft, some families ended up with the best land and the greatest consistent surplus. Those with very poor land sometimes became impoverished, due to floods and other natural disasters. Meanwhile, the families of the big men—who at first were genuine leaders of the clan—became more remote, their time devoted more and more to surplus management, construction planning, conflict resolution, and ritual activities designed to promote the overall productivity of the region.

In contrast to hunter-gatherer in which the impossibility of surplus accumulation allowed no one to become different or elite relative to anyone else, agricultural society, for the first time, fostered the development of classes among the families of any given region. Those without adequate, productive land had no way to survive and were forced to give themselves to a new, initially benign, yet essentially slave relationship with those with enough surplus to put them to work and keep them alive. Thereby freed from the necessity to work their own land, the richest became an aristocratic, slave-holding elite, responsible for general social management, including, when necessary, preservation of social order through a combination of surplus dispersion, court decrees, and force applications. Later, we came to call this structure of social management the *state*. The bulk of the people constituted the peasantry, with the right to work the land of their ancestors provided that they tithed their surplus to the aristocracy and contributed their designated share of labor to the organized communal projects. Gradually, class stratifications and their respective obligations to the overall, ongoing production of agricultural society became calcified and permanent. Eventually, these rules of social conduct were codified as pagan religious doctrine, sanctified by the aristocracy. Metal weapons were perfected, armies were formed, and conquest—to acquire land and slaves—became the order of the day. Such was the process through which the basis of civilization was laid.

Despite agriculture's wrenching cultural transformation, it was the only path ahead for humans in the Middle East who had faced the socioecological catastrophe of overpopulation and the demise of big game hunting. However, the work of clearing, tilling, planting, weeding, watering, and harvesting— aside from the afternoon siesta and seasonal lulls—was steady and hard. It nurtured an outlook of relentless stoicism. When the communal obligations of militia service and the construction of ever more massive hydraulic infrastructure (irrigation systems) are factored in, the work of peasants was often overburdened and oppressive.

The increased burden of farm work must be stressed in order to attack a common perception about the adoption of any new mode of production: that we invent it in our uniquely human, never-ending striving for a better life. Such a viewpoint implies that we "advance" because we "choose" to advance. In fact, the opposite is true. Certainly, the desire for a better life is a significant motivator, but it arises from the despair of a declining or threatened lifestyle rather than a sense that things could be even better than how great they already are. As Ester Boserup (1965) has explained, from the point of view of human society as a whole and the amount of time necessarily devoted to the most basic efforts to stay alive, relative to big game hunting, agriculture was not an advance. We adopted it because we had no other choice. In a desperate time, it was our best option.

Today's transformation, while much different in its particulars, is like those of the past, driven by necessity and independent of human will. Due to the depletion of its most vital resources, destabilized industrialism threatens a full-scale, global collapse of our social organization. We must discover and embrace the culture of service production whose regenerative force offers a new vision and organizational opportunity for the future of social production.

Chapter 1 Response

Am I Alone Out There?—A Skeptic's Last Hope

Charles:

A Model of Cultural Materialism

Cultural materialism, as my brother points out, involves the study of how groups of humans develop social relationships and meaning from the natural resource base that supports them. The theory examines the evolution of dominant modes of production and capital accumulation over time. Karl Marx, a political economist who wrote in the period 1844-1872, long before most of what we consider to be modern capitalism came into existence, proposed that human society had undergone two major transformations in its mode of production. My brother wrote of the first—from hunter-gatherers to agriculturalists ten to twelve thousand years ago—and in Chapter 2, we discuss the second—from agriculturalists to industrialists in the last five hundred years or so, depending on who is drawing the timelines.

These were important transitions because the methods of human production changed, first from seasonal hunting and gathering migrations to sedentary lifestyles of domesticating animals, cereals, and tubers, and then to technological and energy-based mass production. But beyond the changing means of production, major transformations also altered the nature of surplus accumulation, allowing agricultural communities to accumulate both property and stored food and, thus, secure their survival against most climatic tragedies. Industrial communities rapidly altered the environment to produce cities and substantially higher standards of living. The dominant form of social organization also changed with the transformations in production, from communal society to centralized city-states to nation-states. And finally, the culture of the people living inside each of those community types adopted differing sets of values and practices concerning families, authority, individualism, patriarchy, property, political rights, and what have you—the values and norms of daily living and reproduction.

A decade ago, my brother began promoting this idea that today's human society has entered a third transformation in its mode of production, which he then called niche production and which we now call service production. The social transformation accompanying this change was noted not only by him and anthropologists like Harris and social observers like the Tofflers, but by a host of artists, writers, philosophers, and theorists from all sides. But no one had quite described the nature of the new service-led mode of production accurately before.

Service is best provided by trained personnel in specialized fields who meet the needs of specific target groups using their skills in market niches—i.e., well-defined sectors of the economy with a specific set of customers. Mass production continues, of course, at least to the limits that increasingly scarce resources permit. Declines in forests, energy supplies, clean air, and potable water, however, have been precipitating changes that weaken the industrial base of global society, turning it toward the conservation of resources and to service work as the chief forms of employment and exchange. Markets of goods, the centerpiece of industrial capitalism, are becoming much less important, replaced by the marketing of services as the guiding measure of the coming age. If this change of the mode of production is truly a new stage of human social development, then we can expect that the relations of production, the means of capital accumulation, the dominant political structures, and the cultural components of society will also change in the near future. Since the material base more or less determines the rest of these social variables, then, according to my brother, we must now accommodate our culture to the necessities of the global service economy which has exerted itself as the dominant mode of production because industrialism has so efficiently used up the bulk of its energy and biospheric base. A number of scholars, including Jared Diamond and Sing Chew, note that if we fail to meet the challenge posed by industrial-caused environmental degradation, then we can expect a general decline of civilization, perhaps even a 500-700 year *dark age*.

My Undivided Skepticism

I do have days when I believe this scenario. Perhaps, I want to believe that history is a linear timeline of human events, that science is a steady compilation of factual knowledge, that modern society exists as a pinnacle of accumulation of wealth, technology, intelligence, and freedom to speak, to know, to experiment, to innovate. We are the freaking best we can be! That, it seems to me, is the point of cultural materialism.

Then I look around me and I laugh. My skepticism takes over. How can you call this society the pinnacle of anything? My country, the most powerful and wealthiest in history, has been at war nearly every year of my life, each year spending over one-third of its annual accumulated wealth on weapons of mass destruction and its armies. It is run by the "best" academics and politicians from the "best" universities who believe that the "best" economy is one run by gambling casinos (also known as stock exchanges) in New York, Chicago, Tokyo, London, Singapore, and Hong Kong, where speculators drive the price of food, housing, and energy beyond the reach of working people. Every twenty years, during the cyclic crashes of capitalism predicted by Marx, stock brokers and financiers must suck out the savings and other small accumulations (home equity, for instance) of the middle and working classes to bail out their speculation failures in financial markets. The rest of the time, the rich live it up in high style and leave the spoils of their earnings for the rest of us to fight over. The best we can manage, it seems, is a small home on the brink of mortgage failure and weekend shopping sprees among the cheap goods at Wal-Mart. Global population is rising exponentially, just like Malthus predicted 150 years ago. You should be concerned. We are headed to nine billion people by 2050, *if we are lucky enough* to have a sufficient number of natural disasters to keep world population "under control." There's no sign people will willingly do it. Otherwise, we'll have even more mouths to feed. According to a United

Nations report, it is a matter of fact that the U.S. will be the fifth leading contributor to real population growth over the next twenty years, not to mention that Americans use eight to eleven times the resources as the average person in the world and that it would take four-and-a-half earths to provide a standard of living equal to ours to everybody on this planet. I tried four times to discuss American contributions to population with other Americans and everyone said the same thing: "The problem is not 'us' but *'them'*—the flood of immigrants coming into this country. If they'd just quit having babies..." I love denial. Denial always makes "them" the problem.

Let's see. Social inequality, overconsumption, undiminished rate of population growth. What else can I add to the pinnacles of civilization? Assimilation into modern lifestyles and the end of diversity in culture and biodiversity in ecosystems. The militarization of democratic society under fear of terrorism. Religious mysticism at record high levels. Deforestation of both temperate and tropical rain forests. Green revolution pesticide insanity, dead meat culture, maximized transport for commodity markets. I actually remember when fruits and vegetables were seasonal so when you bought a piece of fruit in a supermarket, it had not been picked green and stored to the point of tastelessness and dryness. Fruits used to have juice in them... but then I don't really expect the younger generation to believe it!

I think you're beginning to get the picture. The issue isn't whether the mode of production is changing, but what kind of culture we are going to have when it does. If you are under thirty-five, you better damn well start asking that question...and coming up with answers that make sense. And while you're at it, maybe you should stock up on bags of rice and beans, and canned corn, and seeds for the garden, and maybe a shotgun or two with several boxes of ammunition. Just to be on the safe side...

One thing 9/11 did was unify all the coercive service providers into one single military entity—intelligence, police, army, emergency responders. They now have taken significant control over international development, disaster relief, migration and naturalization, natural resource management, fish and game issues, and public recreation facilities. But none of these should be ruled by fear and guns. They should be ruled by science and compassion, by people who keep their guns in the closet and do not parade them on foreign streets. I generally believe that when poor people resort to guns, they are doing it to protect what little has not already been taken away from them by more powerful people and cultures. Guns are sometimes used by people in defense of their livelihoods, but mostly they are used by governments to push political and economic agendas on to the backs of previously independent peoples. I'm skeptical about big government, big business, big anything. That includes global government, the global economy, and globalization in general.

For me, the real issue is how to do the opposite, how do we not impose our lifestyles and ways of thinking on others? How do we come to trust freedom and democracy enough to let it happen, even among groups of people who see things differently than we do? How do we remain sensitive to other cultures and historical perspectives?

My plan is to promote critical thinking and praxis, practical doubt and collective social action. Liberation is built around people joining with others, comparing their circumstances with others, researching their own problems, and doubting power structures that created the problems in the first place. Teaching one another. Taking stands and fighting back. That is freedom—not tanks rumbling over Afghani mud huts or rockets blasting into Baghdad neighborhoods with their enormous "collateral damage." To be secure enough to act to change our lives, we don't need the global world to be an assimilated whole. We can do it on our own. You get it. Globalization has too many contexts that make me uncomfortable.

I have a couple of stories that relate to this. The first occurred in the department of the Petén in northern Guatemala where I spent a half a decade researching what was happening to Maya communities situated on the fringes of conservation areas. One sultry morning, I hitched a ride on a truck convoy whose mission was to present an eviction notice to an illegal squatter community of K'ekchí Maya that had settled in a recently designated, nationally-protected wildlife corridor. The caravan included vehicles transporting members of Guatemala's National Protected Areas Commission, representatives of environmental non-governmental organizations, a UN observer, the state attorney general who was issuing the order, and forty army recruits to protect them should protection be needed. It took us about eight hours to get there as we had to stop and pull each other out of mud holes or cut logs that had fallen over the road many times. In the nervous two-hour period spent in camp waiting for the farmers to return to the village for a meeting, the K'ekchí women offered us a fire to cook our tortillas and heat the beans we brought for lunch. Most men remained steadfastly aloof, lounging about the camp during the afternoon's torrid heat on their beds—pole platforms tied with vines with a sheet of simple cardboard for a mattress, nestled under a palm thatched roof. There were no modern conveniences that I could see in this village of thirty families, unless you consider worn and tattered T-shirts or dented aluminum cooking pots modern conveniences.

The meeting bordered on the surreal. The K'ekchí elders, all men in traditional style, stood together on the cleared grassy center plaza and refused to speak Spanish, forcing the attorney general to commandeer a conscripted K'ekchí soldier to reluctantly serve as interpreter between the authority of the state and his own ethnic people. It was explained in no uncertain terms that this was a protected area and that the village would have to disband or face imprisonment. The K'ekchí men laughed and seemed amused by the threat. Catcalls and shrieks of derision, in non-traditional style, came from the women who had climbed up on tables behind the elders. Finally a young man, in his early twenties and clearly educated, summed up the villagers' position. "We are K'ekchí and we have lived in this region for over two thousand years. We have always survived by migrating through the forest and making clearings for our crops. Why should we change now? What better life can you offer us?"

I never could come up with an answer to that. I come from an industrial culture that has unsustainably used up its resources and other people's resources in only a few hundred years. Who are we to criticize?

So there you have it. I worry that the rush to find global solutions will only force us to evict more and more indigenous agriculturalists from their historic lands because we, the rich, didn't protect our land and didn't control our population and couldn't ever find a way to stop consuming everything in our path. We go about thinking our ways are so superior and that agriculturalists are so backward and ignorant. I just never found that to be the truth. So, yeah, I'm worried about mode of production theories that don't start with more respect for human foundations and societies that are still with us. All over the globe. They haven't died off or disappeared. I believe they still hold the wisdom we need for tomorrow's world.

I've got this other problem concerning identity politics, political correctness and diversity, be it racial, ethnic, or otherwise. I'm tired of being white. I've got a good friend who's last name is Martin. He got it from his father, his patriarchal lineage, and he's proud of it. For years I have told him I'm just as much a Martin as he is because my Mom was a Martin. But matriarchy in our culture counts for less, and he still doesn't hear me. Obama is lucky. He gets to be black even though his mother is white. I have to be white. I have this wild dream about the future of white people. The world economy collapses, and we are all forced back into being isolated from each other, dependent on our neighbors instead of the global economy. Small white communities are isolated so long that they lose connection, and their genetic inbreeding and cultural selection choices allow them to grow ethnically different from other white folks, like what existed many millennia ago before the mode of production changes that began assimilating us. In my dream—and, in the real world of Australia after the last interglaciation, it only took Aborigines 40,000 years to do it—we deconstruct ourselves into different ethnic groups. The world gets to be different than it is. Black and white get disappeared from the social fabric. I get to be different myself and to share my life with others who look somewhat like me and who practice organic agriculture and share wealth, exchanging knowledge and culture with people I care about. I'm tired of living in cities next to people I don't know and among people who see me as just being white. I didn't do all those things other whites did to other people. Never. I'm supposed to live with white guilt, but I don't do that very well. And that's what's so good about Obama for white youth. They get to be something else, freed of the sins of the father, and mother, and aunt, and...Obama's election offers hope to this country that the future does not have to be black or white.

Please, don't get me wrong. The point isn't that ethnicity is a creation of separatists over time. It isn't and never has been. Race and ethnicity are and always have been mixtures of genes and culture. They always will be. But the difference between assimilation and ethnic differentiation lies in power, control, resources, and authority. *They* get to define what *we* need. That's called assimilation. If you don't think the power of assimilation is strong, think about indigenous people who maintain the right to keep their cultural autonomy and self-determination. Geez, I haven't heard the word self-determination for decades. It used to be important part of the revolutionary vocabulary, the right to determine in conjunction with others of similar history, how you would interact with the political and economic world, the right to prevent others access to your traditional resource base, the right to refuse to develop like they did. I try to talk with other Americans about the right of native peoples to reject or at least limit capitalist modernization while they retain their political autonomy. The response is nearly always the same. "They use toilet paper, too, you know." This comports with "we were justified in attacking Afghanistan because the Taliban wouldn't let children and women get education" and "you can't fight city hall." Well, ghetto children on the lower East Side, or whatever side, don't get good educations, don't have stable family lives, don't have fathers with real careers and investment portfolios. Maybe we should bomb them. If we did, at least we might start a program for reconstruction of their neighborhoods afterwards! The War on Poverty was lost, you know. In America. It was the first war America lost...

My brother wants a global solution, and, you know, I do too. I've been watching civil society fill up with non-governmental organizations, activists, and volunteer groups for a couple of decades. They *are* the hope of the future. Civil society groups represent much of what I care about—the desire and dream of diminishing poverty, empowering the marginalized, opposing war as a solution to anything, learning technology that is useful and putting it into practice, building new lives day by day, restoring the damaged environment. These are not centralized trickle-down programs that come from corporate and state initiatives, but programs built from the strength of grassroots people who care to make a difference. But are they ever hopelessly inefficient and ineffective in the wake of the market economics of the capitalist world structure. Civil society is a nascent social force—it's new but still underdeveloped. Like most of the world's nations. Civil organizations really aren't making the difference they pretend to be making because, in the larger scheme of things, they are pitifully broke and hopelessly mired down in begging for funds from the Rich and Powerful or the Government. They really aren't independent, at least not like they claim to be. But their hearts are in the right place.

Still, in spite of all my skepticism, I'm going to back this global program of my brother, even though I'm not sure where it will go as theory turns into practice. I reserve the right to bail out at any time because I'm postmodern. If I don't like what you are doing, I'll just define myself as something else. But you know, he's got a point. He wants to find a way to capture a share of all those financial transactions that drive up the price of food and energy, timber and mortgages, and use the money to make funds available for an independent civil society to utilize. Tap the global economy to attack worldwide problems through initiatives rooted in local empowerment. Mobilize the global grassroots. I like that idea, so I'm sticking with the program so far. I want us to try it, taking money from stock gamblers and speculators and using it for real things. You know, to actually change people's lives for the better.

Maybe as we discuss it, I'll grow less cynical. Maybe not. But I'm convinced that global warming science by itself can't accomplish a thing, can't save the precious earth and the cultural diversity needed to understand it. Our hope is in uniting with everyone else, of being holistic to the point of error. Let the dialogue between the local and the global continue. Exalt the local-global nexus.

So, the counterpoint to my brother's first chapter on cultural materialism, that begins our story of humanity's third wave transition to the service-led mode of production, has to do with diversity. I love holistic theories, the ones like his that say we are all part of the same mold—the Gaia hypothesis and Alan Watts together, one earth and one people, and one glorious interconnected world. Really, I do. Love them, that is. I just don't like to live them.

I want to be left alone. That's human right number one. I want the right to organize with people I care about to do the right thing. That's human right number two. I want the right not to do what the majority of people are doing. That's human right number three. If I can't be different from you, there are no human rights. If there are no human rights, I will exert the ecological right to fight back until my end. Just like any animal. By any means necessary.

So many of the world's problems are presented in the media as the result of people defending their all too few rights by any means necessary. Those images are bull. Socioecological problems have causes, and those causes are usually based in human groups that think something they are doing qualifies them as victors, as deciders, as governors, as leaders. Calvinist ideology. The theory that marginalizes people who are different as having no inherent merit. Well, we have the right to fight against Calvinist greed, capitalist callousness, the never-ending addiction to power, money, and influence.

My brother has a point. Our solution is and only can be global. Solidarity is international. But we can't confuse solidarity with assimilation, or globalization with the new world order of neoconservatism. Globalization requires an immense respect for the local, for the differences between people that permit choices and freedom of expression and self-determination. It requires self-criticism and social criticism, a willingness not to accept what is happening around us at any cost.

And the cost will be great. Industrial capitalism is driving human society mad. I'm a sociologist by trade and I have read the stats. Eight hundred fifty million people—850,000,000!—do not know where they will get tomorrow's meal. Forty percent of black males in the U.S. are in prison, the most imprisoned society on the globe. Three thousand tragic, innocent deaths on 9/11 have been traded for over 70,000 collateral deaths in Iraq. WWI. WWII. The Korean War. The Vietnam War. The Afghan War. The Iraq Wars, 1 & 2. The Balkan War. Darfur. The War on Terrorism. Mad I tell you, capitalism has driven us mad.

And the most egregious thing to me is the environmental tragedy that goes on under our noses, the one we fail to see because don't want to see it. Global warming. Deforestation. Water pollution. Species extinction. Habitat loss. Smog. Parking lots. Four thousand square foot housing monstrosities. Wal-Marts and Big Macs. Megalopolis. Mad, I tell you, our lifestyles have driven us mad.

We gotta mobilize to change things, and do it soon. We have to stop this insanity.

Or, we can salute and cheer in humanity's next *dark age*. Believe me, the way we're going, it's gonna come.

Chapter 2

Jumpstarting Tomorrow— Turning the Steel Stone

Steve:

Since you're reading this book, chances are you're a thoughtful, socially concerned individual, but you may not know that much about social science per se. The fact is, social science is not well regarded in U.S. society.

Skipping Class in Social Science

Studies show that history is the most hated subject in American high schools. I was a high school social studies teacher, and I can confirm the fact. As an economist by training, I also know why economics is known as the "dismal" science. Suddenly relevant in 2008 (that is, with the global financial crisis), it's usually highly technical, speculative, and boring to anyone who's not a trained economist. Anthropology is old hat—prehistoric and overexcited about the artifacts of lost cultures. Sociology focuses on the minutia of human subgroups and their relations—enamored with endless and less than useful details. Political science looks at government bodies and political parties, and no one holds them in high regard. When it comes down to it, who needs social science anyway?

Moreover, social science seems hardly scientific at all. Rather, it appears as a disjointed assessment of constantly changing things rendered in seemingly random fashion by writers of all stripes and perspectives.

The last thing it does is lead to definitive conclusions about what society can do to better itself. Plus, we all know that social scientists, despite their findings, are complacent like the rest of us. They find fault but don't really do anything about it.

Yet, Charles and I herein suggest that socioecological science is *the key* to making a difference in our world, precisely because it offers a penetrating assessment of the actual forces driving social change and, therefore, provides a basis both to challenge existing political agendas and to define better ones.

The reason our approach outshines the social science you may have previously encountered is its acceptance of one concept that is denied or obfuscated throughout the bulk of western social science: class. Class analysis is the absent element necessary to tie the rest of the social sciences together so that they can render useful assessments of human affairs.

In the first chapter, we explored how the pressures of rising populations in Neolithic settings led human groups to deplete game animals and bring hardship on themselves. Sometimes, the resulting starvation, disease, and warfare decimated human life in the area; oftentimes, migrations to new regions helped resolve the problem. But, at a critical juncture some 12,000 years ago, a confluence of factors produced a socioecological crisis in one region, the Middle East. Because there is no written history from that time, it is difficult to assess the actual extent of the *dark age* that ensued, but humans eventually solved the crisis by adopting agriculture as our way of life.

As we noted, however, the advent of agriculture was not without problems. While it produced surplus food supplies in the form of stored grains and live animal herds, which allowed an immense growth in human population, it also overthrew natural gender relations and created the first class structure in human history. Classes reflect wealth differentials, are inherently unequal, and generally result in domination and oppression.

Necessity compelled that transformation in human culture so whatever objections may have been raised at the time proved irrelevant in history, but many millennia later, in the last half of the 1800s, critics of the then-current class structure—that had evolved in stages from that long-ago start—had reason to investigate and explain the origins and nature of classes. In doing so, they invoked the ire of the "powers that be"—the then-ruling class—and set in motion a process that has undermined western social science to this day.

Up to that time, around 1850, despite the promise of the earlier *Enlightenment* and the democratic revolutions at the end of the 1700s, the Industrial Revolution had brought forth 12-hour workdays, child labor, subsistence wages, recurrent recessions, and bloody attacks on workers who formed unions and went on strike. Cities were fetid pockets of pollution and disease. Rural poverty drove millions of Europeans to emigrate. Taking "enlightened" political philosophy to task, critics—Karl Marx chief among them—articulated the first scientific assessments of social forces, opening the era of modern social science.

Marx broke new ground by demonstrating that (a) the mode of production, itself, creates inherently unequal classes in industrial society and (b) the most economically powerful class—the capitalists—dominates politics, creating a state to manage social and class contradictions, ultimately in its own interest. His conclusion, as we all know, was that the interests of capitalists and workers were inevitably opposed. The vastly more numerous workers could overcome their oppression only through revolution. Hence, *The Communist Manifesto.*

At the time, Marx's critique was a penetrating assessment of the evident inequality and hardship of industrial society. Indeed, it rallied significant support within dissatisfied elements of the working class in many industrializing nations (and, eventually, in many undeveloped nations as well) and was bitterly opposed by the industrialists. Because the United States then was itself a developing nation with a vast expanse of western lands that were offered for free to any who would "go west" and homestead, it possessed a natural "escape valve" for dissatisfied workers arriving from Europe's cities or enduring the hardships of America's own factory centers. With working class suffering mitigated by this unacknowledged escape valve, some American academics and pundits questioned the validity of Marx's critique. Inevitably, they gained favor with American capitalists, and their universities and newspapers received increasing financial support. In the space of a couple decades, a cottage industry of anti-communist intellectual thought established itself.

Certain aspects of Marxist analysis, however, proved difficult to refute, namely, the division of society into classes and the class bias of the state. Adapting to this reality, the anti-communist critics took the view that these class realities, if true, were not so bad or so sweeping as Marx suggested. They pointed out that workers could vote and, thus, control the worst excesses of the state. Further, they advocated a range of social reforms which could ameliorate the extreme disparities of wealth then emerging across society. They spoke of classes as "upper, lower, and middle" without reason for or definition of their boundaries, thus obscuring the power basis of each and creating an impression of easy upward mobility. In the process of intellectual reaction to Marxism, western social science—as we know it today—took shape.

The essence of western social science—particularly, in the United States—is its pragmatic orientation. Unable to refute some basic theoretical claims of Marx, it tends to belittle class theory and focuses on the practical issues and dynamics of social interaction. The father of this school of thought was the pragmatic American philosopher Thomas Dewey, and slowly pragmatism evolved into the dominant paradigm of social science, known as "functionalism." Rather than investigating *why* things happen, the functionalists, in a trend led by the American sociologist Talcott Parsons, contented themselves with careful documentation of simply *what* happens, assuming that because what happened actually happened, it must be superior to other possibilities for social development. Functionalism begins by accepting the status quo.

Throughout the first half of the twentieth century, social science increasingly broke into ever more refined specializations. Every field of study became more widely separated from every other one and more divorced from an overall consideration of the larger social dynamic and its driving forces.

After World War II and, especially, after the Sixties cultural critique of the long failure of functionalism to examine the realities of oppressed minorities, western social science split further into detailed investigation of women, Blacks, Hispanics, Asians, Native Americans, immigrants, homosexuals, bisexuals, and the physically, mentally, and emotionally impaired.

All of this work was and is valuable, but in no way can it answer the question of what is going on it today's world. For that, a holistic assessment is needed, one unafraid to embrace *all* the lessons of human experience, even the class realities uncovered by Marx. A holistic assessment necessitates breaking with the dominant historic framework of most American and European social science—its functionalism and specialization. It demands stepping back and pulling all the scattered insights together into one whole understanding.

I do not mean, however, that we should attempt to establish Marx as the world's leading social science theoretician. Indeed, in its political and social remedies, Marxist dogma is irrelevant to our time. As a theory of the ascendant Industrial Age, Marxism, like other social thinking of that time, suffered from an inability to appreciate the interconnection of our production systems with the natural world and with human population. It failed to grasp socioecological realities. Marx and other philosophers of his day missed the power inherent in industrial development to destroy the environment, human and biological diversity, cultural sovereignty, and human collaboration.

To make clearer the point that we must acknowledge the importance of class analysis, let's return to the cultural materialist examination of human history that we started in Chapter 1. We must catch up on the cultural transformations of industrialism before we move to an assessment of the emerging service class and its future role in human affairs, elaborated in Chapter 3.

Civilization Rises, then Falters

The Agricultural Age began roughly 12,000 years ago, but starting about 4,200 years ago, agricultural civilizations—except in China (see Chapter 4)—endured a number of devastating periods of social and economic collapse, what Chew calls the *dark ages* of civilization. Indeed, after 2200 B.C., periods of stability in civilization—although well-documented by the historians of each—were no more enduring than the periods of their collapse, which, by their nature, lacked historic record-keepers. In the big sweep of history, one can say that agricultural production served humanity well for roughly 8,000 years, only to be followed by more than 3,500 years of intermittent *dark age* collapse and geographically discordant renewals. The

Flipping the Production Switch—Industrial Divergence

Rome collapsed in roughly A.D. 350, and the *dark age* lasted in Europe until about 1500, with a kind of first act revival, known as the Renaissance, commencing around 1300.

Rome had been the quintessential Iron Age empire, having extended the Mediterranean mode of large-scale, irrigation-based agriculture into the far reaches of northern Europe. Chew documents how the Roman Empire's expansion and consumptive practices, along with its militarization of the continent, steadily decimated the forests of Europe, setting the conditions for the ensuing socioecological crisis. By the fourth century, all available land was in production, and the empire's reserves of iron and lumber were virtually exhausted. The combination of population pressure and resource depletion made it impossible to sustain adequate agricultural production. As social dislocation roiled the empire, the aristocracy retrenched on their own estates, cutting tithes to Rome. Infrastructure decayed, peripheral defense collapsed, the "Vandals got the handles," and the Empire was overrun.

Chew's research and theories explain why civilizations reach *dark age* lows—characterized by warlordism, fragmented social structures, loss of knowledge, and steep declines in population—and, thus, do much to illuminate our present time on earth, a time also characterized by extreme deforestation and widening social unrest. Over the last century, population has exploded while our available supplies of agricultural land, fossil fuel, clean air, and potable water were reaching the limits of their exploitation. Accordingly, social discord, war, genocide, and terrorism increasingly define human relations.

However, Chew's theories are less useful in delineating the forces that either overcome centuries of *dark age* stagnation (which we may face) or, despite seriously threatened sociological conditions, might somehow allow us to avoid such a fall in the first place (as we hope for our time). The Tofflers, Harris, and Marx help fill in this blank.

Taken together, they suggest that whenever the mode of production shifts, an over-arching social and cultural change also begins which ultimately unleashes fresh human ingenuity in the face of the encroaching crisis. While human innovation and agency play some role in the emergence of the new mode of production, the driving force, as explained by cultural materialism, is *necessity*—the inadvertent response to economic and ecological hardship. It is beyond human will that the emergence of a new mode of production begins the creation of new classes of economic and, ultimately, political power in society, setting the stage for a cultural struggle of revolutionary proportions. Where human innovation and agency ultimately play a more decisive role is in the definition of alternative values and political agendas and the creation of social structures and political organizations that finally overcome the old social order and accelerate the new mode's development.

The key issue is whether human ingenuity intervenes early in or, better yet, on the eve of an impending social collapse or comes through the difficult trial, error, and hardship of a prolonged *dark age*. The latter path is well-illuminated by an examination of civilization's recovery after the collapse of Rome, and it sheds light on the ways a contemporary *dark age* might be averted or, at least, ameliorated.

While the collapse of the Roman Empire threw Europe into an extended *dark age*, the impact was less pronounced in the Middle East, always the backwater of Roman prosperity due to its already depleted natural resources. The empire's collapse opened a new center of power in Constantinople, which sustained a modicum of imperial power through its northern conquests into the unexploited regions of modern-day Russia and Ukraine. This Byzantine Empire, however, was short-lived, uprooted by the combination of Mongol invasion from the east and Islamic insurgency in its south which, together, eventually produced the Ottoman Empire, an ossified but steady agricultural economy dependent on the same large-scale, irrigation-based production that had sustained life in the region for millennia.

In contrast, in the western Mediterranean and northern Europe, the collapse of Rome initiated a *dark age* in which agriculture reverted from large-scale, irrigated farming which supported relatively massive populations to small-scale, marginal farms that could support only a tiny fraction of the former population. This was because the collapse of the Roman state eliminated the mechanisms that society had evolved to organize itself for the construction and maintenance of hydraulic infrastructure, including its protection by a large military complex. In the steady development of social collapse, in the disarray of widespread starvation, disease and social migration, population dropped precipitously, allowing irrigated farmland, increasingly abandoned, to gradually return to forest. After 800 years, around 1150, a new, bottomed-out equilibrium between population and forestland resources was reached.

No sooner was that equilibrium reached, however, than the pressures of population growth returned, knocking the manor-based agricultural system for another loop.

According to Harris, wheat prices tripled between the late twelfth century and the fourteenth; the resulting malnutrition greatly raised everyone's vulnerability to the Black Plague that swept across Europe in the mid 1300s; the sex ratio reached a peak of 130 males for every 100 females, evidence of extreme female infanticide employed in desperate attempts to control population; messianic movements, witchcraft, massacres of Jews, and the Inquisition arose as people and authorities reacted and over-reacted to the crisis; and the Hundred Years' War (1337-1453) engulfed the region as people fought for a way to survive. "[T]he intensification of the manorial mode of production had reached its ecological limits..." (Harris 1977:259).

Europeans found two ways out of their crisis. Influenced by cultural exchange and trade with Ottomans and Arabs that developed in the aftermath of the ill-fated Crusades, manor elites on the Italian and Iberian peninsulas—where larger-scale production required irrigation—marshaled peasants to begin reconstruction of long-dilapidated dams and aqueducts. But, in the rain-soaked climate of northern Europe, something different emerged. The Industrial Age was born.

According to Harris, because adequate rainfall in northern Europe made agriculture sustainable without irrigation, no urgency encouraged the reformation of the large-scale social organization necessary to rebuild irrigation systems. More fundamentally, without the same reconstruction financing made possible by the trade surplus that accumulated in the south after the Crusades, the northern aristocracy could not undertake large-scale construction even if it had wanted. Instead, northern Europe's aristocracy favored social organization only to the extent necessary to protect themselves, their manors, and their peasants from the incursions of outside invaders. While returning population pressure drove the Italian and Iberian peninsulas to an agricultural- and trade-based *Renaissance*, that same returning pressure in the north—with its more marginal farm economy—simply dragged the region to the brink of another socioecological collapse.

Necessity Intervenes for a New Social Contract

A particular but seldom appreciated facet of the feudal obligations that governed the relationship between peasants and aristocracy on northern Europe's manorial estates was the duty of the peasants to farm the land and deliver the harvest's surplus to the lord of the manor in exchange for his obligation to store and return the surplus to the peasants as necessary for their survival in times of crisis. Accordingly, the land was technically held in common, and both classes were tied to the particular land of the manor. Neither could leave, as much due to the morality of patronage culture as to the lack of any other potentially arable land to which to migrate.

As the crisis worsened through the fourteenth and fifteenth centuries, landlords with depleted land found it impossible to sustain their growing peasant population. Facing widening starvation and renewed social unrest, and without a way to extract more from their land, desperate lords sought other ways to be productive. Seizing opportunities provided by the trade routes inching northward from southern Europe's *Renaissance*, lords with land alongside rivers augmented traditional flour mill operations with wool spinning and weaving operations, which, up to that time, had been local craft enterprises of peasant households. By opening textile mills, marginal landlords were able to employ their peasants, using the trade economy to sell woolen goods, produced much more abundantly and cheaply than could be done in homes. The new income stream allowed them to meet their patronage obligations and, thereby, sustain their class privileges.

As the practice of commodity production succeeded, landlords across northern Europe fenced their land, converted it from farming to sheep grazing, and invested heavily in the expansion of mill operations. Dislodged peasants were forced to abandon farming in favor of day work in the mills—selling their labor for wages as their best way to survive. Mills quickly diversified from woolen goods to an ever-growing array of commodities. Towns—which had had little purpose during the Middle Ages except as cultural centers for the Catholic Church—now converted into market and trade centers for commercial agents of the millers and, later, into concentrations of mills themselves. Steadily, the balance of power in northern Europe's mode of production shifted from agriculture to mass production.

As the mode of production shifted, cultural and political struggle unfolded. A split opened between the two wings of the aristocracy as the traditional landed gentry endured rebelliousness from their more desperate peers now forming as a new class of mill owners along with their commercial and financial allies—together known as the bourgeoisie (town-dwellers in French) or capitalists (its later English variation). The bourgeoisie legitimized the enclosure right of landlords to take land once held in common with peasants as their own private property, now to be used, fenced, or sold as landlords alone saw fit. At first, more prosperous lords, ruling kings, and the Church resisted such change, but the march toward industrialism ultimately left the landed aristocracy in a subordinate social position.

The advent of commodity production, essential for support of northern Europe's expanding population, compelled a *new social contract* based on private property. Compared to farming, industrial production was fast-paced and required organizational flexibility; the industrialists needed complete control over their land, raw materials, and capital. They also needed, as Marx explained, control over labor power to keep the industrial mills working. Thus, peasants had to be "free," at least free in the sense of leaving the land of their impoverished heritage to adopt roles as wage earners in the new industrial cities. Necessarily, the patronage system and other feudal obligations collapsed.

By concentrating large numbers of workers in mills and in the mill towns that sprang up across Europe, the new mode of production reorganized both work itself and the society that surrounded it. While creating two major new classes—the bourgeoisie and the proletariat—mass production also steadily differentiated ever more specialized roles for bankers, traders, shop owners, land speculators, scientists, educators, and government bureaucrats, all of whom filled the strata later labeled as the "middle class" that now forms the bulk of the rising service class in today's economy.

Industrialism transformed social relations. No longer were the main productive laborers scattered on landed estates, remote from each other, where they worked side by side with generations descended of the same family. Now, they were brought into urban life and introduced to a mass of compatriots enduring the same dislocation, reorientation, and generalized poverty. Eventually, proletarians would also begin to see themselves as a class, compelled to unite in self-defense against the industrialists' constant drive to keep wages at subsistence levels through the hiring of replacements from among the unemployed streaming into the cities. From this awareness, the union movement got its start.

But the development of class consciousness among workers trailed that of industrialists who recognized early in the social transition that they shared capitalist interests, interests that were unique and in opposition to those of the ruling landed aristocracy. The success of the new mode of production was founded on its reliance on natural resources other than just land. By employing energy—first from water power but later from steam and electricity driven by wood, coal, oil, and natural gas—mass production created a new class of energy, industrial, and transportation owners which gradually became conscious enough of its own unique interests to organize itself in political struggle. In the process, it espoused a new social contract, nurturing its insurgent values and radical formations and broadening support among potential social allies. Steadily this new class asserted itself and, in various forms along differing national trajectories, fought for political power against the decadent, dynastic regimes of the feudal era. As it triumphed, it forged a new cultural mainstream, restructuring social relations and norms to serve the new mode of production. It created states that conformed to industrial interests, marshaling national resources to define, compete for, control, and conquer commodity markets. From these beginnings, European imperialism—and its offshoots in America and Japan—colonized and dominated most of the world's people by the twentieth century. Indigenous groups, ethnic minorities, women, and children all fell prey to the demand that lives be sacrificed in factories in the name of expanding global production.

It is important to note that the triumph of mass production did not mean the end of agricultural production. Rather, the *social system* was transformed, through investment and social reorganization, from one in which aristocratic landlords exercised decisive cultural influence to one in which that influence was transferred to the owners of energy resources and mass production facilities. Dramatic events characterized the industrial transformation to capitalist states—the American Revolution of 1776, the Napoleonic conquest of Europe, and Britain's more gradual series of political shake-ups from the Magna Charta on. Through it all, agriculture adapted, learning to operate within mass production as a vital economic appendage tied into exchange through increasingly complex commodity markets.

Production and Crisis in Human History	
Time Frame	**Events**
200,000 YBP* to 12,000 YBP	Neolithic Age (subsistence production - hunting and gathering)
Circa 12,000 YBP	Neolithic *Dark Age*
12,000 YBP to 4000 YBP	Bronze Age (agriculture - farming and herding)
4200 YBP to 3400 YBP	Bronze-to-Iron *Dark Age*
2900 YBP to 350	Iron Age (agriculture - farming and herding)
350 to 1400	*Dark Age* of Antiquity (Middle Age)
1400 to 1950	Industrial Age (manufacturing - mass commodity production)
*Years Before Present	

Sunset for the Industrial Age

That same fate will now befall industrial relations and their corporate forms as they lose predominance in the emergent service-led mode of production. Population growth and industrialism's mass consumption have depleted the world's supply of clean air, clean water, and forests. They have also depleted fossil fuel, driving the cost of commodities far beyond the means of most people. The Industrial Age—including its mass consumption, its class elites, its corporate forms, and its nation-states—is obsolete. As with food, we will continue to manufacture the goods necessary for effective human exchange, but agricultural and industrial processes must now be reorganized and adapted to the social contract of service-led production. Either we take that collective step, or the *dark age* of industrialism will wreck global civilization.

Class analysis—with due regard to Marx for his insight—is the key to identifying the most fundamental interests that fuel the necessary cultural struggle through which our new social contract must be forged. With class analysis, we can examine our new service-led mode of production and discern its rising class interests. With these interests in mind, it may be possible to formulate a political agenda that, *by actually serving the only interests that have a sustainable future*, can guide us in the cultural transformation we so desperately need.

We will turn to that task in Chapter 3, but just in case our line of analysis tweaks mainstream political thought enough to stir a debate, let me first vet myself. We've all noticed, of course, that vetting is *de rigueur* these days, and if you aspire to be more than a momentary blip in the public discourse, you better be prepared to endure full disclosure of anything you've ever done in your life. While many object to this fact of contemporary public life, I consider it a worthy feature of the new, service-led economy. Service requires the free flow of information. The information age does not abide hoarding or hiding. Transparency trumps all.

Vetting about Leftist Roots

So, yes, in my youth, I was influenced by Marxism and even considered myself a communist. That was a long time ago. Yet, as noted, I am the son of a U.S. Air Force officer and attended the Air Force Academy, so I didn't start out a radical.

But the war in Viet Nam, hopeless as it was, dragged on unmercifully, long after most of my generation—and, frankly, a large portion of the rest of society as well—realized its futility and stupidity. Eventually, I came to protest the war and found my peers labeled "communists" by then-President

Nixon. I witnessed the reaction of the government, including the killing of protestors at Kent and Jackson State and police attacks on protesters in Washington. I was radicalized.

Later, I came across some Marxist literature and was surprised that it wasn't as incredibly bombastic and superficial as I had been led to believe. Reading Marx and thinking about my experience as a protester, not to mention the on-going war and continued hardships of women and minorities, I began to understand something that I'd never been taught in all the economics and political science courses I'd taken in high school and college—I began to understand the concept and power of class.

Afterwards, that's when I went to the extreme. I joined one of the new left's many Maoist-influenced communist parties and put a few years into efforts to build a revolutionary movement among workers in the U.S. But it didn't work. Our group eventually summarized that some kind of change was taking place in the country's class structure, that proletarians were being replaced by a different kind of worker. We never asked why, but we called them "knowledge workers." And, somehow, we realized our communist party was hopelessly irrelevant. Within another year, we disbanded and dissolved. A few years later, under the leadership of Gorbachev, the Soviet party rattled down the same path.

It's been a couple decades, and, now, it's far easier to see what was going on back in the 70s and 80s, that humanity's mode of production had undergone its third great transformation—this time, from mass production to service-led production—and was creating a new structure of classes and class interests. In retrospect, we were wise to abandon our communist-inspired fantasy of proletarian revolution. I've long-since dropped any pretense of overthrowing the state, whether through violent or peaceful means.

Marx's nineteenth century political program thus rejected, his appreciation for the role of classes in society remains highly relevant. Face it, political power *is* a matter of access and money. We've all got some of those things, but some people have more than others. We can choose to be vague about why this is and where the boundaries exist, or we can deal with the fact that real classes exist, based on ownership or control of resources vital to the mode of production. It's not to say those with such ownership or control are evil, only that they possess a different extent of potential political power. And sure, some individuals in this class may choose to act on behalf of those in other classes or to abstain altogether from political action, but, in the big picture of things, it's inevitable that most will pursue the effective management of society as they best believe necessary. After all, they need and want social stability. Inevitably, their class interests, since they are backed by the most wealth and access to power, tend to prevail.

That is, of course, except at those times when a socioecological crisis exists, when problems proliferate and social harmony unravels, when a new mode of production has emerged and begun to develop the power base of a new, rising class. In such times, the power of the long-dominant class will be challenged. Eventually, it will be overcome, again, not because of intrinsic goodness of the insurgent forces but because of intrinsic social necessity and opportunity. In a socioecological crisis, the only way out of the *dark age*—or the only way to avert it—is for the forces of the new mode of production to triumph. And, as the old way of life falters, people have reason to align with the leaders of the new.

Today, globally, we stand at the precipice of industrialism's *dark age*. Yet, for roughly the last fifty years, a new mode of production—service-led production—has emerged and established itself. It has begun forming a new class structure, and it is beginning to assert itself culturally and politically. It is upon this developing foundation that we can have hope for our future, hope that we can avert the *dark age* by appreciating and advancing the rising interests of the service class and its developing mode of production.

However, the key to success is understanding the nature of those interests which, inevitably, *are distinct from those of industrialism and the capitalists*. Western social science, in its failure to recognize the role of classes and class struggle, is hopeless to this task.

Of course, more is involved than class alone, and we will get to the other factors as we move through our analysis. But, heaven forbid, Marxism provides the key link! Pull your heads out of the sand, you western academics. Let go of your fear! The communists are no longer a threat. Even those in China are capitalists these days.

Chapter 2 Response

What We Choose to Do Matters

Charles:

The general skepticism expressed by my brother of Western social science leaves me uncomfortable. I, too, passed through a revolutionary stage in my youth when I accepted Marxist class analysis as truth and Maoist peasant self-reliance and resistance as a model to be altered to urban struggles. But believing in theory or ideology as truth has its downside—it makes us blind to the essential biological requirement for diversity and the needed differences upon which to build tomorrow's future. We come to accept, as Derrick Jensen (2006) notes, too many cultural lies and justifications. But that's also as true for patriotic nationalists who wave flags instead of criticizing the role their country plays in global socioecological disasters as it is for dogmatic, self-proclaimed revolutionaries.

I remember a discussion I had with a radical friend around 1976, when the civil rights, anti-Vietnam War rebellion was experiencing the end of its days. He was a mechanic, and some neighborhood gang members had broken into his garage and stolen all his tools. So we gathered at his house to plan a fundraiser to replenish his shop, not really considering chasing down the culprits. We didn't trust cops either. He laughed at my mention of revolution. "You don't get it, man," he said to me. "Real revolution is a new way of thinking. It's cultural, not political. We gotta have a whole different way to say things, to express life. Your protests and demands for socialism are dead, man. You'd only fuck things up if you got into power with them. People have to change how they see and express life, and that's it."

Well, maybe my friend and Jensen are right, real change can be measured only by how much our values and visions reflect something other than what is. My brother's vision of the rise of a global consciousness movement to effect change is an example of this. What makes his vision and my "utopian socialism" of the 70s different is that material conditions have changed. We've added a couple billion people to the planet, deforested hundreds of thousands of square miles of forests since then, both in the U.S. and the tropics, and devoured so many resources that warfare over what is left drives millions to migrate across borders hoping to find change in their lifetimes rather than in those of their grandchildren to come. And society has reorganized to address those problems, albeit unconsciously, developing the knowledge, communication networks, and global service skills that many put into practice in development and entrepreneurial systems throughout the world. But then, that's where theory comes in, and that's where dogmatic ideas and ideology must be left behind. We need ideas to lead us forward, but we also have to leave the process of development spontaneous and open to change. I didn't get that as a kid.

The problem is that Western social science has tossed out the baby with the bath water. It has forgotten the Marxist essentials of class, social structure, and critical social science, allowed them to get put in the closet and be forgotten. We've lost the essential tools of change because we let them get dull and chipped, like an old carpenter's chisel that can only butcher the hardwood object of its desire. Theories are not dogma. They can be refined, resharpened, and redirected. We do that in this book: refine, resharpen, and redirect Marxist concepts for today's world. We aren't ashamed of reusing other peoples' ideas. That's essential to any science. But we must account for new conditions if we are to dispel the cultural lies with which we have learned to live.

Socioecology as science acknowledges that the nature and type of resource used by a society affects how that society is structured because how it is used and what can be achieved using it determines the society's options for actions. Furthermore, since one resource use affects others, social structure (i.e., habitual social interactions) develops around complexes of resources, not just a single one. For example, firewood gathering for meat cultures may not need extensive regulation because meat cooks rapidly and hunting game requires migration, so wood supplies generally remain abundant. But a bean culture needs substantially more wood due to the extended length of cooking times for beans. Concerns about wood supplies also heighten because agricultural communities are more stable, and surrounding firewood is inevitably depleted. With agriculture and larger populations, property rights to land and wood resources proliferate, reflecting difficult but vital decisions that involve class privileges, ownership of land and resources, community norms, and enforcement capabilities as well as complex marriage arrangements and dowries. Hence, even without full resource depletion, increased population tends to add complexity to social organization. After millennia of resource depletion over and over again, I guess we end up with what we have—an immensely complex global economy geared to sucking up resources and cultures at every edge of the planet.

My brother should not be so insistent in his critique of Western social science. It's been using the last fifty years to study and teach us about the complexity of social structure and the stagnancy of cultural logics. Social science offers critiques of systemic problems and offers evidence to help us find ways to resolve them. Because change involves global alterations of values and goals along with the creation of new social organization, greater collaboration, and an all-out effort to protect diversity in all forms, we will need that knowledge to reconstruct our futures.

Increased complexity of social organization is accompanied by increased specialization, such that today most of us know very little about how our lives are actually produced or where the products come from. Sociologists have long studied how the industrial revolution introduced entirely new levels of specialization such that capitalist society had to cope with increasing interdependency and solidarity between diverse groups and production enterprises worldwide. Central control of social development became virtually impossible, and the nation-state, the form of government that came to dominate national politics under capitalism, became a regulator of the economy rather than its ruler. Under national direction, legal, labor, and subsistence systems developed that extended the power of corporations, as Marx predicted, but also extended global commodity markets and worker benefits, which he did not. The structure of the capitalist economy promoted international competition and imperialism that led to warfare between nations over markets and resources. Lest you forget, the twentieth century was by far the granddaddy of militarism and innocent civilian deaths. The collateral damage champion of all centuries.

Furthermore, the impoverishment of non-industrialized countries, which found their labor and natural resources exploited, became the operative rule under imperialism even as the internationalization of capital brought great wealth to industrialized nations. Until WWII ended, capitalism was closely associated with ethnic and racial violence, the exclusion of women's rights, unfair class differentiation and inequality, and market militarization. I get tired of people extolling "free enterprise" when its costs measured in human suffering are actually so high.

But by the way imperialism forged international networks and revealed the competitive potential of serving culturally-sensitive market niches, the imperial era was also the harbinger of the global era.

The global nature of today's financial networks, the linkage of world markets, the spread of human rights issues, and the need for international development programs all figure in the trend known as globalization. Globalization is material and cultural; that is, it is based in changes both of technology and of knowledge, applied science and theory, productive processes and communication. But the central feature of globalization is social—it is making our former forms of social structure and national preferences outdated. Patriotism and nationalism are vestiges of a dying order. Today, most people believe in human rights, not class, racial, or ethnic assimilation. They support international financial investment, not investment in national isolationism. They travel widely, hire people from multiple countries, buy goods produced all over the world, and enjoy movies from every society. They volunteer money and labor to help people suffering natural disasters, and they send their military on missions to protect human rights. An honest look at the home front reveals that it was not produced at home, it is not oriented toward resolving problems at home, and it is not determined to secure advantages against other people in the name of national pride. The world has gone global, and we haven't really noticed.

But how that has happened still needs further illumination. We offer two theoretical solutions in this book toward understanding the new global contexts for our world—socioecological science as political advocacy and service class consciousness as necessity. While we may disagree on the utility of Western social science, my brother and I can at least agree that social science and class, the heart of Marxist analysis, are not yet dead concepts.

I think I figured out that environmental issues were really social issues a long time ago. But I couldn't do much with that knowledge. I just wasn't a very social person. I grew up a loner and have stayed that way, a product of shyness and an angry critical eye toward others. Maladjusted might be the word to describe my life. Living on the political fringe, never fitting in too well, and constantly moving from place to place to avoid too much familiarity—these are measures of my own life. Most of you will not understand me, because, in reverse, I cannot understand anyone who actually knows a home and gets to grow up there. What does it mean to keep the same friends for more than a few years? My Dad was military, and home was a set of family relationships that survived wherever the military displaced them. We grew up as military refugees inside of America.

But in some ways I was lucky, and mostly that could be said in an environmental sense. I walked through orange groves to attend elementary school and later lived near a lake and wilderness; I got to hug redwoods as a child and drive in weightless leaps over rolling North Dakota roads, float through the Ausable Chasm, and see the Grand Canyon and Bryce National Park long before they became so trendy as recreation destinies. For a shy kid in the back of a two-toned mid-50s Oldsmobile, this was the life. There wasn't any emptiness in nature that I could find; it filled me with life.

I was never the boldest of my group, whatever group that was, but I always recognized the need for association and collective vision. My social connections began as childhood cliques that sought out salamanders and poisonous copperhead snakes with equal abandon, skinny dipping in moonlit lake waters with the girl down the street, and starting fires we were lucky enough to put out. The environment was a place to take risks, but not a place to use up. In college I joined political collectives that smoked joints and talked strategy in philosophy offices at the university by night while organizing all manner of wild protests in the streets by day. As a young adult, my friends and I formed a tree planter cooperative that spent months in the woods amid snow and mud, exchanging critiques of government management of our national forests around starlit campfires, sharing Bob Dylan and the Clash before setting out at dawn to reforest America's gaping clearcuts even while the logger "locals" belittled us as "dirty commie bastards." I stayed in the background most of my life, and my few attempts at leadership failed miserably. So I learned to watch, to record, to study, to theorize about fellow man and the environment. Using lessons from life and the environment, I became a socioecologist.

And I think that's the key for all of us. I know it's egotistical to a fault, but *you all* have to become more like me. This separation between all the social sciences has to end, and the separation between life sciences and social sciences also has to end. Both separations are artificial products of capitalist specialization, and neither will work for tomorrow's world. We have to attend to both environmental problems and social problems at the same time, and do it together.

But that's where Marx comes back to haunt us. Tomorrow's solutions cannot come through the big corporations becoming greener, through greater governmental regulation to the point of the strangulation of innovation, through greater investment in imaginary money markets and imaginary profits that do absolutely nothing for real people. Solutions will come through initiative, collaboration, and independence from the status quo. From new vision and new social structure. That means we need new habits, not reformed old ones; new social ties and not greener old ones; a new sense of social justice built on a global scale, not fairer nationalist ones. Politicians should be careful when they use the "change" word. Because the ride from here on out is going to be so different in so many ways. When the service class decides to lead instead of follow industrialism's old order, our lifestyles will be whisked away, becoming archeological remnants of today's rotting structures. In that old 60's phrase, "You're either on the bus or off the bus," I'm buying my ticket right now. Want to come along?

Chapter 3

Conjuring Up Ghosts—Some Things Must Be Believed to Be Seen

Charles:

During crisis eras faced by our ancestral forbearers, human societies discovered new modes of production that greatly altered socioecological relationships afterwards. As game disappeared, cooperative hunting and gathering gave way to stable agriculture communities; then, farming lost its dominance as commodity production and trade expanded into industrialism. Each step improved the ability of human populations to survive, reproduce, and, ultimately, expand civilization to new frontiers.

Contradictions Push a Social Transformation Forward

Today, we are on the brink of another great transformation in human relationships, instigated by the rise of the service-led mode of production. In the service economy, investment decisions that guide development are properly no longer based in mass production and capitalist accumulation but rather in the promotion of niche markets, diversity, inclusionary politics, and social responsibility—using one's skills, training, education, and opportunities to assist others to achieve their goals. The rise of the service class to dominance means that a new value system will replace the one we are currently familiar with and that a cultural transformation will restructure social relationships, economic organization, and political power in modern society.

But we have also learned from Chew and Diamond that when faced with socioecological crisis, civilizations may well fail to account for the environmental impacts of their existence. Social chaos unfolds, and the collapse of civilization into ruins becomes irreversible. If expanding social chaos marks the first stage of collapse, the disappearance of prevailing civilization from our collective memories is the last. The lessons of lost civilizations are forgotten, only to be reconstructed generations later by archeologists. I wonder about that sometimes. Will global warming and exponential population growth induce a crisis so immense that we, too, will one day be forgotten, our cities abandoned, our lessons lost as small remnants lose touch with their past in the struggle among themselves for survival?

"Ridiculous!" you say.

Christians believe in Armageddon. Native Americans talk of the three former collapses of human life and of an imminent fourth demise. The Maya predict a world turning in 2012. Ruins abound across the globe—signs of great human ingenuity meeting an all too early demise. What happens when humanity is a global culture and neither diversity nor isolation can protect any of us from the flames of overconsumption and blind faith in our own infallibility? Global warming scientists have let loose a clarion call: We are approaching a dramatic ecological crisis if we don't learn to curtail our civilization's impacts soon. Calamity will ensue. Sociologists have issued their own warnings: We are not in the least ready to deal with the social crisis that will accompany major ecosystem failure and social change. In spite of our general belief in human infallibility, the world capitalist system has not reduced social inequality. Many have benefited from modern finance, production, and consumption, but all told, global industrial relations have increased poverty to new levels and the phantom of daily misery now envelopes more people than ever before. The specter of social chaos has not been driven away by free-market capitalism even though the world has accumulated previously unimagined wealth under industrial leadership. Fear haunts us more than ever, and the world's middle class rarely sleeps contently for very long.

I never put too much stock in human infallibility. History reports that all too many of us will persist in our ignorance, retaining patriotic fervor toward past glories regardless of early warning signs of global disaster. We have problems looking ahead even when we must. But I do find considerable hope in human agency and ingenuity, in the ability of humans to make change through collective choice and directed social action. Social philosophers call that "praxis," linking critical perspectives of society to choice and action. The question remains as to whether we can harness the willpower to make the choices that experience, including scientific evidence, tells us we must make. Our system, as Chapters 1 and 2 presented, has always come up short of the expectations it set for itself and believed. Five *dark ages*. But there is hope. There are other ways.

For the last forty years, the signs of a great transition in human productive relations have become more evident with each passing year. The old order, the industrial mass production era, is passing away. Resources are being used up by exponentially expanding human population, species are rapidly disappearing, and ecosystems are failing; climate is changing faster than scientists can predict it, and world poverty has reached new heights. War, criminal violence, terrorism, and genocide are also on the march. Necessary solutions no longer fit the values and constraints of the industrial mode of production.

More production may offer some type of hope, in the form of factory jobs, to the impoverished, but it also assures faster global degradation. The great contradiction of the modern industrial age is that more ultimately means less. We can't afford greater military operations on every front to protect our own energy supply lines for our overconsumptive lifestyles. We can't stop the migration of people seeking opportunity and escaping hopelessness in a world divided between developed and underdeveloped countries. We can't even figure out whether we should invest in science or ignore its conclusion that we are causing the greatest of threats to our own lifestyles—global warming. We know solutions exist, but we can't stand the idea of doing with less. Industrialism was the theory that by marshalling labor in dehumanized situations we could create more products for everyone. It has turned into a nightmare of foolish consumption and extravagance for many, and lost hope for the rest.

In contrast, service is the willing assistance given by one to another to help the latter achieve his or her goals. Think about that for a moment. In the service-led mode of production, we produce to facilitate the livelihoods of others. In the process, we earn our own rights and standards of living, but the core of our daily work is to yield to the dictates and desires of others, not as slaves, but as people whose skills, training, education, and experience can transform knowledge into effective, goal-oriented service. I wonder what a world would be like if people received wages based on the effectiveness of their service to others. If human society survives the coming crisis, we will find out.

The new mode of production carries a new set of values and norms of behavior for its members, families, social groups, and production crews. Industrialism was based in individual property rights, inheritance, and wealth for those who applied science first to mass production and who, in that application, could enlist the largest possible workforce at the lowest possible wages. It was based on unwise profit rationalization that sanctioned the abuse of land and labor power. Industrialism grew through the drive to gain more of everything from monopolizing knowledge, markets, and opportunity. I find it a mystery how the service-led mode of production could even blossom in such stultifying conditions. But it has. Like the forest phoenix that follows a wildfire, seeds of renewal arrive when the moment is most bleak. For those willing to look at the world with a critical eye, the moment of change is at hand.

The service-led mode of production rejects much of what the previous one held dear, not because a bunch of people met together and decided to attack the system, but because the possibilities created by industrialism inevitably generated more demands from humanity than mass production could ever fulfill. Industrialism could change its technology, its sector investment policies, even its global location, but it could not change the cultural basis it was built on. To survive, industrialism and green revolution agriculture—that is, agribusiness and chemical- and oil-based agriculture—needed low-paid workers, cheap resources, public subsidies, and mass markets to counter diminishing profit margins. To achieve their production goals, industrialists naturally spurred ethnic and racial divisions, nationalism that allowed foreign exploitation, state tariff and tax protection from competition, a military for conquest, and a police back-up when times got tough and workers too rebellious.

But service providers demand recognition of their skills, respect for their ethnic identity, rights as individuals (human rights), and health care and retirement benefits distributed society-wide rather than just for accomplished special interests. The service economy needs negotiation and peace to maintain access to niche markets in a highly competitive world. It needs shared information and collaboration between user groups. It requires that the opportunity structure be open to all because service needs the best minds and most skilled to rise to the top, not just the well-connected sons and daughters of the rich. The service economy demands public scrutiny over government and corporations. Service values are ultimately incompatible with industrial culture, but because one mode of production arises from within the other, it is often hard to distinguish between the two during the development phase of the new mode. Now we must. Our world is threatened.

A new mode of production produces new class relationships. That means that stratification in society takes a different form than it did in the past and, therefore, that power, wealth, capital, and knowledge are distributed along different lines and for different reasons.

Marx established the baseline theory for analyzing social strata. His was the first voice to make the case that class interests in modern society and the industrial mode of production were characterized by a contradictory dialectic between wage workers and capitalist owners. Capitalism maximizes profits by keeping labor cheap so, Marx thought, the central capitalist contradiction could not be resolved without restructuring society and social relationships in favor of workers. He promoted the necessity of socialist revolution—the overthrow of the capitalist state and its replacement with one in which the means of production are owned, through the state, by the working class.

Yet, history reveals that years of revolutionary activity by workers, peasants, and intellectuals failed to restructure the class contradictions of industrialism. Socialists became leaders by taking on roles in government and industry not all that different from those in capitalist nations. Cultural materialism suggests that conditions at any given time limit the choices that leaders of a society can make, so it is no real surprise that socialist efforts to reform capitalism proved unsuccessful. Industrialism in the twentieth century was still expanding, gathering momentum, and sweeping more and more countries into its international web. During the internationalization of capitalism—the Marxists called it imperialism—only a small portion of social surplus was invested to ameliorate social inequality. Most of the accumulating wealth was absorbed as private profit-taking, and while a few became rich, most of us in the imperial nations simply found it easier to get by.

But along that path toward relative well-being, often labeled the middle class lifestyle, we lost our way, became complacent, and failed to extend those benefits to others. Why? Because most of us came to believe in the culture of inevitable growth. More resources, more goods, more commerce, more gain. Eventually everyone would benefit, so there was little reason to worry or care. Yet today, as the frontiers for expansion rapidly shrink, we already know that everyone didn't share in the benefits of growth. Industrialism's day is done.

Or at least, it should be. You see, the choice is ours. We can let industrialism drive on to its own inevitable collapse into its own *dark age*, or we can embrace the new mode of production and restructure human society around it.

What the Marxists could not know in their time is that a new social contract—in their dream, socialism—can only be forged on the basis of an emergent, developing mode of production. Further, new modes of production only arise when a socioecological crisis—the contradiction between rising population and depleting natural resources—force their inadvertent emergence. In the hundred years from 1850 to 1950, when socialism built its case and practical momentum, industrialism was always ascendant, and its class realities were inherent. The mere desire of the socialists to transcend this reality could never, in fact, surmount it. Despite their ideals, they succumbed to the same imperatives as the industrialists in capitalist production and society. Ironically, it was Mao who first acknowledged the phenomena when, in the mid-1960s, he labeled Khrushchev "a socialist in words, an imperialist in deeds." Yet, despite efforts to overcome the historic imperatives set by capital, Chinese production and finance have increased their ties to international capitalist markets since that time, not reduced them.

Today, due to the crises of population growth and global natural resource depletion, a new mode of production is emergent. Indeed, it developed in the aftermath of WWII, during post-war Pax Americana and the Cold War. Faced with the impossibility of ever competing successfully in the international commodity markets of the 50s in which the U.S. and the U.S.S.R. were hegemonic, recovering capitalists in Europe and, especially, Japan opted to serve various niche markets that the American mass producers ignored. The classic example is the small, fuel-efficient automobile (VW's, Nissans, and Toyotas), but the Japanese made all kinds of inexpensive, innovative products in order to regain a foothold in international manufacturing markets. In the process, they discovered niche production and the service-led economy, leading the world toward global restructuring.

Niche production is not about hegemony. Of course, every producer wants to serve as large a market as possible, but investors in niche production have no illusion that they someday will control and dominate extensive markets. Rather, they embrace the reality that they will always be adapting and moving on to new niches. They build their enterprises with the necessity of flexibility firmly in mind.

Today, the stark difference between mass commodity production (industrialism) and niche, service-led production is obvious to anyone who looks for it, but old frameworks die hard. Despite the clear changes in the production model that attracts investment in today's world, economists, politicians, and social activists persist in viewing these as mere quantitative developments rather than a qualitative change. This failure is fundamental to their inability to grasp the way out of today's financial debacle as well as the larger socioecological crisis.

In 1915, Lenin explained how the interests of industrialists and bankers had merged, forming what he called finance capital, a coalition that dominated international politics and economics in the last century. But today we need to rewrite his thesis. The interests of the banks and the industrialists are diverging. Industrialism—mass commodity production—is strategically unsustainable. Naturally and inevitably, investors are moving their money into other channels—service-oriented development, niche production, and speculative finance markets.

Who makes the capital investment decisions in our new global economy— and in what they invest—has changed, demonstrating that a new mode of production has taken root. Real industrial investment has been negative in developed countries for decades, surviving in the underdeveloped world only through labor exploitation and resource degradation quite equivalent to industrial practice in Marx's time—grossly dehumanizing yet still providing liberating opportunities for poor workers and peasants. Industrial development in China, India, Mexico, Brazil, and Indonesia represents the growth of the multimodal global industrial economy that is no longer centered on American production.

In place of real industrial investment, however, global investment from developed nations has diversified. Much of this investment supports advanced systems of information exchange, communications, inventory management, real-time production facilities, alternative energy, scientific research, and human capital, including global public health and the steady expansion of civil society. However, a huge and decisive amount of investment—concentrated in consumer credit, banking, insurance, mortgages, and stock, bond, and money market transactions—takes the form of speculative financial investment. It serves no purpose other than self-centered accumulation for a relatively small subsector of the economy. Many of the investment firms bailed out by tax-payers in 2008 and 2009 were lending thirty dollars for every real dollar behind their transactions, and some 50 percent of loans went to finance debt repurchasing schemes rather than to any investment at all. We are watching the roots of those greedy and wasteful private investment gambles unravel today.

Let's look further at that contradiction in investment strategies, the one between real and speculative capital investment. The finance sector of the service class takes decentralized working class and service class earnings and turns those into speculative capital, using savings deposits made in the day to finance buyers and sellers in foreign stock markets, in futures markets, in currency markets, and in international bond markets at night. Most money is never "saved" nowadays, just placed into an endless and seamless system of financial transactions that moves money from low return accounts to higher return accounts whenever possible. Low-return accounts represent the savings of workers and professionals in retirement funds, money markets, and checking deposits. Finance managers reinvest this money in riskier, higher rate global funds in hopes of making a profit for private investors and investor organizations before depositors need their money returned. As long as the global economy is growing, the risk is not particularly high, and the deregulated (since Reagan) financial sector can gamble away on speculative stocks, bonds, and investments using other people's money. When the system fails—as it did in 2008 and has done at least twice every decade for the last forty years—depositors must bail out the risk takers. There's no more spectacular example of this practice than the current financial crisis that cost U.S. tax-payers nearly a trillion dollars to stabilize.

Beyond the obvious direct, taxpayer financed government loan guarantees is another critical, yet often overlooked practice. Risk takers must find real wealth to liquidate as fast as possible to buttress their illusionary wealth with real value. When the specter of financial retraction sets in, investors scramble to gather funds to protect their own resources through a rash of speculative buy-outs of companies with real resources with the goal of rapid liquidation. Logging in the Pacific Northwest has been a good example. Over the last few decades, financial speculators in trouble found a goldmine of cash reserves in the old growth forests whose harvests kept them one step ahead of their own creditors and their own credit noose. In the process, the world lost much of one of the world's greatest ecosystems.

Neoconservative ideologues were successful in separating investment from its responsibility to protect national industries in the 1980s. They successfully globalized currency, using their financial might to punish rogue nations who were experimenting with socialized investments and to bring them into the global capitalist fold under strict policies of the multilateral institutions—the International Monetary Fund, the World Bank, the Inter-American Development Bank, and the World Trade Organization. Currency, banking, and trade policies were systematized worldwide. Unable to survive open global competition because of their high-priced labor pool, industries in developed countries found it cheaper to export factories than products, sending the jobs that went with them to cheap labor markets in Mexico, Southeast Asia, India, Pakistan, and China. Into the political and economic vacuum came financial capital—banks, insurance companies, stock brokerage firms, accounting firms, investment managers, and other service professionals—whose role was to use money to make money without investing it in an intermediate level of real goods production. Finance capital replaced industrial capital at the helm of governments around the world.

Industrialism floundered, with most surviving companies making it not by the profits of their production, but by diversifying holdings to include high-profit finance and credit operations. General Motors proffered its own auto loans and Home Depot its own credit cards to capture additional profits. Manufacturing became secondary. Service-led production—unfortunately, dominated by its most self-centered sector—had finally become ascendant.

The Service Class

Understanding this systemic change is central to understanding the choices before us now. The nature of the service class and the character of its own internal contradictions determine what we can do in the near future for social development—both for the social justice necessary to prevent widespread social rebellion and for addressing concerns of global warming and ecological diversity.

The new mode of service-led production is strange fruit. It's been able to operate with very little scrutiny because no one developed a theory that pinpoints its strengths and weaknesses, its contradictions, and its classes. With society failing to comprehend its make-up and character, the default leadership of the service class—the financial services industry—has avoided critiques that suggest that the way service is currently organized is neither beneficial to society at-large nor to the interests of small capital accumulators—workers, homeowners, small business, even most service professionals. Small capital accumulation interests are distinguished from finance capital by the following.

- They save money based on real earnings in the field of mass production and direct service, *not in servicing finance exclusively.*
- They invest in projects that generally have lower rates of return and usually involve forms of real property.
- They generally have little knowledge of international finance regulations and practices and commonly rely on others to invest what savings they have.

- They are more risk aversive and less likely to want to invest in speculative finance.

- They are decentralized and independent of other investors.

All of these factors indicate that when we talk about service, we must differentiate between different levels of financial service on the basis of who is serviced and how detached their investments are in terms of real property and real lives. We must differentiate between servicing speculation and servicing real social investment.

Let's start with my brother's assumption—further elaborated in his response to this chapter—that all service providers are part of the same class, the service class. To clarify the assumption, the professional who works everyday as the CEO of Fannie Mae is part of the same class as the worker who provides assistance to you when you buy a new cell phone or dine at an ethnic restaurant. They are united in that they bring personal skills and education, known as human capital, to the economic arena, and they use those talents promoting the health, welfare, income, and property of others. Their possession and development of particular forms of human capital—including college and business school education as well as other avenues of personal talent development—allows them access into the opportunity structure of society where they sell their skills in a highly competitive labor market. In fact, the transformation of the economy into a service-led one means that these skills will continue to have enormous value because they already are essential to global market continuation and expansion.

But the service world is global, not national, and its workings are inherently inclusive. Anyone can play, if they have the talent and skills. The capital flight of industry has served to vastly accelerate the growth of economic centers beyond the U.S. and Europe, opening competition for service jobs to an increasingly global service workforce. In the service-led mode of production, neither jobs nor skills can be protected within national boundaries precisely because neither production nor finance nor knowledge knows boundaries anymore. We can feel sorry for those who are losing their jobs and livelihoods to globalization, and we can and should support significant investment to alleviate their circumstances, but we cannot stop the inevitable process that drives recurrent industrial unemployment. Instead, we need to understand and adapt to the changes around us.

Service work has inundated our lives. Health care, entertainment, banking, international development, and peacekeeping—they all fit the basic service description. So do teachers and foster care parents, stock brokers in Hong Kong and London, computer technicians virtually everywhere. They all are compensated to keep our business and lives going smoothly because they have the goods—the knowledge and networks—to keep us afloat. So much diversity. That's a lot different than industrial roles where someone told employees what to do every minute of the day or where a salesperson sold goods so someone else could make a lot of money off their work.

Service providers in general, and service professionals in particular, demand flexibility and control over their knowledge and training, at least in a general sense. When they don't get it, they move on, leaving employers stranded or with substandard workers. Not surprisingly, service providers have enforced new work disciplines that include flexible hours (even though they often work more hours in a week due to their incessant work regimes), greater benefits, higher salaries, and less domination by bosses. They like teamwork and networking because individual skills can shine at the conference table. These are not small things—they will become increasingly standard for workers throughout the world. In fact, I personally dream for American businesses to adopt European work standards as part of the global service work regime—shorter work weeks and longer vacations periods, even the right to take extended vacations without pay without losing one's job! In Europe, rising service demands for workplace flexibility could build on previous left-wing organizing in the industrial mode of production. In the U.S., anti-communist ideological dominance squashed union importance long ago and left many of its major social aims outside of daily political debates, forcing, as seen in the current debate over health care reform, a reinvention of the wheel rather than a logical path toward progressive and fair health care system.

Of course, you are beginning to doubt my rationality, because many service providers don't come close to having all the rights listed above. Nurses work long hours with few benefits, a bit like Catholic nuns, and have considerably fewer opportunities to jump ship to another hospital with better working conditions than do better paid finance sector workers. It's true. Not all members of the service class operate on the same plane. This is a product of a service culture still in its infancy, of industrial mentality still ruling our lives in spite of the fact that it is essentially spent. We must remain sensitive to differentials between service providers because the differences go a long way in explaining why, in spite of a new mode of production, we still face a looming crisis of human and ecological survival.

Marx talked about a "class in itself" with class consciousness. Among other things, he said, a class in itself is one that has developed historically to the point that *it no longer just serves the interests of other classes, but has learned to reproduce itself and its own class culture.*

The service class has achieved this reproductive capability. Business schools produce corporate managers, bankers, accountants, stock brokers, and monetary fund regulators, and sociology schools produce social workers, international development consultants, and, even, their share of lawyers. Private technology institutes yield computer graphics designers and advertising specialists, while religious organizations fill volunteer organizations with well-meaning assistants. These schools serve as examples of creeping prowess in the reproduction of service culture. Moreover, none of the above schools and training programs enrolls exclusionary clientele—they are open to qualified personnel of all classes and ethnic backgrounds. That violates the essence of industrial culture that divided people by class, race, gender, and age. What they do is teach, first and foremost and very subtlety, the service-led culture of inclusion.

A second part of Marx's definition of "a class in itself" is more difficult to assess and comprehend. To be a class, he said, *a class must have self-consciousness about it, a sense of belonging, a sense of responsibility to each other, and a sense of duty in terms of the larger class culture.* It must appreciate and pursue its distinct interests as a class (which may also advance the interests of other classes). That clearly does not exist today, anywhere, in service class centers.

The reason that the service class lacks self-consciousness and, thus, the capacity for collective conscience in terms of its responsibilities in wider society is a matter of contradictions. The ultimate contradiction among all people is to believe we are independent actors and thinkers just because our minds and bodies are our own. Cultural materialists laugh at the thought of individual independence, Ayn Rand and Roark be damned. From birth we are socialized into our society, taught that its values and norms make sense and that its history is valiant and significant. Believe me, as an American, that's a lot of story to accept outright! Most of us never learn to look at our own lives critically, and many that do end up alcoholics and drug addicts. These people often tend to appear as our voices of conscience, our poets, our radicals, but only rarely as our leaders.

Contradictions in the service class are three, at least three principle ones.

First, the class is so diverse and so distinctly divided by its roles and benefits related to compensation and investment that it's pretty hard to imagine it ever acting as a single group. Dreams of class solidarity never seem to materialize as reality. But if we think about this for a moment, we realize that feudal lords once felt that serfdom suited peasants quite well enough; colonialists enjoyed the fruits of slavery for centuries; capitalists accepted child labor without qualms. Oppressors have developed cultural rationalizations, called *logics*, for their class positions, and we grow up socialized and educated to embrace these views. But even socialization can be countered. Workers organized for revolution for a hundred years to gain a better standard of living; peasants organized to overthrow government after government that dared try carry feudal relations into the twentieth century. Class consciousness is a real social force and has been for centuries. This century will be marked by the growth of service class consciousness.

A second contradiction is that a service class with self-consciousness would have to put down nationalism and accept global responsibility for providing service. It would have to renounce inequality, political repression, and poverty as inimical to the values of service work. What would be the point of service work if it did not leave the client better off than before? It's not like nations or national cultures have to be abandoned. Chicanos—who always have been American citizens (being born and raised here)—need not reject their Mexican and Indian roots, quit speaking Spanish in the home, nor denounce people fighting ethnic injustice and for immigrant rights, and nationalism is similar. Nationalism is just reduced in importance, and many of the regulatory roles of present-day government will be passed on to civil society organizations that tend to carry out programs with far less racism than the industrial-based state ever did. Global holism is a practical necessity, not a religion.

This brings us to the third major contradiction, the question of speculative investment in securities markets versus real investment in civil society organizations—known as non-governmental organizations (NGOs)— that deal with business development, scientific research, urban renewal, or environmental protection. The first lives off gambling addictions, using other people's money to, hopefully, cash in on high, short-term profits. Think about the recent and on-going speculative crises—the sub-prime mortgage crisis brought on by speculation in the housing market, the energy crisis brought about by speculation in the oil futures, and, upcoming, the speculation on the value of American currency that will ultimately produce a devalued dollar and erode the earning power and savings of Americans. Believe me, other speculative crises have occurred over the last three decades. Speculative investment, such as the risk taking associated with unproven technology, is helpful to innovation and technological change in some situations, but hardly to the degree and breadth that its self-touting media message accords. Mostly, speculation is a wealthy man's gambling activity that Congress, government officials, bankers, and money managers accept because they, too, are trained to rely on it. They are addicted to it. The rest of us can just guess what's really going on behind their closed doors. What makes speculative investment so criminal is that 'they' take risks using *our* money, knowing that when the die is cast—which it *always* is—we'll have no choice but to ante up to cover their bets.

Speculative service activity runs contrary to service values, to the idea of helping real people with real problems using specialized training and education. The service class needs a conscience as much as it needs consciousness. It must recognize its own value system and demand that this value system take command of politics and the global economy. When we talk of a cultural transformation under the service-led mode of production, we emphasize the need for a different value system and its importance to future global decision-making and solutions.

The dichotomy between speculative and real investment finds its expression in the rise of civil society and its wide range of non-governmental organizations that promote human rights and the empowerment of the marginalized in global development, that is, development from the bottom up. Civil society represents a mode of production refinement of freedom itself, an acknowledgement that in a scientific world any individual and group may have the tools to make capable management decisions. The days of science being controlled by industry technicians and government agencies are over. Modern education has given rise to scientific wisdom outside of imperial agencies. Citizen science, that of self-educated community investigators and the science of independent professionals, has already proven its importance to political decision-making, revealing gaping problems in communities with chemical pollution, ecological destruction, global warming, and oil energy dependence. Advocacy science has also demonstrated its positive propensities through investigations and work projects that prove the potentials of alternatives that favor habitat restoration, renewable energy, and responsible social action. We call this ground-up science *socioecology*.

Civil society has become the conscience of the service-led mode of production, the voice of reason in discussions on where and how society must develop in the future to protect human survival. Civil society is horribly underfunded at the moment, and it must constantly fight for legitimacy against government and corporate hegemony. As such, non-governmental organizations, though they have the answers or, at least, know what direction to advance, are never strong enough to adequately deal with the nature of the problems they face. When we finally find a way to fund civil society and to give it the political power to make those society-guiding decisions that will be necessary to deal with global warming and global social inequality, we will be able to say that the service-led economy has finally reached maturity. Service workers and professionals will be self-conscious of their role and value in society, and they will have a collective conscience to guide their actions. A new social contract will have formed.

Much of what passes as civil society work now is supported by private contributions, foundation grants from corporate profit accumulations, and government assistance programs. To date, NGOs have been extremely good at pinpointing solutions to problems from the perspectives of the victims of political persecution, economic stagnation, and ecological disasters. But competition for funding is so ruthless that most programs lose funding after a number of years, and even those with sustained funding find themselves overwhelmed by the need for their services. Furthermore, since their funding comes from the centers of wealth and power in our current society, the independence of their work is often compromised and questioned. Rarely are they allowed to advance recommendations regarding the necessity of major restructuring of the global political-economic system.

The call to restructure the global economic system is part and parcel of an effective program of political advocacy in the course of this century. Systemic restructuration is needed to unleash the power of the service class. As much as anything, the recent, almost ludicrous profit-taking by oil companies and the speculation of investment banks demonstrate the need to reorganize how socioeconomic relations work. Letting the same people who have facilitated the massive overconsumption of society and who have been responsible for cycles of global financial failure to continue making decisions for us makes no sense. Barry Commoner (1990) has for years advocated that the economic realm needs control by civil society in order to turn investment from processes threatening ecological health to restorative programs. But as long as non-governmental organizations are tied to the purse strings of business-based philanthropy and government, they cannot fulfill their necessary role as social critic. Establishing a source for the financial independence of NGOs through a global commercial transactions fee is one of our major proposals.

Adding a Cautionary Voice...

Well, that's more or less the rudimentary theory of the service class. I wrote it, but I am not quite so sure what to do with it. I have lingering questions about both the nature of the service class—you know, its make-up including the assumption that it is only one class—and whether it can actually lead us anywhere forward and at a pace necessary to fix global problems before it's too late. I suspect you feel the same ambiguity. These questions relate to just what service values are supposed to replace the gross profiteering and accepted suffering under industrial capitalism and just how science, which has largely been industrialism's servant, must be adapted to actually help the planet survive.

My vision of the ultimate service provider is the auto mechanic that services your car. I mean, even without union protection mechanics have carved out a marvelous spot in our social structure on the basis that they know something we do not: auto diagnosis, car parts, and their replacement. But far beyond the simple payment for their labor, you might notice they command high wages for their services, often $35/hour, even in remote rural areas. That's a product of their training and experience and their ability to use a niche market. True enough, mechanics were critical to the functioning of industrial capitalism, so there is no claim here that skill-based service is new or that niche marketing of that service capability was absent under the former mode of production. In fact, mechanics bolster the argument that the service-led economy is the birth child of industrialism.

But then, nagging doubt has a way of creeping into my own version of reality. While I have had great success learning car mechanics myself, so as to avoid the usual pricey auto maintenance work for which most of you pay, I have been stumped a few times and forced to trust my vehicles to a mechanic. I haven't fared well. One year I paid out $900 for front-end repair on a Toyota station wagon and a new front seal in a Mazda pickup, and neither fixed the vehicle's problem. But in both cases I had to pay the mechanic for the labor of his work, anyway. I found that vexing, paying for pricy services not rendered in a sufficient manner. That's a problem with service. It doesn't always perform the way we want or produce the results we desire, but we have to pay for it anyway. I once had a broken tooth, for example, that two dentists concurred had to be pulled. The third scrunched up his face at that and said, "Better dentistry through chemistry." He rebuilt my tooth. Not all service providers are worth their mettle. So I'm a bit worried about the customer in service transactions and the tendency for service providers to charge without having to prove their worth. I worry about hype and arrogance, about just what values the service workers are bringing to the table.

I have become a skeptic about service work, not because it isn't essential to my livelihood, but because I rarely have the personal expertise to judge the expertise of the person from whom I require service. We're all specialists nowadays, so how can any one of us know what's up with other specialties? To some degree, we rely on professional associations to police their own members or schools to offer the proper training to students or the mysterious labor "market" that supposedly pays more adept providers more for their skills than less skilled service professionals. But don't count on it. Sometimes, when I find I have to go to some service provider or other, I wonder if the used car salesman culture hasn't pervaded the entire service industry! Sell 'em a bill of goods, not service that really helps!

Another doubt I have with this theory is that I don't think I am particularly qualified to talk about service culture or what its make-up should be. I have lived a life way too independent from modern economics to pretend to understand how the whole system works. But I know that when it comes to service, the client has a fair right to have an opinion about it, and when things do not go well, an established right to jump ship and choose another service provider. Thus, the marginalized people of the world find themselves with more voice than they ever had under industrialism which merely barged in and took their labor, resources, and lands for private profiteering. Service must yield results, better results, and if it doesn't, then clients have not only the right to find another provider but, also, to advise others against the failings of the first. That rarely happens today, mostly because the costs of advertising are such that only the wealthy and the large companies can afford media propaganda. But in a service-led mode of production with conscience, the right of critique will be guaranteed. And as women and blacks have demonstrated, there ain't no rights unless we also have the means to use them. In the Information Age, for example, we must not allow the Internet to be controlled by fear mongers or corporations who restrict our right to transmit criticisms of their weak performance.

One of the problems we have is that many end results of service actions are the products of very vague forces, so that even when we employ science to make better decisions, we sometimes cannot predict outcomes. Thus, when scientists try to measure global warming, they often find themselves relying on models they, themselves, created rather than on carefully collected environmental data. That sounds fishy to those of us who are not scientists. But there are reasons behind this. Data collection itself is often whimsical and is done only if a particular researcher chooses to research the problem in the first place and then can devise ways to research it thoroughly. All data is necessarily fragmented and partial when describing real conditions (Pielou 1991). Financing for research is capricious, dropping some lines of research and favoring others because of donor or industry preferences, national fears, and lobbying strength, not because researchers think it best. And finally, science is not just fact finding. As often as not, science is the process of tying together multiple sources of diverse information into a single theory, and this takes a special talent and some plum luck on the part of the scientist. Most of us don't have the time to accomplish such things, so we leave theories to academics and research institutes. But sociological studies of natural resource issues make it clear that most of us are unhappy with that scenario (Bocking 2004). We want to command our own knowledge, not rely on others. Service-led production faces a natural animosity among most of us, even as we rely on it.

The diversity of agendas of different special interest groups makes the service-led mode of production difficult to guide. Global warming, water pollution, massive deforestation, hunger, and poverty—these are important problems to be addressed, but they are quite literally of interest only to a small number of us. In fact, many of us profit from and enjoy amenable lifestyles because we support and work in the status quo, energy-intensive economy that produces greenhouse gases and massive social inequality in the first place. We don't want to hear about restructuring our world for ecological preservation or for the betterment of others.

Global warming science shares the same problem that revolutionary socialism and population science have faced—too many people gain by the status quo even though it's not good for the majority of people. We need global warming science that involves political advocacy for real change. Such science should permit a rising standard of living and greater security for most of the world's people. Successful climate change science will keep population growth in check and people out of sensitive ecological zones. Most climate change models used by scientists don't even consider these social variables, discounting them as irrelevant or secondary to biological and physical models of earth systems. Last year, I read seven of the most recent books on global warming and came away horribly disenchanted. It is time that socioecologists lead climate change science. Socioecology does not pretend that we're all in the same boat, all with the same interests. When people acknowledge their differences, we come to understand that simple technological solutions just aren't the answer. Social restructuring is also necessary. We need to argue out differences in public, and that requires that media access be opened up to critical viewpoints.

So maybe we need new types of political advocates, too, to go with the expansion of the global service field. All the scientific data in the world by itself will not bring social forces around to slowing capitalism's use of energy and natural resources. As my friend said in my comments in the response to the last chapter, that's going to take a whole new perspective on life, a new vocabulary of cooperation, a different value system that begins by helping people and ecology.

Throughout this book, we look for answers to the dilemma of science in the service-led economy. Neutrality and objectivity only go so far. Useful change demands debate, critique, struggle, and the willingness to put some ideas aside and to guide people into working for others. This is the nature of socioecology. We all must learn its lessons and take a stance in this new service world we live in.

Chapter 3 Response

Servers of the World, Unite!

Steve:

In 2000, at the urging of my son, I invested in a new business he wanted to establish in Myrtle Beach, South Carolina. The region—the most remote and last-developing beach economy on the east coast—was then in the midst of a twenty-year boom. The area was awash in new construction—homes, golf courses, retail outlets, entertainment centers, roadways, and bridges. My son and his partner, both truck mechanics in Maryland, thought they could get a new lease on life by opening a big truck—cement mixers, dump trucks—repair shop in Myrtle Beach.

Their business plan was simple, and it would have worked well except for one thing they didn't anticipate. They thought they were opening a truck repair shop, but it turned out they were actually opening a small lending institution.

No sooner had they signed a lease, purchased initial inventory, and put the sign on the shop than the customers came running. They were excited. But there was a catch. No one wanted to pay cash. Everyone was used to credit, and the new business had to offer it.

No sweat, it seemed. The repair shop's suppliers would sell to them on credit, too. It seemed simple. Buy parts on time, then sell service on time. It'd all balance out in the long run.

But, no, it didn't balance out at all. My son and his partner were mechanics, not credit managers, and the learning curve was sharp. A few customers filled out the credit application, got the work done, and just never paid. Ouch. But, worse than that actually, it soon became apparent that most of the paying customers wouldn't pay on time. Thirty days passed, and some accounts drifted in. Another thirty days, some more. The last few came at ninety days.

Parts vendors weren't as kind to the business as it had to be to its customers. To keep our credit good, we had to pay vendors on time. Nine months into things—despite a growing customer base—the business was in trouble, which means I, the investor, was in trouble. Our entire cash reserve had been consumed in credit extension. And to take advantage of the opportunity in the market, that is, to expand as far as the potential customer base appeared to allow, the business needed to extend even more credit, an average of about sixty days worth on every account. My son reported, "Dad, we've got nothing left. If we're going to make it, we've got to have more capital." A few days later, we were back at the bank, increasing the size of our start-up loan by a whopping 67 percent. Not money I had intended to guarantee, but there seemed no way back. And, the bank was more than willing. What, borrow almost twice as much, just six months into the business plan? No trouble, said Wachovia (which was one of the first to disappear in the 2008 crisis, bought out by a larger competitor). It was all easy, too easy.

This is the way things worked, back in the go-go 90s and a few years afterwards, before the financial bubble burst. We just wanted to provide truck repair services in a growing construction market. As it turned out, we had to become a mini-bank in the process. No doubt we weren't the only ones. Seems like, these days, the whole economy is run on the credit-debt cycle. Everything works on a line of credit, and nothing is ever fully paid off. No one ever really has the desire or chance to actually save something for a rainy day. Under modern rules of trade, you either play broke, or you don't play at all.

Today, I'm resentful of this because, eight years after it started, my son's business has gone bankrupt, and I'm the one who guaranteed the loan. In retrospect, it's easy to see what happened. In the late 80s, Myrtle Beach began to fill in with retirees seeking a cheaper alternative to other more highly developed enclaves along the east coast. In the 90s, on the basis of this rising demand and Clinton-era tax "reform" that made mortgage interest on second homes deductible, the area boomed to prominence on the strength of the housing market. Developers went wild, building acres of new homes and retail centers to service the mushrooming retirement and vacation economy. By the time my son picked up on the opportunity, the boom was in full swing. But, only seven years later, in 2007, the bubble had burst.

The sub-prime mortgage crisis of 2008 brought the bubble to everyone's attention, but nearly a year earlier, our business was among the first to notice problems. Unfortunately, in the first quarter of 2007, just before the crash, we committed to a second loan to purchase land and build a large new facility of our own. The month after we bought the land, there was a sudden, precipitous drop in our monthly revenue. We were shocked. We put an instant hold on the construction phase…and lucky we did. That was the first month of what became a persistent decline in sales and revenues. Construction in Myrtle Beach ground to a halt.

More than half of the customer base went bankrupt or closed. Without construction, the big trucks left the area. At first, we shifted into the box trucks of companies that serviced the local economy, but, with a surplus of delivery trucks relative to their own declining sales, companies starting pulling any truck with major repairs off the road. Soon, the only work we got was oil changes and minor repairs, not enough to sustain operations. Gradually but steadily, we laid off all our employees. By the end of 2008, my son and his partner, the owners, were the only ones left to turn the wrenches. Saddled with mounting, unpaid customer accounts, the business was unable to pay its own vendors so its vendor debt went way past due. Forced into a cash-on-delivery program with its suppliers, the business then required cash from its customers. Taking that as a cue, another round of customers retreated into the "underground" economy, leaving us with their accounts receivable. In January, 2009, we faced the music, shut the doors, and entered bankruptcy.

I'd feel better if I had been one of the "big boys" who rode the bubble up and, now, must endure its puncture. But, like so many other small businesses, I didn't ride it up. Foolishly…well, no, I don't buy that we were foolish, but in retrospect it sure looks that way…we bought into the boom (who knew?) way too late to get anything out of it. We just borrowed and lent because that seemed the only way to make the business work. So, here I am, the chief investor in a business, the guarantor of its loans, and it has gone under. Our business was hardly unique. Ninety percent of businesses in the United States employ less than twenty workers, but, together, they employ the vast majority of people. Across the country, these small businesses have gone—and are going—bankrupt like nobody's business. And nothing in the bailout or stimulus packages is helping at all. Those are start-at-the-top plans, designed to make sure the biggest banks don't collapse. The big boys have a real problem, but they're the ones who created this bubble and collected their profit as it expanded. And tax credits for small business is a Republican hoax. Most small businesses don't make enough profit to pay much corporate or business tax; instead, they support the government through their payroll taxes and collection of sales tax. We need a stimulus plan that gets to the economic grassroots, not by trickle-down, but by real, direct support and investment. It's outside the box, but it could be done. Why not set up local development committees, including local banks that depend on small business, to distribute stimulus money to local operations?

Hell, yes, I hate the banks. But, "don't get mad, get even," someone once said, and I sure hope I find a way. This book would love to spark a prairie fire of resistance against both bank and federal ineptitude in managing our economy. Today, we have no effective social contract, only lip service to the dead New Deal contract of the 1930s. Security for small businesses, their owners, and their workers is a thing of the past. Collusion between government and corporations is blatant, and the government is first committed to the big banks. The Supreme Court kicked off the 2010 election campaign by guaranteeing corporations the right to invest as fully in politics as they wish. How obvious does corporate hegemony have to get for politicians to support their own citizenry?

Service Age Social Security

Clearly, we need a new system, based on a new social contract, one that turns the corner from supporting mass industry to creating new space and stability for smaller enterprise and which strengthens our social security networks. Specifically—and appropriately for these times—let's look at the question of personal and family security, comparing the nature of security in the industrial era to what the service era has to offer.

Security is a basic human need, so the culture of every age must have a way to address it. During the Agricultural Age, the ethics of feudal relations obligated both the lords and peasants of the manor to watch out for each other and the land; in times of crisis, they had to pull together. Not so in the Industrial Age. Under the reigning principles of private accumulation, whether an industrialist or a proletarian, each individual is "free" to pursue his or her own security through savings, investment, or, if feasible, the exploitation of others. That process was never fair nor meant to be so.

With the individual so supremely enshrined in the mythology of industrialism and its framework of citizenship, the potential of collective and negotiated security arrangements was constantly derided. Only in the last century of the Industrial Age did experience and insight develop enough among proletarians for them to create unions, bargain collectively, and, eventually, forge the social consciousness to demand that states provide some measure of "social security" for all citizens. Nevertheless, whether under socialist states like the Soviet Union, China, or Cuba or under capitalist states and their social welfare programs, real security for most people remains to this day largely a private matter. As the present financial crisis again makes clear, even in developed nations, security for each individual or family is ultimately a personal concern.

Just as earlier ages had their own way of providing security, the Service Age will surmount the lagging failures of the bureaucratic and centralized welfare state to create its own. Its security system may become known as "network security."

Network security is the kind of security that comes from being part of a well-run, well-established, service-exchange network. As my brother noted, in the emerging service economy, humans will ultimately survive by exchanging services with each other in a vast, highly complex, global web. People, communities, commercial enterprises, states, international federations, and civil society entities are nodes in this web, linked through connections of all sorts. Because this global network is relatively new and, so far, one-sidedly dominated by the power elites of the last era, it is but a skeleton of what it can and must become for successful survival in the epoch ahead. Though life and work in this network today appears far less secure than, say, a good job at GM in the 1950s, the full development of service production in the decades ahead will eventually provide more and broader security than the industrial era could ever contemplate.

Getting there, however, isn't going to be easy, as evidenced by governments' response to the current financial crisis. As noted, during 2007 and 2008, the most recent and worst speculative bubble of the Industrial Age exploded, this time rooted in mortgage speculation. For a week or so in September, 2008, the entire system wobbled, threatening a full-scale collapse. Comparisons to the Great Depression were common, and governments were aggressive in asserting a "take charge" attitude. Nevertheless, all they really did was ensure bank liquidity by pouring a trillion dollars into the system, buying time for the big banks to sort through their mess and weather the storm. The storm's still blowing, but, meanwhile, no fundamental change in the system or in the opportunities of banks to speculate was made. The wobble was steadied, but the underlying issues remained unaddressed. Two years later, as we go to press, the on-going effects of speculation in home mortgages has rippled through Iceland, Greece, and Ireland and now threatens Portugal and Spain.

Meanwhile, with so much money already spent on the banks, governments are vulnerable to rightwing charges of "excessive" spending, and they are currently conforming to conservative rhetoric that their debts are too high relative to their gross domestic products (GDPs). Despite the fact that debts relative to GDP still lag significantly behind the highs of the Great Depression/World War II era, by curtailing spending instead of raising revenues, today's governments are actually compounding the depression for small businesses and the general population by cutting government services, forcing layoffs, and trimming demand.

As bad as the conservative remedy is, the liberal remedy doesn't appear much better. The liberal answer to the crisis is more of the same Keynesian programs that helped western nations get through the Great Depression. Famously, Keynes argued that governments should spend freely during a depression to dampen unemployment and put spending money in people's pockets. While government debt will pile up, it can be repaid through tax revenues after the depression ends and economic expansion returns.

A key problem with Keynesian logic today is that the world's economy is service-based and service-driven. Commodity production, of necessity, has been consigned to the back seat. Moreover, the service mode of production is global, not merely an international patchwork of industrially-driven economies. Most fundamentally, however, today's crisis is not simply another, if larger, cyclical crisis of mass production, such as was that of the 30s. The world got itself out of the Great Depression by (1) using Keynesian spending to ride out the worst, early years, (2) blowing up about half the world's entire industrial capacity during the war, and (3) launching a massive industrial expansion after the war to rebuild Europe while drawing the remaining undeveloped markets of the world into international commodity exchange.

Today's situation is much different because expanded commodity production is not sustainable, which is why the service mode of production came into being in the first place and assumed leadership over global production. Thus, the remedy to today's crisis cannot be the kind of industrial expansion that restored prosperity after World War II.

Nor is the world's industrial capacity currently destroyed, so its re-creation is not going to be a source of growth.

Further, in today's global economy, China dominates commodity production. A nation like the U.S. cannot borrow to keep its people working in expectation of paying off debts through taxes on a future, expanding manufacturing base. Such taxes would have to be collected by China and transferred to the U.S.—and that's not going to happen. Here in the U.S. and in other nations, taxes would have to be levied on more limited, local, but desirable commodity production and on services, which would impose taxes and a regulatory hodgepodge on the global, service-based economy.

Finally, while it is true that the U.S., Britain, and, perhaps, a few other powerhouse nations could expand domestic spending by simply creating funds on account—no real savings is required—they can do so and still command respect for their currencies only because they are at the top of the economic heap. Financial might makes right. But, to expand the U.S. money supply in a globally responsible manner, the Federal Reserve cannot pursue a we'll-pull-you-up-by-the-bootstraps program that, objectively, puts U.S. national interests ahead of the rest of the world's. Instead, it should recognize the superiority of the interest of the whole world over of the American part. That notion, of course, sounds far worse (to Americans) than it should owing to the incessant, narrow nationalist jingoism of the right, but the fact is that America, now, *can best achieve its interests as a nation by pursing them entirely within the framework of holistic, global problem-solving.* Yet, post-nationalism—and its most consistent representative, former U.S. President Jimmy Carter—is consistently bested by the rhetoric of American exceptionalism. Given America's nationalistic framework, it's hard to see how Keynesian spending in the U.S. is going to make the world a better place.

Meanwhile, because currency speculators have become major players in global economics, poorer nation-states and their national currencies would be savaged by speculation if they tried to emulate the U.S. and unilaterally expand their money supplies.

The Keynesian security plan certainly appears more humane, inclusive, constructive, and secure than the all-private, me-first, get-government-off-my-back, hoarding model of the financial conservatives and free marketers. By itself, however, it can't break the critical, mounting logjam of global crises. Nor does it meet the Simultaneity Principle because, unless deeper issues of economic restructuring and economic democracy are first addressed, its contemplation of a future, expanding industrial tax base stands in opposition to restoring global ecology. And don't yelp about how we'll get "back" to the environment after we get out of the immediate crisis. There is no separation between this immediate crisis and the larger one.

Given the forces of the new mode of production that must be liberated and advanced to avoid the coming *dark age*, the only way forward is to invest first and foremost in globally-networked service production and new forms of social organization to make our new mode of production even more expansive, efficient, and effective.

What services? Alternative energy research and development; mass transit design and construction; health care, sewage, and sanitation systems; education; and infrastructure maintenance and repair that aids service expansion. Though food and commodity production is required to sustain the people who provide these services, it is the provision of the services, themselves, that directs changes in other production areas. Take health care as an example. Many health products companies and pharmaceutical giants manufacture things (e.g., bandages and pills), but currently they reach only a portion of the potential market because so many people do not have adequate access to health care service. If funding were channeled to the creation of a global health services program—in which thousands of young people in the developing world (and the inner cities of the developed world) were trained to be community nurses, physician assistants, or barefoot doctors—we'd soon have real medical people providing real services in all kinds of places that currently have none. Along with the development of the services, the manufacture and sale of the products would go hand-in-hand. But the service side has to lead.

Thus, humanity's current task is to forge a new network of global security by constructing a system of global problem-solving in which any of us—indeed, most of us—will be participants. Despite the despair and desolation of our present situation, we must find a way to achieve household and community security in the areas of food, health, energy, communications, and ecological and personal safety. Without ensuring a modicum of personal security to everyone in the world, it will be impossible to create the social cohesiveness necessary to sustain a global effort that confronts and handles the global crisis for decades to come. One-time solutions are no solution at all. The next thirty years will involve critical decision-making over and over again. A good start makes future strategic success possible, but if we fail to put in place mechanisms that enhance network security for those who lack resources and skills, the struggle of desperate families and their "protectors" to ensure survival through private aggrandizements, hustles, and the use of force will accelerate the general slide into socioecological disaster.

Through the steady unraveling of the New Deal social contract since 1980 and with rapidly advancing globalization on all fronts, the service economy nurtured civil society to address vital problems left unaddressed or inadequately addressed by the fraying international order. Civil society organizations know how to solve these problems and—along with the corporate-based philanthropic sector—have developed the beginnings of the networks needed to attack them. Yet, it is woefully underfunded for the task. Civil society needs money and, also, far broader popular support and participation. We need a movement that promotes increased recognition, authority, and resources for its mission (we offer our suggestions for this in Chapters 8 and 9).

I very much like what my brother has written about the service-based economy and the rise of the service class. I especially like how he's elucidated the question of "service class ethics." If we're going to lead humanity into its future, we need to clean up our class. In particular, we need to focus on banking and financial services. As long as that sector defines the basis, scope, and content of service class ethics, we're in deep, deep trouble.

Though I'm less skeptical than my brother about the potential of the service class to build a political movement for its own interest, it *is* troubling that he and I, both far removed from practical power or moral influence in American culture, are currently its best champions. The service class has a long way to go, and time is short.

The biggest intellectual problem in today's world is the failure of opinion leaders to grasp the transformation in the mode of production. Today's leaders are thinking in the past, circa 1940, but I don't expect most politicians or bankers to get it. Vision and new direction are not part of their job description. But, among political progressives, those who profess the need of real change, I'd hope for better. But still we wait, and I join my brother in this book in order to engage progressives, to transfer onto any willing shoulders the responsibility for making service values the basis of a new, global social contract and for building a progressive movement for effective crisis management in the difficult era ahead.

Accepting that the accelerating and deepening crisis of industrialism lays the foundation for a class-based progressive movement of some sort, my brother and I assert that it can be coaxed into existence now, but only through the articulation of a *practical* agenda for change that umbrellas the interests of the diverse progressive forces in today's world. A sound agenda will rally support—eventually financial support—from many sectors, and a global consciousness movement can mount the world's stage.

Clearly, no such agenda exists today; otherwise, we'd see the shoots of a popular movement. We think the problem is the failure of critical thinking, the lack of a sound theoretical foundation upon which a practical agenda for restructuring the global economy can be formulated.

My brother and I preach *that the mode of production has already changed, and a new class structure has begun to emerge.* Therefore, human salvation, such that it is, rests in promoting the class interests and culture of rising service production and struggling against the dominant class interests and culture of the Industrial Age.

One Class or More?

A question we have discussed but not yet resolved is whether the service class is a single entity (though, perhaps, with distinct strata within it) or whether service production creates more than one new class. Since it doesn't matter for the primary point of our presentation—defining the kind of political agenda that would allow service culture decisive mastery over industrial culture—we're working on the assumption of a single class.

I've worked among service providers all my life—as a community organizer, as a teacher, as a social worker, as an issue advocate, and as a communications professional. In every realm, the work is intellectual and social, dependent on knowledge, good communications, and effective, collaborative problem-solving. This is distinct from work on an assembly line, the essence of industrial production. That work is rote and physical. Today, of course, even factory work is evolving rapidly, what with robotics and real-time production, and today's far fewer factory workers focus increasingly on production problem-solving while their machines do the heavy work. I would argue, however, that this change in factory work is a manifestation of how service production is transforming industrialism in its own image.

To be more specific about how today's class structures and boundaries are changing, let's examine the development of one of today's most notorious figures, the corporate CEO.

Early industrial enterprises were family-run businesses, but, through the 1800s, as the scale of industrial production grew ever larger and more complex, more capital was needed to expand operations. Eventually, in the mid-1800s, the corporation was invented. Initially, despite the presence of outside investors, corporations remained under the practical control of the small family groups that created them. But around 1890, something began to change—professional talent among managers emerged as a social force. As Peter Drucker pointed out, the evolution occurred between 1895 and 1905.

It distinguished management from ownership and established management as work and task in its own right. This happened first in Germany when Georg Siemens, the founder and head of Germany's premier bank, Deutsche Bank, saved the electrical apparatus company his cousin Werner had founded after Werner's sons and heirs had mismanaged it into near collapse. By threatening to cut off the bank's loans, he forced his cousins to turn the company's management over to professionals. A little later, J.P. Morgan, Andrew Carnegie, and John D. Rockefeller, Sr. followed suit in their massive restructuring of U.S. railroads and industries (Drucker 1992:356).

In ensuing decades, management science developed to the point where it became unimaginable that a large corporation could be run by the owners themselves. Unable to run their own enterprises, owners became dependent on professional management for their profits. They ceased to play active roles in daily corporate leadership. Yet, even though managers were increasingly compensated with company stock and, thus, became partial owners themselves, they too could not pass control of the corporation on to their own heirs. Being an heir to ownership or managerial wealth may be a sure path to a palatial income, but it no longer makes one qualified to manage a corporation. That right goes to those who dedicate their lives to acquiring the skills and networks that are vital to management success.

Thus, while today's inheritors of industrial wealth and social positioning have many social advantages, in the new markets of service production these advantages are fleeting and dependent on efforts of each person to augment and enhance them. Even with such efforts, heirs can be rather readily surpassed by talented, hard-working professionals starting from almost anyplace in our society. Indeed, to a large extent, the accumulated wealth of industrialism survives only because a financial service stratum has risen to guard and invest it on behalf of its owners.

We can now see that corporate CEOs—and other corporate managers— were among the first of what can now be called the service class, dependent for their position in production on the strength of their professional talent.

Banking and merchant accountant roles go back many millennia, as Chew demonstrates, but the service class appears only within mature industrial class relations whose growing dependency on the service sector unleashes a service class consciousness that contends for cultural dominance in society. As long as mass production dominated, the independence of the service class was curtailed by the larger industrial bourgeois reality. In the last five decades, as service production supplanted mass production as society's primary mode, CEOs gained incredible stature both as founders of enterprises in the new economy and as leaders of old enterprises making the transition to the new economy. Their compensation has risen accordingly. Too much so, many of us believe.

But what in the rise of CEOs reveals something more general and significant about this new class of service providers? What is it that distinguishes this class of people from previous classes—from peasants, slaves, the aristocracy, industrialists, and proletarians?

Keep in mind what defined all those other classes. Because every mode of production has certain natural resources that are vital to its function, the most powerful group of people is the one that owns or controls these resources. This control is what defines the boundary of the dominant class. Other classes are also defined by their less powerful but nevertheless specific relationships to these key resources. To appreciate the nature and boundary of the service class, we have to ask what is the key natural resource in service production. This brings a rather stunning and illuminating rejoinder.

The key natural resource in service production is human capital itself, that is, the knowledge, intellectual talent, social skills, and networks possessed by individuals. That's what the first professional CEOs brought to the table. The fact that this key resource is actually owned, more or less equally, by everyone is immensely empowering.

Which, unfortunately, may be another way to say that we've reached the bottom of the barrel, that we've depleted so much of what nature had to offer that all that we have left to proffer is ourselves. We have nothing more from which to extract value except ourselves.

But we've got plenty of ourselves. Indeed, we've overpopulated the planet. Relative to the planet's reproductive capacity, that is, relative to the other remaining natural resources, the supply of ourselves is excessive.

Inevitably, given the truth of supply and demand, the compensation for putting ourselves to work for each other isn't going to be too much. Actually, until we reduce population substantially, for most of us, it's not going to be much more than what it takes to survive. On the other hand, out of quantity comes quality, and we have a lot of minds to put to work on our behalf.

Moreover, even in our depleted and overpopulated world, survival needn't be as difficult as it is today for the vast majority of the world's people. Here, I depart, I think, from the Libertarian tendency that my brother sometimes sees in my discussion of the character of the service class and the empowerment of individuals. CEOs to the contrary, most service providers are dedicated to the service of other people or people-oriented enterprises, not corporate profit. On this basis, I believe the service class as a whole will embrace global infrastructure and human capital development programs that enhance the quality of life for the vast majority of people—even if such programs do not substantially improve personal income—because they vastly enhance network security.

And, let me note before I go on, many of today's corporations are, themselves, service-oriented enterprises as well. Consider, for instance, Disney or CNN, Verizon or Microsoft. Indeed, there is nothing inherent in the corporate form that requires it to exploit workers or consumers. Rather, greedy corporate behavior is, I suggest, a remnant, not yet superseded, of industrialism's hegemonic competition for markets. More generally, greed is the outgrowth of any system in which the key resources of production are monopolized by a small minority of people, yet all people struggle for survival due to the ongoing depletion of these resources. In such conditions, those in positions to seize and hoard resources will do so. In the last century of industrial production, it was mainly corporations through which exploitation and hoarding was conducted.

In the service era ahead, despite individual differences in talent and connections among us, all humans will own an essentially similar piece of the key natural resource—ourselves. It cannot be hoarded or monopolized. Moreover, our very diversity is vital to addressing the particular local and regional conditions of our crisis. As the values of the service era congeal, struggle will be raised with hoarders and speculators. A new global social contract will be forged in which most corporations will recontextualize their profit-making goals to fit within the new constraints. Exposed as they will be by investigative reporting and mass communications and subject to the pressures of shareholders who, increasingly, will be service providers and civil society institutions themselves, corporations that do not constrain their greed will not survive.

The emerging social contract is about serving each other for our common well-being in a world enduring a long-term socioecological crisis. This is not merely an individual effort where we each offer our services in the global market with all its local and regional diversity. More than that—much more than that—the new social contact involves a commitment to the creation and development of new *social systems* that holistically enhance our common life on the planet.

For individuals, productive work will increasingly be based upon the conscientious development, over the course of a lifetime, of one's knowledge, skills, and connections so that we each can play more valuable roles in enhancing the quality of life, thus securing our individual position in the local-global nexus of the service economy and earning a stable livelihood. For corporations and other business enterprises, profit will accrue from the successful organization of employee talent to provide constantly evolving service in the marketplace. For NGOs and civil society agencies, the work will involve enhancing expertise and efficiency in particular areas of social problem-solving and mobilizing community and business collaborations to help resolve these problems.

As a whole, individuals, families, communities, businesses, corporations, NGOs, and new local, regional, and global structures of civil society will evolve a new system of flexible, fluid problem-solving that will be the structural core of the service era's social contract. As the general purpose of nation-states also entails management of social problem-solving, albeit at the national level, we might call this new system the *global state,* but we're likely to find a term less associated with bureaucracy or the historic use of monopoly force and more associated with flexible collaboration. In any case, the emergent value system will empower a class of service providers to pursue their own success and survival in the context of working with peers and other class allies to ensure the survival of the whole.

In conclusion, I return to the question of whether the service economy creates more than one class. In the discussion above, I go far out on a limb that's been sawed off before—toward the end of class society. Marx argued wrongly that proletarian revolution would lead eventually to the withering away of the state as the working class suppressed the bourgeoisie out of existence and even the peasantry transformed into farm proletarians. He thought the need for a coercive state would eventually disappear, replaced merely by a benign administrative body. He never imagined that socioecological crisis would intervene, creating an entirely new mode of production and a different path of human development.

Here we are, however, and it looks like—as far as the primary factor in class definition goes, that is, ownership of the key resource—all service workers are alike in owning their own human capital, however different from one another their actual talents may be. In regard to secondary relations in production, however, groupings are apparent. For instance, in a law firm, everyone contributes on the basis of their intellectual and social talents, but clear strata exist: senior partners, junior partners, paralegals, and support staff. Their compensation systems are different. Some may be wage workers; others earn salaries; still others also get profit distributions. A look at any service-oriented enterprise, for-profit or non-profit, displays these kinds of strata.

However, upward mobility in these strata of service production seems mainly an issue of life-long learning and the development of one's personal networks. While individual interests and talents vary, and hard work and luck play important roles, in the service economy more senior positions are going to tend to be occupied merely by older, more experienced, and more mature individuals. Of course, there is never going to be as many positions at the top of an enterprise as at its base, so levels of reward and compensation are bound to differ. That said, the difference seems not one of class but of the inevitable fact that social structures have leaders. While the socioecological crisis unfortunately ensures that the next epoch will not eliminate human hardship and suffering, it seems likely, at least, to witness the progressive elimination of its 12,000-year-old, class-based inequities.

Our task, as I said at the opening, is to stimulate a cultural transformation to assist the empowerment of the service economy against the interests of the old industrial elites and empires. Today's political and cultural opinion leaders are thinking in the past, constrained by the weight of centuries of competitive, nationalist ideology. It's not merely, as they suggest, that our wondrous system of free markets and democracy has hit a stumbling block, encountering obstacles and groping for a way forward. No, a whole new way of life is trying to open up, and it's being strangled at birth by a stagnant, decadent, corrupt, overbearing, entrenched, fortified, and deeply institutionalized past.

Our future rests in service production. We can be liberated only by serving each other and ourselves. To avert the *dark age* of industrialism, we must embrace this path, investigate its necessities, and discover its possibilities. As Marx might say were he alive today, "Servers of the world, unite."

Chapter 4

Population Paradox—Improve Human Welfare, and Fewer Will Come

Steve:

A woman I know well works for the White Ribbon Alliance (WRA), a network of organizations in mostly poor nations that want the world to do something about the fact that more women of child-bearing age die in childbirth than from any other cause.

The Global Curse of Maternal Mortality

To me, this is a startling reality. In the U.S., my friend tells me, one in 4,000 women die in childbirth. In Sweden, it's only one in some 17,000, but in sub-Saharan Africa and south Asia, the rate is more like one in 800.

While these data say something about the difficulty of childbirth, their disparity says a lot more about inequity in global society.

The root cause of these disparities is difference in access to medical care. In Sweden, there seems to be no acceptable reason for a woman to lack adequate maternal care. In the U.S., though no one wants to say it like this, being a poor or minority woman is just your own tough luck. Though the U.S. ranks forty-first in the world of nations in maternal mortality—a shameful statistic for the world's largest economy—data demonstrate that non-Hispanic, white women have little chance of death in childbirth. Black and Hispanic women are the ones who are dying.

In the U.S., access to health care is a matter of money. If you can afford it, you can get care. As Americans know, however, many of us can't afford it. In 2008, some 47 million people (one in six) did without health care coverage (the recent passage of health care reform remains largely promise, not yet actual change). In developing nations where half of all women give birth alone or with a neighbor, it's less a matter of cash and more a question of whether adequate medical facilities even exist…or, if they do, whether rural, birthing women in stress can get to an emergency care center in time. Women everywhere need a functioning health care system before, during, and after giving birth.

Another factor in developing countries is the cultural oppression of women. In impoverished circumstances, for instance, families sometimes marry off or abandon daughters at very young ages, and, either through marriage or youthful prostitution, they embark on lives of serial pregnancy with short birth spacing. Without adequate nutrition and care, their health fails, and they eventually succumb to the hardships and hazards of natural childbirth. In other circumstances, the failure to produce male offspring makes women unworthy in their husbands' eyes, so little effort is made to find help if their birthing goes awry.

Maternal mortality is a good proxy for global social and economic disparity because nothing is so basic to human life as reproduction. With Sweden's example, it is clear that humanity knows how to prevent these deaths; we just aren't doing it.

But the WRA is doing something about changing that fact. It has networked or developed activist groups in more than thirty countries to pressure their governments to invest in community health. The target goal is fifteen percent of their national budgets. Moreover, knowing that poor governments lack the resources to build the medical facilities, roads, and communications networks necessary to overcome maternal mortality, WRA is also pressuring wealthy nations to meet the Millennium Development Goal (MDG) they set for themselves in 1990, to reduce maternal mortality by 75 percent by 2015. With only five years to go, this is the one MDG on which *no progress* has been made. So far, not a single wealthy nation has come anywhere near even once meeting its pledged financial obligations in the eighteen years since the goal was set.

If real progress is going to be made on this goal, it will have to be because women insist that social institutions reflect the needs of birthing women. Despite the long failure to date, recent indications are that women are going to spur real global change. With a tiny amount of seed money from the Gates Foundation, the WRA has made a good start in a short time. The WRA initiated a campaign to raise social awareness in developed countries through media-savvy challenges aimed at assembling IMF, World Bank, UN, and G-20 leaders. Through these activities, they attracted interest from a number of celebrity women to serve as patrons, and they've activated social networks and the blogosphere to their cause. Now, continuing the efforts to raise global awareness, they are seeking resources to strengthen their in-country alliances and activities. The global campaign unleashes the power of women to network in their own behalf on this most basic of women's needs.

Over the years, I've been involved in a lot of local community organizing, but the WRA's global challenge takes grassroots organizing to a new level. While the lack of quality maternal health care is experienced at the private family and local level, its systemic provision is, and can only be, a global matter because:

- Solutions require substantially greater financial support than local communities can provide.

- Technological assistance and exchange is required between developed and underdeveloped countries.

- Changes in dominant social attitudes and cultural values in recipient countries are needed to grant women greater status and access to medical attention.

This is what we mean by the local-global nexus—using modern service-led technology, funding, and organization to meet local needs in new ways. In achieving the goal of community revitalization, the service class—and women, in particular—will play the decisive role.

I've worked in the service economy all my life, and in every situation— the antiwar movement, a food co-op, nursing homes, family services, state government, high school, an on-the-job safety organization, and a couple service-sector labor unions—women service-providers outnumbered the men. This is no accident. Women are leading the economic and cultural transformation of the Service Age. Indeed, throughout American non-profits as well as global NGOs women are predominant. I wish I could say, in terms of genuine gender equity, that women are the actual leaders of major service-oriented corporations or that they, in general, now earn the same for similar work as men. We're not there, yet. Few corporate CEOs are women, and women still earn only about 76 percent of what men make. This compares to about 60 percent in 1980. Still, in the U.S. at least, a greater percentage of women than ever occupies middle to top managerial posts in the corporate world, and the number of women in high political posts creeps steadily upward. In contrast, in the entrepreneurial service economy, women already dominate, leading significantly more small businesses than men. We expect these trends to continue.

Women around the world have much to gain from the advent and development of the service mode of production. It is no wonder that they gravitate to it. Sociobiologists point out that, due to genetic make-up, women generally bring a more complex and effective mix of social, emotional, and communicative skills to production than do men. Similarly, sociologists also have documented the particular talents learned by women in childhood relative to men—social interest and networking—that make them especially capable in the new economy. Social contact, social interaction, social introspection, social planning, and social implementation are central to service negotiations and the collaborations necessary for modern socioeconomics. As the service-led mode of production blossomed over the past four decades, women, once they received the opportunity for training and education, took advantage of service positions in record numbers.

Moreover, leaving aside their role in production, the role of women in society in the arenas of reproduction is much more significant than men. As a result, the expanding economic empowerment and elevated status for women in Western nations is already manifest in changes in sexual relations, parental and family relations, and overall population management. Similar cultural challenges to gender relations have arisen around the globe, though the cultural response to women's entry into service-led production is as varied as the cultures that inhabit the planet.

From Infanticide to Unrestrained Population Growth

I welcome the widening domain of women's power in reproductive matters because overpopulation of the planet is a root cause of our socioecological crisis. It is something we must learn to control. When I think of this, I'm always reminded of two geckos my daughter bought as pets when she was in middle school. We put them in a terrarium we made from a six-gallon glass aquarium. Geckos eat live crickets which we began buying in small batches from a neighborhood pet shop. But, after a few trips to the shop, I realized this would be a relentless duty. Thoughtlessly, I proposed buying a larger quantity and just storing them loose in the terrarium with the geckos. The geckos could eat them as they wished. Two days later, responding to her shriek, I rushed to my daughter's bedroom. The crickets had attacked and all but devoured one of the geckos.

The terrarium was a tiny environment, but I realized what an overpopulation of crickets could do. On another level, Diamond writes about Easter Island, a remote place in the Pacific that was first settled by rafting humans about a thousand years ago. Originally, the island was entirely forested. However, due to the growth of population and the adoption of agriculture, the colony completely deforested the island, and its small civilization eventually collapsed. Did no one see it coming? Or was population control just too overwhelming for the social capacities of the people?

Our terrarium and Easter Island were closed systems, meaning they had finite limits on the natural resources required for survival. It used to be that the socioecology of human society was an open system, that plenty of unsettled regions and unexploited resources remained for human use. But those days are gone. Today, human society is global, a closed system, and it is increasingly overpopulated. Global warming is unambiguous on this point. We must reverse this trend.

How can men and women unite, worldwide, in a concerted effort to control our numbers?

First, we have to accept why reproduction is out of control. It is not a matter of bad intentions or, like me with our geckos, mere thoughtlessness. It goes right to the root of human sexuality and the way our species ensures its reproduction. As we all know, it is a matter of our genes. For us, sex *is* pleasurable, and, generally, that's why we pursue it. Inevitably, that leads to pregnancies and births. For various reasons, other species also pursue sex, but they don't overpopulate—except in temporary situations—because natural forces (disease, predators, resource depletions, and natural disasters) restore the necessary balance. For the past 12,000 years, human ingenuity allowed us to escape such natural constraints. As we alluded in Chapter 1, however, the ingenuity that invented agriculture also replaced matriarchal family and social structures with patriarchal ones and imposed social dysfunction on our mode of reproduction. With men largely in command of reproduction structures and the economy that stems from them, with one unsatisfactory exception, we have never been able to control of our numbers.

The one exception was China during the 4,000-year epoch from roughly 2000 B.C. until the arrival of European imperialism in the late nineteenth century. Because of the stability of the Chinese dynasties and the meticulousness with which they maintained population records, it is clear that China maintained zero population growth—and avoided a *dark age*—after its agricultural economy reached its ecological limit. How was this achieved? Through female infanticide. Hundreds of successive generations of Chinese parents accepted that no more than one of their new-born daughters could live. The others, of necessity, had to be exposed to the elements or simply starved until they died. As Harris documents, the practice in China was hardly unique, only more systematic and sustained. Many other cultures in human history display aberrant male-female sex ratios, clear indication that female offspring were denied life support.

Under the male-dominated social logics of the Agricultural Age, there was a certain rational quality to female infanticide. It both reflected and contributed to women's devaluation in society, a result of their relative unimportance in farm production relative to their prominent role in hunter-gather production. Anthropologists note that female infanticide constricts population growth without limiting male sexual satisfaction—at least for wealthy males, though the poorest often must do without wives—and it preserves the maximum number of men for farming and warfare. We can only speculate, but if women had been in charge of Agricultural Age value formation, they might have found other ways to constrain population growth, such as less frequent and more carefully limited coitus, controlled by women.

Speculation about how decision-making by women would impact population control may get a full-scale, global test sooner than we think. There is no question but that, to avoid a socioecological collapse, we have to mobilize humanity to reduce global consumption and waste during the lives of the next few generations. One way to do that is to constrain current standards of living, particularly in the more developed economies of the world. Another way—really just a temporary escape valve to buy time—is to facilitate population-resource balance through more open immigration policy in relatively underpopulated regions (such as the U.S.). A third way, the best and most strategic way, is to reduce global population. Fewer people mean fewer mouths to feed, fewer jobs to sustain, less need for food and commodity production, and less waste and pollution. However, we can be certain that female infanticide is not going to be the preferred method of population control in the era ahead because women are gaining so much power and influence as the service-based economy predominates over industry and farming. If we're going to make gains in controlling population, it will have to be women's values that direct and manage the process.

Industrialism, actually, is the material basis for, the cause of accelerating growth in human population, which has tripled over the last 120 years. This is because, under the pressure of industrial competition, mass producers constantly invest in new technology to reduce the per item cost of production. Aggregately, however, for industrialists as a whole, this leads to a falling rate of profit. Thus, to sustain overall levels of profit, industrialists constantly seek to control larger markets. A hundred years ago, this was achieved through war, but as competing industrial powers fortified themselves, conquest proved increasingly difficult. The one sure way to ensure expanding markets was population growth, and the developed economies and political forces of the industrial era did nothing to hold it in check.

Women's Liberation and a New Vision of Population Management

The service-based economy, potentially, has both the will and the means to rein in and eventually reverse population growth. The will arises from the fact that service producers have no need for ever-growing economies of mass consumption, yet have a real need to curtail ecological destruction. The means arises from the growing power of women, a process that incubated during the Industrial Age but, as we have noted, is accelerating rapidly in the dawning Service Age.

For its first 400 years, industrialism did little to advance the status of women that had so degraded during the Agricultural Age. Men's strength was still fundamental in most industrial production—garment work was the primary exception—and women's propensity to become pregnant and, then of necessity, to be devoted to childrearing kept most of them from attaining economic independence from men. The rigid gender division of labor—men in social labor, women in household labor—remained largely intact, and cultural norms of male supremacy remained entrenched. Except when extreme market competition or war made women a useful, temporary substitute for men, industrial work remained the sole province of men.

Around the turn of the twentieth century, the first signs of service-oriented production developed in corporations facing the increasing complexities of large workforces that required growing numbers of information-processing workers in the lower levels—accounting, retailing, and credit operations. At first, these jobs went to men, but the combination of competitive cost pressures and the work's minimal physical demands—along with the occasional war—encouraged the turn to lower paid women as office workers. At the same time, some of the more oppressive aspects of industrial era gender culture came under question due to the growing number of wealthy, bourgeois women who were raised in privileged nuclear families and who managed to gain training and education as a result. In particular, the Suffragette Movement demanded the right of women to vote and hold public office. These developments reached a zenith during the Roaring Twenties when the "pink collar" workforce—underpaid service jobs dominated by female employees—aligned with the struggle for women's rights to launch the Feminist Movement.

Massive unemployment during the Great Depression forced many women out of the workforce, but WWII pulled them back, this time into the factory jobs of wartime production. After the war, men returned to industrial employment, and women were shifted back into the home.

In the 1950s, however, the service-led economy began to challenge industrial power, taking giant steps forward as service jobs, values, and volunteer ethics began spreading throughout the global economy. By 1956, the majority of employees in the U.S. worked in service-based jobs.

Rising global competition—manifest both in the Soviet bloc's early entry into space and in the spirited, innovative product lines coming out of Japan—spurred American investment in public education in the post-WWII period and accelerated the transformation of gender relations. As the poor, minorities, and women were allowed access to higher education, they demonstrated their capabilities as service workers, intellectuals, and political leaders. As Baby Boomer women came of age in the 1960s, they went off to college and career in record numbers. At the same time, the perfection of the birth control pill and access to abortion made it possible for women to assume full control over their reproductive capacity. The service-led cultural transformation moved into a higher gear.

The Sixties are famous for the Sexual Revolution—the sudden openness of society to sexual expression and examination—but the more fundamental part of that departure was the women's liberation movement. For the first time in thousands of years, substantial numbers of women asserted control over mate selection. Dowries disappeared, and the rights of divorce and child custody for women were won. A generation of young American women entered the professional workforce, filling the rapidly expanding demand for service workers of all types. In the process, they achieved financial independence from men, establishing the basis of a self-sustaining movement against sexism and male chauvinism and for the opening of all economic opportunities to women as well as men. As the global service-based economy developed rapidly over the last decades of the twentieth century, its need of skilled social facilitators, communicators, and specialized experts in niche marketing spread tentacles of liberation for women to all corners of the earth.

These developments bode well, not only for women worldwide, but also for the effort of humanity to gain control of its reproductive splurge. As modern demographers point out, when women are given education, rights, and jobs, the birthrate drops. This is because a woman's own interest as a person and potential parent comes into play. For women, children are expensive. Each will occupy the woman's time and attention for most of two decades. When women have opportunities for jobs, income, and rights, they also acquire the possibility of comparing the high cost of childbirth and childrearing to the low cost of working and earning an income. Although in most cases, the number of children remains a household decision shared by husbands as well as wives, the combination of financial independence and emerging cultural support for independent women means more women marry at an older age, don't marry at all, or decide to have fewer children.

In some countries, such as Japan, this development is extremely pronounced, and opinion leaders, realizing that the country soon will not have enough young workers to support its aging population, have articulated two distinct reactions. The more regressive one is to encourage more Japanese children by forcing men out of their offices—in Japan, corporate employees typically work exceedingly long days in what is, generally, a hopeless effort to climb the corporate ladder—and into more engaged relations with their spouses. The thinking is that this will lead to more sex and more births. The other response is more progressive. It involves encouraging immigration of younger workers and families from poorer nations. If adequately supported in Japan, they bring their proclivity for larger families into the national workforce. Of course, eventually, immigrant women, too, employed in Japan's large service-based economy, will decide to reduce family size, like their Japanese peers.

The reality is that service-based production, rooted as it is in the empowerment of women, frees society of the need for large families. While this may be a problem for national chauvinists in Japan and elsewhere, for the world as a whole, it represents an important path out of our socioecological crisis.

Though the character is vastly different, the empowerment of women in service-based production reintroduces a change reminiscent of the matriarchal power of women in Neolithic societies. Its redevelopment in contemporary form in the decades ahead promises elimination of the social dysfunction that was imposed on human society by the adoption of agriculture some 12,000 years ago (see Chapter 1).

Retro Reaction to Population Control

However, the reemergence of a human society built around women in social leadership—and, thus, responsive to women's needs—continues to face substantial opposition. In the U.S., this is most evident in the power and influence of social conservatives and Christian fundamentalists who reasserted their moribund values in the cultural backlash of the 1980s and 90s. They consciously tout subservience of wives to husbands, and, under the Pro-Life banner, they demand that the government re-outlaw abortion, restrict sex education, block distribution of birth control information and technology to teens, block availability of the morning after pill, rescind funding to foreign governments and NGOs that provide abortion counseling, and promote abstinence programs as a means to curb unwanted pregnancies.

The desperation of any social system nearing the end of its time is manifest in the most outlandish advocacy of increasingly backward ideas. A Pro-Life movement that lacks population control measures is characteristic of such a philosophy. The need to control global population dooms Pro-Life policy as a regressive cultural trend. Though ultimately inconsequential to the service-led mode of production, its continued prevalence in American politics hinders effective action to confront the world's socioecological crisis.

A more substantive, yet backward commentary on the advancing liberation of women is that launched by Western intellectuals—conservatives and liberals, alike—on China's one-child policy. The policy grants state support for a family's first child but not for other children, allowing social norms to flourish that criticize the thoughtlessness of parents having multiple children. If the communist government of China hadn't had the foresight to advance this policy way back in the 1960s, China's population would be double what it is today (2.6 billion!), and the rest of us would have long-since run out of oil. Few countries in the world are so enlightened on reproductive policy, least of all the so-called liberal U.S.A.

A few other nations have also achieved remarkable success in family planning. One is Costa Rica which reduced the average number of children per woman from seven in 1950 to three today. This was achieved through public and private sector investments in sanitation, public health, and family planning services. In Sweden, close relations between family planning agencies and schools ensure a highly aware population in sexual matters, and the nation enjoys one of the lowest rates of young adult pregnancy in the world. Many of the world's indigenous tribes have adopted social and sexual norms that support far less sex in general with a resulting limitation on tribal growth.

These examples demonstrate the impact that the service-based economy can have on population management, provided outdated religious and industrial era sexual mores and population doctrine are cleared away. They also demonstrate that real crisis management leadership can come from anywhere in our world. If a global consciousness movement gets off the ground, the United States and its conservative culture will be compelled to follow suit.

The White Ribbon Alliance is one of those global NGOs that is breaking new ground through its practical organizing and promotional activity—advancing the day when a progressive movement reflecting feminist ethics can gel worldwide. Like most global NGOs, WRA operates on a shoestring budget and has no money or time to work outside its specific mission. Nevertheless, it is uniting women to advance their own cause and helping them acquire the resources to make a difference in their own behalf. Through practical work and concrete actions, they also restructure our ideas about what is possible in the fight against social inequality and injustice. Through the service-based, local-global nexus of contemporary exchange, what is learned locally through problem-solving activities becomes important global knowledge that aids solutions elsewhere.

The WRA demonstrates the ability to organize women of all walks of life, worldwide, in rich and poor countries, to end the travesty of maternal mortality. If WRA succeeds on a large scale, it also will save millions of children who die in childbirth or who must survive alone, without a mother to nurture them. To achieve this goal, the women of the WRA must overcome the deeply ingrained and deeply oppressive cultural conditions of women's lives, and they must find an effective way to mobilize billions of dollars for investment in sanitation, roads, communications systems, and medical facilities in undeveloped regions. They also must find resources to train and supply a global army of community medical professionals, the lifeblood of health service.

Most strategically, if the WRA achieves its goal, it will empower women to take control of their lives, their communities, and their relationships with the rest of the world. Self-liberated, they will also claim control of who they want as a mate and if or when they will become pregnant. Finally, the capacity to control and reduce human population will be within our grasp.

That sounds like a daunting task, and, indeed, it is. But necessity makes it possible. How can it be done?

Gaining Control of Our Numbers

Most fundamentally, financial support for NGOs like the WRA must be raised to unprecedented levels. Yet, we've already seen how governments in wealthy countries have failed to meet the foreign aid goals they set for themselves almost two decades ago. While I see merit in fighting for governments to step up to their self-defined obligations, I have doubts about whether they ever will. After all, in the competition for government dollars, domestic interests consistently trump foreign or global ones unless "homeland security" or "national defense" drives the decision. Though many civil society groups wax eloquent on the claim that HIV/AIDS, climate change, or some other global concern will undermine national security, my brother and I find that line of reasoning merely the re-affirmation of the narrow nationalist, hegemonic orientation that is the problem in the first place.

Another way to pursue the struggle is to acknowledge and assert that impoverishment in the developing world is to some significant degree the result of a century or two of imperial exploitation by industrial enterprises of the developed countries, thus deserving of reparations. But that is a hard argument to sell to most citizens of developed nations since, unless they were corporate stockholders, the average person didn't benefit directly from imperialism. Denizens of developed nations rarely accept guilt by association no matter how strong their life's comforts were linked to their nation's political-economic dominance over others.

A better argument is this: If wealthy countries don't help poor ones, then the disparity—accented by global telecommunications—is going to invite criticism and social unrest, even terrorism. Global markets will be further destabilized and a broad, irreversible crisis could set in. While one way to handle such unrest is to stomp down hard on resistance, we now know—after the test of the Bush Doctrine in the War on Terror—that suppression can be extremely costly, not very successful, and never ending.

The on-going collapse of global financial institutions and the resulting global depression confirm a message, obscured by the former administration's reaction to 9/11, that developed nations need to hear. Terrorism—bad as it is—is merely one manifestation of the catastrophic polarization that is intensifying social crisis all around us. Perhaps, it would be cheaper, wiser, and more effective to do as the WRA and the rest of civil society have asked—just invest in the millennium development goals.

But, as I said, I don't have much hope that the political elites of the wealthy nations of the world are ever going to take this route, no matter what the rationalization. Operating under industrial era values and politics, individual nation-states implement population policies based in their national interests rather than global necessities. For the most part, they implement none. Whatever foreign aid is distributed for family planning and global health depends entirely on the good will of individual states, their domestic politics, and their rivalries with each other. Each state decides what it will support and how it will do so, so genuinely coordinated, comprehensive international programs are difficult to mount and hard to sustain.

The scale of investment required to contain maternal mortality, much less stabilize and reverse more general social polarization, is immense, yet the beneficial impacts of such investment would be great. Global investments in hydraulic and electrical infrastructure would improve health and advance local economies, creating much needed jobs. Right away, the plight of women and children would sharply improve. Global investments in education and health care training would create an army of self-supporting young health service providers qualified to serve families and communities. Most of these would be women.

These efforts should be augmented by the establishment of a global, community-based, microlending program for every adult. Under such a program, individual and family opportunities to participate in economic ventures would expand through the provision of credit to purchase technology, forge social organization, or conduct other start-up business activity. Again, the main beneficiaries would be women.

In addition to general investments in infrastructure and human capital, specific programs should bolster family planning. It seems reasonable, for instance, to provide an annual stipend (cash incentive) to every woman of childbearing age who passes another birthday without giving birth. Let's put our money where our mouth is. Let's also widely disseminate sex education and birth control technology.

In each of these proposals, the goal must always be to empower women and local communities to control their own lives. It should go without saying that programs must be implemented in culturally sensitive manners with local control over the content and practice.

So, yes, there is a way to constrain population and avert the *dark age* of industrialism, and it is rooted in unleashing the long-trapped power of women. We need women to resume control over human reproduction, and, for that, they need power. The service-led mode of production has laid and is expanding the basis of that power, but the cultural shackles of patriarchy remain to be broken. The task now is to elevate the collaborative culture of service-based production and, in the process, rewrite civilization's social contract to embrace women's power.

Chapter 4 Response

More Headaches for the Skeptic in All of Us

Charles:

For years sociology books and journals have recounted all the reasons why Paul and Anne Ehrlich and their predecessor Robert Malthus were wrong with their population bomb theories. "Catastrophe looms!" the doomsayers cried. "Natural resources will disappear, and the planet's life-support system will fail!" It became very chic in academics in the 80s and 90s to denounce population scientists, whose arguments portended the collapse of civilization from its own sheer success at reproduction. "All bunk," said so many sociologists.

Then, I look at the United Nations' population curves, and all I see is exponential growth from humanity, the U.S. among the top five major contributors. We are soon to be nine billion! Should we be proud parents or humans scared to death? "They" say that green revolution agriculture, with its tractors and oil-based pesticide and fertilizer culture, can provide food for eight times the current world population, so really there's no cause for worry. But then, one out of seven people in the world already faces hunger and impoverishment with no way out of his or her dilemma—ever. I can't resolve the facts and fictions of the case.

I know I don't want to live in a world with 40 billion people! I have a hard enough time wanting to live in this one with 6.5 billion. I love to drive off into the forest and camp in isolation by a creek, but it's getting hard to find a place you can do that without some yahoo on a four-wheeler, a family with six yelling kids, partying teenagers with their stereos blaring, or a rifle-shooting nut just a little ways away. Listening to silence in nature has always been my most precious experience. Now, it costs money—to park, to hike to a peak, to sleep under the sky.

My wife and I never paid to sleep out until fate and pure tiredness from driving caught up with us about five years ago, and we gave up five dollars to the state of Oregon for the privilege. No, that was $7.50. Oregon charges out-of-staters more than in-staters. That has become a more frequent exercise for us ever since, paying to sleep out under the stars, although I still like to tell my fellow citizens that you have the right to camp out on National Forest lands for fourteen days if it's not posted otherwise. Do it—for free. But in a country where people pay $85 or more to sleep in a motel bed (my county commissioners averaged over $110/night for the last five years), they think fifteen or twenty bucks a night to camp out is cheap. I'm hopelessly outnumbered by slackers who give in to governmental miscreancy and economic markets.

The government should have been protecting our resources for the last three post-Earth Day decades, but it hasn't. It's been in the business of helping companies serve themselves to low-cost raw materials. It's also been helping farmers lap up the public dole, and, while the argument might hold some validity that it should be the small farmer we are helping, most public farm subsidies go to rather large enterprises. And the rest of us rarely get a chance to get our hands on any of the public dole, so for those of us outside the money stream, it all looks like a corporate welfare stream. Or rather a river. I doubt this nation could exist without our kinds of work, but the corporations get most all the welfare as if their defense projects, sacred cows, and pesticide residues earn greater merit. I'm not sure why.

As a people, we are horribly modern, urban, and used to exchanging things. We love commodities and are so accustomed to buying them that we really don't even care if goods last very long anymore. As long as we have cheap replacements for them, all the better. We love to go Wal-Marting. All four billion of us (the other two and a half billion really "don't count" because they don't have enough to even be considered consumers in the traditional sense).

But then, that's the problem, of course. It would take four earths the size of this one to produce the necessary natural resources if everyone on earth shared Americans' penchant for goods. The average American consumes between eight to eleven times the resources of other people in the world. Since America's poor actually consume energy and goods on par with rest of the world, it's most of us middle income people who actually must bear the blame for environmental problems, including our mountains of waste—you know, the billions of throw-away plastic bottles with natural spring water that make us so green in the first place. Ever feel there's a bit of contradiction in the way we see ourselves?

The picture isn't pretty, and neither is the thought of a whole world of people like us. An expanding number of us. An exponentially expanding number of us.

Population's a problem, and the way we eat up resources is a disaster!

I realize I am being intentionally caustic, but I started thinking about this fact about thirty years ago and I constantly hear NPR reporters talking like being green is a new thing, as if the concern for global warming, overconsumption, and overpopulation has just been discovered! Old hat, I say. The issue isn't the pollution or resource use; it's our systemic inability to deal with our unsustainable lifestyle. From a resource viewpoint, industrialism failed. Utterly.

Ever ask yourself how it is that we can live such denial and not have it bother us? Just after the turn of the twentieth century, in the early 1900s, a sociologist came up with the idea that he could encourage consumptive needs with advertising science. Yeah, social science put to economic work. By introducing people to the idea of buying, by making purchasing seem sexy or colorful, by making goods standardized and commonplace, business could count on sales, sales, sales. It worked. The culture of capitalism established itself in the minds of the masses. We need more! We need more!

Sometimes I think I can hear the poor and marginalized, the workers of underdeveloped nations, chanting that mantra. The UN estimates that 853 million people live in abject poverty with perhaps two billion more suffering relative deprivation. Relative deprivation is where people receive enough income and support to live simply and reasonably securely, but at a standard of living way lower than normal for their society. People in abject poverty have little guarantee that their next meal is coming, often finding themselves in refugee camps and slums, living without hope. They need the services of the service-led mode of production—food aid, emergency health care, family planning, education, jobs training, and farm extension programs. For most of these people, more economic exchange of goods takes a back seat to more services. So servicing the needs of humanity is not a hollow political slogan but a social imperative. Providing for livelihood improvements for half of humanity is a real goal that must be accomplished in the next fifty years. Truth be told, capitalism and financial speculation have no solution for inequality, hunger, and poverty. They survive by exacerbating difference, not by resolving it.

But the other extreme is also problematic. Ignoring difference within communities and assuming that all NGOs share goals and methods is simply false idealism. The world, wherever we look, is filled with conflicts and contradictions, inequalities, and differences of opinion and interest. While books like Paul Hawken's NY Times bestseller *Blessed Unrest* detail the myriad of categories filled by the world's burgeoning NGOs, they do a poor job of relating the lessons learned from the last thirty years of NGO work on community development and ecological protection. Hawken leaves the reader with a false sense of unity and purpose in development activity, and you'd never get the sense that what is development for one group is quite often oppression to another.

One reason we need socioecological science is because it does not ignore complexity in the brief history of civil society. That history is full of social antagonism and signs that even the goals of NGOs are often out of sync with desires and needs of communities themselves, not to mention that NGO actions are caught in a web of governmental and multilateral complicity that makes it difficult to meet objectives due to regulation, financial limitations, and outright institutional competition for the hearts and minds of local people.

The question of gender in development programs is all important. One of the most important lessons we have learned is that development for men is not at all necessarily development for women. In the feminist movement, development goals have switched from Women in Development, which saw development in terms of women entering the economic and decision-making playing field on equal terms with men, to Gender and Development, which demands empowerment for women in their traditional roles. The first is simply economic in nature, while the latter suggests political and cultural empowerment for women who, under earlier manifestations of development, found themselves saddled with increased household and agricultural duties while men participated in development programs. We have learned over time that the areas of production and reproduction cannot be separated from one another, particularly in assessing the consequences of economic change as it affects women. The White Ribbon Alliance example used in this chapter points the finger at cultural issues as key to successful implementation of development initiatives, for many countries and programs spend substantial funds to train and equip male-dominated sectors and leave areas of traditional women's participation and employment outside of the scope of assistance.

Beyond gender considerations, there are other considerations that key authors on civil society have avoided discussing. I don't want to step on the toes of war heroes, but I think we need to strip the military of its international reconstruction activities. Soldiers may be macho machine gun and missile experts, but they don't know a damn thing about social restructuring and never will. They have no training in economics and development, in cultural sensitivity, or in appropriate technology. They have never even supported a culture of democracy among their own ranks. It's inimical to believe that people who work in a hierarchical military institution can produce democracy in civil society. The military has no institutional memory for development work. It's irrational to believe that the hundreds of thousands of people who have studied development and political problems in college can only be an effective force for change if they put on a military uniform. The military has a term for its reconstruction programs in foreign countries: full spectrum dominance. Does that sound like international development to you?

What's so odd about American foreign policy now is that NGOs have flocked to work with the military, so that our foreign policy now is to declare war on another country, attack and destroy, and then pay civil society service workers to train the locals to be like us—all under the control of generals and colonels. Yeah, there are three tiers of international workers now—soldiers who are underpaid but highly esteemed, military contractors who are overpaid and contemptuous of the rest of us, and NGOs that live off the spoils, devoting their good hearts to work among all those who are victims of the first two.

I just want to ask what happened to the sociologists. I spent ten years studying rural sociology and international development and couldn't find a job with the military if my life counted on it. I'm a leftist, have long-hair, and I don't believe "collateral damage" is an adequate rendering of the thousands of innocent lives lost under military barrages over the past five decades. Derrick Jensen is right. We do lie to ourselves—it's the first act of denial. The world needs development, but not under the banner of guns, guns, and more guns. You can't make other people look like you with weapons. That's a policy that has never worked.

We will lose Afghanistan and Iraq once we leave.

An international core of civil society workers, independent of western military force, will soon revamp the world's economy or else…but that won't be an easy task. It will require educated, youthful generations in developed nations who leave their country with the proper tools to join their generational peers in helping marginalized people everywhere gain control over their lives. Not the life we envision for them, but the one they choose for themselves. We need service workers, not the propaganda managers and carpet baggers that have flocked to Iraq, Colombia, Afghanistan, and Bosnia. We need people who go to share their skills rather than make money off them. The future of humankind rests in collaboration and sharing, not in force and its legitimation through Calvinist, god-fearing discipline. How old capitalism and its stale state politics have become.

There are too many people in the world. I confess to moments of wanting to withdraw to my place in the mountains and let them all suffer the consequences of their own situations. After all, I am more Hindu than most care to admit, life being suffering and illusion rolled into one. Why should I care? But I have always revolted against the concept that it's ok to be born into injustice. Even Gandhi didn't buy that one. Yet, every day, millions are born into situations where the color of their skin, the religion of their parents, the poverty of their community, and the particularity of their culture leaves them outside the flow of global goods, social equality, and opportunity. Each year, the earth has to provide sustenance for some eighty million more of us than last year. I still haven't seen signs in the younger generations of developed countries that they are willing to take on the task of real world development.

The Food First! organization (Boucher 1999) has carried out a number of international studies that demonstrate that population control is first and foremost an issue of food security. Communities that are food secure have lower birth rates. Add that to the fact that girls who get education grow up to have fewer children, and you have a formula for the international development program that the service world needs. Food and education. Nothing equates democracy or military intervention with lower birth rates. Nothing.

Food security, however, is not measured by how much *international* food aid reaches an area. Rather, food security is a *bioregional* solution. Food aid must come from the locality in which it is needed, not from pesticide-ridden North American grain fields. As it is practiced today, food aid disrupts social structures in receiving zones, overthrowing centuries of social relationships to favor gangsters and ruffians. Ultimately, it makes people dependent on food stuffs that rapidly escalate in price during emergency situations. Food aid weakens people and local communities. We must quit patting ourselves on the back for our Christian response to people's suffering. We need real investment in making people independent and capable of handling problems with their own solutions. My brother and I think only civil society is up to that task.

The world's population problem will be a multi-generational problem. Right now, our investment schemes and retirement practices ensure that if population declines so will the wealth of people in those countries. Capitalism lives on expanding mass markets, not shrinking ones. We need more! Of everything! Under industrial culture, there is no solution to exponential population growth.

Thankfully, the Industrial Age is ending, but the task before us is great. We must cut the number of people born on this earth. We must expand the local food security of bioregions throughout the globe. We must share technology and information in ways that make people independent of us and capable of making their own collective choices. We must face the rigors of a contracting world economy.

Got an economic theory for that one, Ivy League graduates? We need to listen to centers of intelligence far away from those who have paraded their stuff for the last hundred years.

Chapter 5

Social Contracts Are Really Generational Things

Steve:

In late September, 2008, a seismic tremor tottered the world's financial system, nearly causing a global economic collapse of catastrophic proportions. For three days, it looked like the system might topple. In that brief interlude many American political and economic observers wondered if the time had come *for a new social contract*.

But the moment passed, and the old social contract built during the New Deal—as tattered and flailing as it was—remained in place. More than two years later, it's still there.

Yet, certainly, we are not doomed to endure the regime of that antiquated bargain forever. In the previous chapters, my brother and I have shown how the mode of production has changed and is now pressing for a cultural transformation. We've shown that a new class—the service class—is rising, beginning to challenge the class biases of the last era. We've shown that women are ready and able to assume vital, expanded roles in social leadership.

So, with all this in place, what is the prognosis? When will change come? What forces shape the tipping point when people suddenly let go of their old ways of being and energetically embrace the new?

The Temporality and Tipping Points of Social Contracts

It turns out that social contracts change every 80 years or so, the outcome, each time, of an era of social crisis. The first social contract of the United States was created out of the American Revolution and the adoption of the Constitution, which rewrote the social contract with English authority and codified the new arrangement. That social contract was torn up and rewritten by the Civil War and its aftermath, officially sealed by the resolution of the nation's electoral crisis in 1876. That contract, which gave northern capitalists most favored status and allowed Jim Crow in the south, was shredded by the Great Depression and World War II, which produced the most recent social contract—the New Deal—in full fruition when the war ended in 1945.

Each of these contracts lasted in the neighborhood of sixty years before their gathering disintegration invoked social crisis and, after twenty years or so of unrest, the forging of a new social contract. It has now been more than sixty years since the New Deal. Are forces in motion, now, that are could forge the next social contract in the years just ahead?

Al Gore had long advocated the fight against global warming, facing near constant derision. Suddenly, in 2006, his message was heard worldwide, and he won the 2007 Nobel Peace Prize for demanding social action against global warming. Had climate change suddenly worsened? No. Something else tipped the balance.

Take the question of the Iraq war and the American public. Despite substantial opposition all the way through, Bush and Congressional war supporters were consistently re-elected. Why did the voters turn against them in 2006 and, despite gains in Iraqi stability in 2007, dismiss McCain's view in 2008 that "the surge" was working?

What about big cars and the price of gas? In high school in 1965, I remember paying twenty-five cents for a gallon of gas. I remember the first Toyotas in 1969 and the invasion of Hondas after the oil embargo of the 1970s. Still, despite rising prices and clear options, Americans opted for the SUV explosion of the 80s and 90s. All of a sudden, however, in 2008, the inappropriateness of gas guzzling sunk in. Why now but not before?

The world is full of problems. Wars are always in progress. Suffering is immense and never ending. And, due to the media, we know all about these things. Gore is an example of a person who has worked long and hard on his issue. Every important issue has people like him, people who research problems and solutions and others who organize and advocate for change. Some social change agencies even are institutionalized, as is the case of many of today's NGOs. Yet, most of the time, these efforts don't matter to most of us, and no fundamental change occurs to society at large.

Think back over your own lifetime. If you're an American Boomer, you lived through the Civil Rights Movement, the Viet Nam war, the Sexual Revolution, and the Reagan Revolution. Lots of things have changed, but most of the old issues are still with us. If you're a GenXer, you grew up under the relentless attacks and counterattacks of social conservatives and liberals, but did anything significant come of it? Not really. Our lives continue pretty much like they did twenty-five years ago.

Yet, as the history of the American Revolution, the Civil War and the New Deal show, momentous shifts *do* take place. In each case, a crisis arose not from a single traumatic event but from a long series of similar problematic events, ongoing for decades, that for some reason marshaled in a shift in mood only at a certain moment in time. Something in our mass psychology, our group consciousness, seemed to snap, and, suddenly, we were ready for change. And when it snapped, change couldn't come fast enough. Suddenly, we were disgusted with ourselves and our leaders, with our culture and our institutions, for holding us back. Suddenly, we all became creative thinkers, imagining new directions and, in whatever ways we could, pushing to bring change about. Suddenly, in the space of a quick twenty years or so, we turned society upside down, shook it out, and laid it down again in a fundamentally different arrangement, pointing off in a completely new direction. We adopted a new social contract.

Every eighty years or so. If the pattern persists, we are indeed fortunate right now because it suggests that society is ripe for another transformational shift.

But, why sometimes and not others? Why now?

This is a matter of *mass psychology*, another force greater than any of us as individuals, yet decisive to our potential for the kind of cultural transformation vital to successful management of the world's socioecological crisis. How does it work?

Mass Psychology in Social Development

As cultural materialists, my brother and I recognize that the ideas, values, thoughts, and emotions of people are formed by their experiences in life. Every individual is different and creative in his or her own way, but our outlooks on and reactions to events are largely framed by forces greater than ourselves. Much of how we think and feel is no accident. This accounts for the general similarity in perspective across the broad spectrum of societies in any particular epoch of history. For instance, in Neolithic times, whether in Africa 200,000 years ago or on the American Plains in 1600, women chose their mates and tribal culture taught every child from the moment of birth that that was the way it was, plain and simple, no debate. During the agricultural era, whether in ancient China or on the Yucatan Peninsula in A.D. 900, people accepted the need for sedentary lifestyles, adopted patriarchal family structures, and unquestioningly followed the lead of religious leaders. Later, wherever and whenever it developed, industrialism raised the importance of scientific thinking, encouraged a more secular society, and eventually forged the nationalist consciousness that is so prevalent today in countries around the world.

When we dissect the forces that shape people's outlooks, it is easy to spot the larger elements. As members of families, races, genders, classes, nations, and other special groups, we are socialized through experiences which bind us by common perspective to other members of the same groups. These outlooks have both an ideological (intellectual) and a psychological (emotional) character. In both cases, we are largely unaware of the specific slant of our perspective, but, taken in total, our social relations and experience circumscribe the limits of our personal outlooks.

Ideology is our *pattern of thought* or way of assessing things. It shades each individual's intellectual analysis and engagement. For instance, how should today's crisis in world financial markets be addressed? That is an intellectual question, and people of different ideological make-ups will approach it from entirely different perspectives. A financier thinks most fundamentally about credit, liquidity, and bank stability while homeowners think more about their wages, their mortgage payments, and the value of their houses. Each may address the other's concerns, but they come at it from different perspectives and with different priorities.

Psychology, on the other hand, is our pattern of *emotional* reaction to the world. While it also derives from our broad experience in life, psychology, much more so than ideology, is *primarily* shaped by our experiences *as children* in families run by parents and in societies run by adults. Abnormal psychology deals with situations where genetic conditions or trauma create an individual of extraordinary and, often, debilitating emotional character. It also deals with situations in which a person, deprived of vital childhood nurture, grows up emotionally defective and unable to cope with typical social problems. Societies in all times and places have had individuals who were unable to cope, and they have been handled in different ways, including banishment, imprisonment, therapy, and indifference.

Normal psychology deals with the range of human emotional behavior that derives from the upbringing common to a given society. The most crucial aspect of psychological development is an individual's relationship with his or her parents, since they provide the nurture and guidance which most influence early childhood development. Other childhood relationships also play a role. The first three years of life are the most formative; as time passes, our psychological state coalesces and further development is limited. The character of emotional energy displayed and dispensed by parents is of decisive influence.

Individual psychology governs our emotional reaction to social phenomena. One person might be shy in reaction; another bold. One might tend toward anger; another toward frivolity. The range of emotional possibilities is endless. Leaving aside abnormal psychology, differences in psychological reaction have different strengths and weaknesses, but, overall, they are just different, not one better than another except in relation to the needs of a specific situation.

Mass psychology appears to be some kind of amalgamation of individual psychology, but the nature of the amalgamation has puzzled observers. Wilhelm Reich first identified the phenomena in his groundbreaking 1933 work, *The Mass Psychology of Fascism*, in which he struggled to understand why much of Germany's numerous and intellectually-developed working class nevertheless embraced Nazism rather than Marxism. It was a matter of collective psychology, he asserted, only to be expelled from the Communist Party for deviating from the party line that recognized only class consciousness, not underlying psychological phenomena, as society's driving force.

After WWII, historians remained intrigued by the apparent phenomena of psychological eras (e.g., Erich Fromm and David Riesman), but no cogent theories explained their basis until the mid-1990s work of William Strauss and Neil Howe.

Strauss, Harvard-educated, had worked on Capitol Hill before the 1980s when he founded the *Capitol Steps,* a satirical, political cabaret. Howe, a demographer, is a historian and an economist by training.

In *Generations,* published in 1992, they explained why troubling and controversial events in history sometimes provoke profound social transformations while similar events at other times engender only patchwork reform or mere distain and dismissal. It is not so much the actual, on-going, underlying events that provoke change but, rather, a cyclically recurring psychological mood.

In their study of history, Strauss and Howe observed that modern societies pass through a psychological cycle of four phases, each about twenty years in duration, which they labeled according to their respective emotional moods: High, Awakening, Unraveling, and Crisis. Every eighty years or so, a Crisis mood leads to a profound reordering of social priorities, and a new social contract forms. Their analysis suggests that society has entered a Crisis era and that the resolution of our current struggles will set the framework of social problem-solving for decades to come.

After the present phase of turmoil and struggle, a High will form, reflecting the adoption of a new social contract. A High is a time when, despite the problems that continue to plague society, most people feel satisfied with the ways things are being addressed by society's dominant forces. With satisfaction running across the board, parents of a High convey a sense of calm security to their children. With that feeling imbuing children throughout society, a generation with rose-colored glasses takes shape. Strauss and Howe called them Idealists.

An Awakening is a period when some elements of society begin to question the values and structures of the High, which, after twenty years, is showing signs that it is not quite the end-all, be-all that it had been touted to be. Serious criticism and disruption ensues, sparked mostly by the coming-of-age Idealistic generation, but no fundamental social shift—a new social contract—follows because young adults do not have enough social power, relative to their entrenched elders, to force such change. However, in raising their rebellion and focusing outward, young adult parents pay relatively less personal attention to their children, who, as a result, grow up more alienated from society and more self-reliant. Pragmatists, according to Strauss and Howe.

An Unraveling follows an Awakening as the Awakening's critics carry their resentments and dissatisfaction into the mainstream of society's structures and values. A cultural war unfolds in which contending political sides undermine social confidence in the existing regime, yet, neither, in the polarized society, can marshal adequate consensus to address underlying problems. The social contract frays. Problems fester. Meanwhile, parents focus on conveying their social mission and values to their children, thus nurturing a generation with strong social purpose: Civics.

As the Unraveling reaches its nadir, the mood shifts again. Sixty years or so after the last High embarked, its social contract has been thoroughly discredited. Meanwhile, due to the neglect and failures of the dilapidated order, social problems are intensifying. A series of catalytic events pound the social psyche, steadily forging a Crisis mood. Children of a Crisis are protected but kept in the background, less nurtured. They are: Adaptive.

Strauss and Howe showed that these four successive social moods are caused by the evolving cycle of generational character types advancing through the four, twenty-year stages of life (see table). When a generation of a different psychological type becomes society's elders—and different psychological types move up in life's four phases—a new constellation of social mood forms.

Successive Social Moods			
Life Phase	**Generation Type**		
Youth	Idealist	Pragmatic	Civic	Adaptive
Rising Adult	Adaptive	Idealist	Pragmatic	Civic
Mid-Life	Civic	Adaptive	Idealist	Pragmatic
Elder	Pragmatic	Civic	Adaptive	Idealist
Mood	**High**	**Awakening**	**Unraveling**	**Crisis**

Because of this cycle, societies adopt a Crisis mood roughly every eighty years, and the struggles during these Crisis eras produce new social contracts. Inevitably, the new social contracts reflect the balance of social forces as it has evolved since the last contract was created, eighty years earlier. Some class, gender, and social forces drop out; others come in. To the extent that the necessities of rising social and class forces are addressed in the new social contract, society can look forward to twenty solid years of advance before the next round of Awakening, Unraveling and Crisis unfolds.

Based on Strauss and Howe's analysis, we can expect that the present sense of crisis—shared by people around the world—will resolve itself the next decade or so as global society forges a new vision and social contract.

Mood Swings in the Post-War Era

To illustrate, consider the situation in the U.S. after WWII. The country had escaped from depression and world war and entered a new era of seeming stability. Major problems— segregation, high unemployment, and a looming Cold War—still existed, but exhausted from two decades of hardship and struggle and revived by the stability of the New Deal's social contract, most U.S. adults refocused their lives and embraced a confident, new mood. Much of the rest of the world, also exhausted from depression and war, embraced the same post-war High.

Most people over fifty can remember that time. The world was divided between two systems—capitalism and socialism—and locked in an arms race between two superpowers. Within each camp, cultural conformity was the rule of the day, and the authority of the state, church, and social institutions was unquestioned. In each system, government was empowered to make all things right while the citizens went about their daily business, largely unengaged by politics. In the U.S., the values and initiatives of the New Deal were enshrined in a modern but massive social support system. The military-industrial complex quietly extracted huge profits through construction and maintenance of unprecedented defense systems. The oil and auto industries spurred construction of the interstate highway system, and every family was encouraged to get a second car. Disengaged politically, yet trusting wholeheartedly in their government, the taxpayers paid for it all.

Yet, twenty years later, as the idealistic children of the High—the Boomer generation—came of age, the mood began to shift. I was born in 1947, my brother in 1949. In general, anyone born after 1944 (until 1963) is considered a Boomer. Raised in stability by parents that believed in the greatness of the post-war High, we Boomers accepted our parents' uncritical but warm feelings about post-war stability and how it had overcome so many big problems of their youth. The world wasn't perfect, they said, but it was getting better all the time. We believed them. Of course, believing was different if you were Black, Hispanic, Native American, woman, or gay. Everyone's experience was unique; yet, across it all, Boomers believed as we were taught, that if we just did the things we were supposed to do—if we just fit in and worked hard—things would be fine.

For me, as I've said, the Cold War was a pressing background anxiety because it threatened to take my Air Force father on a mission to near-certain death. And, later, when angry whites denounced racial integration in Little Rock, I was surprised as much by the existence of a social problem as by the problem itself. Overall, however, I got through the 50s and high school in the early 60s without too much angst. When I resigned from the Air Force Academy in 1967 after two years of study, I was still pretty jaunty about the prospects for me, the nation, and the world.

Then, on January 10, 1968, I showed up at Georgetown University in Washington, DC. What a rude awakening!

Three weeks later, the Vietnamese launched the Tet Offensive, proving to American youth, at least, that all the talk of inevitable victory in Viet Nam was just hype. Suddenly, Eugene McCarthy's quixotic anti-war campaign—

announced a few months earlier—caught fire. In March, he almost beat the sitting president in the Democratic primary in New Hampshire, and a few days later, Bobby Kennedy announced that he, too, would challenge Johnson. On March 31, LBJ went on national television to say he was sending more troops to Viet Nam but, also, that he had decided not to seek re-election in the fall.

I listened to Johnson's speech in my dorm's television room and felt an urge to go down to the White House to cheer and jeer his decision. When I did, I was surprised and elated to see that several hundred other young people had done the same. At that moment, I sensed I was part of something bigger than me, that I was being swept onto a path different than the one I'd been on the day before. My awakening had begun. Our Awakening had begun.

Aside from my assigned Georgetown roommate—who flunked out of school a few days after we met—the only person I knew in DC was my cousin from New Jersey, same age as me, a student at American University. I'd heard through the family grapevine that he'd signed up for ROTC. Soon after I arrived in town, we crossed paths—literally and figuratively—at the Tombs, a Georgetown student hangout where he tended bar. I was out of the Academy and entering civilian life. He was quitting college for the Army. I told him I didn't think he was going to like it. A month later, he was on his way, ultimately, to Viet Nam.

Before he left, he gave me the phone number of his cousin (other side of his family) who, eventually, would get me my first job in DC. I interviewed for the job—a message boy at what I now know was the granddaddy of K Street lobby firms, *Corcoran, Foley, Youngman and Rowe*—on April 4, the same day that Martin Luther King, Jr. was killed. K Street was gridlocked with fleeing professionals in cars. Forced to walk, I was nearly late for my appointment. When the anxious switchboard operator paged the executive secretary who was to interview me, she came charging out of her office with her bag over her arm and burst out, "You've got the job. Come in when your schedule next permits. Now, let's get out of here!" She joined the staff rushing for the elevators.

The city was shut down for the rest of the week. Even when I showed up for my first day on the job, national guardsmen patrolled every corner.

A few blocks away, buildings still smoldered. In the Black community, the Boomers' youthful awakening to the fact that America's social problems remained intractable had clearly taken a more angry form than my own.

The political season was unfolding. I resented Kennedy for jumping on the antiwar bandwagon only after "Clean Gene" proved it was the way to go. In those days there were fewer primaries, and Kennedy won all but Wisconsin. Yet, McCarthy fought hard, almost winning in Oregon. Taking up Johnson's fallen banner, Vice President Hubert Humphrey, a supposed liberal, eschewed the primaries but announced his intention to seek the nomination at the Democratic Convention. In June, at a victory rally following the California primary, Kennedy was assassinated.

My awakening continued a few weeks later when the Democrats held their convention in Chicago. A variety of anti-war groups urged young people to come and set up a protest camp in Grant Park. Chicago Mayor Richard Daley forbade the gathering. In a showdown that Walter Cronkite called a "police riot," Chicago's "finest" beat young protesters with clubs in the street outside the convention while the nation's television cameras recorded the scene. Meanwhile, the delegates inside handed the nomination to Humphrey. In November, he was trounced by Nixon—later known to my generation as "Tricky Dick"—who claimed to have a "secret plan" to end the war. What bull! But the voters went for it. Personally, though entitled to vote for the first time in my life, I joined a large part of my generation that stayed home.

So that was 1968, the beginning of my political awakening. When you factor in cultural changes like pot, Yippies, hippies, the Summer of Love, and women's liberation—*sex, drugs and rock-and-roll*—it was quite an Awakening.

And it was a generation-wide, global phenomenon. Most young people were aroused by the times in some way, and not just in the U.S. In Paris that May, students rebelled and shut down the city. In Prague in January, the younger generation challenged communist authority only to face an invasion of Soviet tanks in August. In China, the Great Proletarian Cultural Revolution rose on the energy and dissatisfaction of youth. Everywhere, young people questioned authority and the old, established social regime. The hair grew longer. Bras were discarded. Electric music filled the air.

Despite its energy and spectacle, however, the Awakening's questioning was everywhere conducted by a rising adult generation that lacked the social positioning and power to institutionalize its critique.

In China and Czechoslovakia, as in Chicago and Alabama, force was employed against awakened citizens. In the U.S., the Reagan "Revolution" rode to power by channeling one element of the Sixties' critique—the rejection of big government—into a general social backlash against the critique itself. Once in the saddle, Reagan exploded the federal budget in an all-round effort to revive the tarnished luster of America's loss in Viet Nam. Renewing Cold War rhetoric and appealing to the fearful sensibilities of Christians whose religion was losing its dominant place in American culture, Reagan counterattacked against the values of the Sixties—of minorities, women, and youth—and launched an era of state-sponsored cultural warfare against change. Meanwhile, deploying theories of market fundamentalism, finance capital began a re-negotiation of the New Deal social contract and its bank regulations that had long-protected the economy from the kind of market excess that had caused the Great Depression.

For myself, idealistic to the bone, I clung to a vision of "changing the world" even as the Awakening started to peter out in the late 70s. I continued to seek jobs that I thought could contribute to social change. Many others did the same, but given the waning protest movement, no one was going to do much to "change the world." Eventually, like most of my generational peers, I settled down with family and tried to find a career path.

Yet, we settled in without faith or confidence in the system. I watched the social conservatives hurl their ideological bombs and endured the indignity of the nation's cultural counter swing. The Unraveling had set in. Without clear intent and certainly without any conscious organization, the deflated idealism of Boomers—in all its political currents—began undermining the system from within. Slowly but steadily, the Boomers' loss of confidence was spread throughout the land.

As the cultural malaise spread (Reagan's cheerful homilies to the contrary), the more practical forces in the economic base steadily advanced their cause. U.S.-based financial institutions fought steadily for—and won—looser regulation and, each time a speculative bubble burst, they managed to enlist the Feds to bail them out. Cutting social welfare programs as much as possible, the government instituted the most extensive incarceration policy in world history. Inevitably, minority youth bore the brunt of the assault. Finally, in 1992, the overt alliance of social and fiscal conservatives—backed quietly by the U.S. oil monopolies—gained control of the Congress. They leveraged the Clinton Administration and financial capital to the right. A few years later, in 2000, the neoconservative alliance won the presidency. After that, people who overtly favored shrinking government were put in charge of most government agencies. The capacity of government to address real social problems sunk to a post-Depression low.

Today, after more than two decades of unraveling social cohesion, respect for social values and institutions has hit rock bottom. Indeed, the glorification of "me," the deification of markets, the saturation of debt, the triumph of speculation, the toleration of greed, and the embrace of hoarding are all signs of the collapse of our *social* values and the nearing end of the New Deal social contract. Government and politicians have never in our lifetimes been so disrespected.

Yet, even as we write, the plodding of generational progressions is changing the social mix. Boomer idealists are ascendant as society's new elders, steadily replacing the adaptive, older generation that "managed" society during the cultural wars. Whatever our shortcomings, we Boomers believe not only that we know what's right (however, different each of our perspectives may be from each other's), but also that it is both our destiny and a social necessity that we resolve the great issues that were churned up but left unresolved in our youth. When a generation like this reaches elderhood—and faces its last chance to get things right—it inevitably stirs a mood of urgency and crisis.

The Fourth Turning Has Begun

Ominously, Strauss and Howe coined this mood shift *the fourth turning* and summarized it like this:

> A Crisis arises in response to sudden threats that previously would have been ignored or deferred, but which are now perceived as dire (103). Sparks in a High tend to reinforce

feelings of security; in an Awakening, argument; in an Unraveling, anxiety. Come the Fourth Turning, sparks of history trigger a fierce new dynamic of public synergy… Each of these sparks is linked to a specific threat about which society had been fully informed but against which it had left itself poorly protected. Afterward, the fact that these sparks were *foreseeable* but poorly *foreseen* gives rise to a new sense of urgency about institutional dysfunction and civic vulnerability. Out of the debris of the Unraveling, a new civic ethos arises. One set of post-Awakening ideals prevails over the others. People stop tolerating the weakening of institutions, the splintering of the culture, and the individualizing of daily behavior…Instead of downplaying problems, leaders start exaggerating them. Instead of deferring solutions, they accelerate them…Leaders energize every available institution and direct them toward community survival. Thus invigorated, society starts propelling itself on a trajectory that nobody had foreseen before…Societal problems that, in the Unraveling, posed insuperable dilemmas now appear to have simple if demanding solutions. A new resolve about urgent public goals crowds out qualms about questionable public means (257).

If you've been around since September 11, 2001, you've certainly noticed this kind of shift. For Americans, 9/11 was the first "spark" of the Fourth Turning. The Iraq War was the next. Katrina was another. 2008's housing, gas price, and credit crises added to the contagion. Suddenly, Al Gore's climate change complaint makes total sense. Suddenly, Neocon logic is obviously befuddled. Suddenly, the SUV has got to go. Suddenly, we hear talk of a new social contract.

Now, the battle of "post-Awakening ideals" rages in earnest. In office on 9/11, the Bush Administration got the first chance at defining that agenda. Its program, amounting to little more than a grab for Iraq's oil, was embellished with the idealism of neoconservatism—the assertion that deployment of the U.S. military would unleash a long-awaited Islamic Democratic Renaissance.

Under pressure of the terrorist assault on the World Trade Center, many Americans, grasping for answers, were lured by this vision. But it didn't work. Visions are valuable, but only if they conform to the potentials of history. Grabbing oil—whatever the stated camouflage—is a dying strategy in today's world.

Neoconservatism's failures now propel a broader search for "change," and Obama was elected to pursue it. What vision can guide that change? From where will such vision come?

Clearly, America's mass psychology is well into the Crisis phase, searching anxiously for change. We have embraced the fact of a real crisis that demands powerful action. Moreover, Americans are not alone. The same psychological constellation prevails in all the world's industrialized and industrializing nations (as we finish this book, the Egyptian revolution provides stark and inspiring confirmation). Moreover, today's generations, all over the world, were raised in the era of global telecommunications. Like never before, human society is united in its near-intuitive grasp of our mutual interdependence. Worldwide, we know our fates are tied...and in jeopardy.

Forced first by terrorism and the unilateralist American war in Iraq and now by the global financial meltdown, world leaders—few of whom appreciate, much less acknowledge, the world's socioecological crisis—are desperately seeking remedies to the more immediate crises at hand. In a fortuitous coincidence, the developing Crisis phase in global mass psychology can now enable and accelerate humanity's first steps toward addressing our looming socioecological catastrophe. As the class- and gender-based transformations in the economic base—elaborated in Chapters 3 and 4—open potential for a new, globally-oriented social contract, generational forces are also shaping mass psychology to unleash the cultural transformation now vital to strategic survival.

As social elders worldwide, the Boomer generation is positioned to define the agenda of change. Inevitably, its vision will be shaped by values that were uncorked during youthful years of awakening and experimentation and then forced back into the bottle by market fundamentalism and social conservatism. The progressive Boomers worldwide have scores to settle with their rightwing peers. Our vision is peace, not war; love, not hate; sharing, not hoarding; cooperation, not competition; nurture, not oppression; us all, not us and them; and trees, not concrete.

Beyond vision, the agenda of change will be rooted in the interests of the emergent service class and the liberation of women. It requires the empowerment and substantial bolstering of civil society to capture the pragmatic, problem-solving spirit of GenXers and the sharing civic spirit of Millennials. The means must be found to sustain a vast new, NGO-community partnership network to attack world problems along the local-global nexus of human cooperation and exchange.

GenXers hardly care about politics and cultural warfare; indeed, after twenty years of listening to social conservatives and media know-nothings assess public affairs, they consider politics and politicians the scum of the earth (a lot of us Boomers share that view, but we *believe* in our souls that we can make the world different). Many GenXers disrespect institutional remedies and are highly individualistic. Yet, mid-life GenXers, staring the socioecological crisis in the face, will take the progressive agenda articulated by Boomers and provide the will and ability to make sure it is carried out. No generation is better prepared to implement a social restructuring program than this pragmatic, GenX cohort, raised on Nike's energetic directive: *Just Do It!*

From today's civic generation—the young adults now moving through their late teens and college years, the oldest about thirty—much will be asked in terms of sacrifice. In most past Crisis moods, the resolution was reached through warfare—that is, through international, industrial era competition carried to its most extreme. Already, we see plenty of that in the current one. But, if humanity succeeds in facing and starting successful management of the socioecological crisis at hand, today's youth will have to make a great sacrifice by becoming the first generation in human history to consciously embrace and implement a global program to reduce human population and contract the global economy. And while they greatly slow population growth in their time, they must also serve as the foot soldiers in civil society's cause of worldwide, socioecological, crisis management.

We don't need more national duty and larger armies. We don't need another "Greatest Generation" that gives a great portion of itself in international war. What the world needs is a globally-networked, youth service corps through which young people can work along the local-global nexus to help their families and communities manage the socioecological crisis. Let them earn the equivalent benefits of the GI Bill in doing so—the right to a college education at public expense and family medical assistance for life, Service Veteran's benefits. We need health workers, midwives, teachers, technology nerds, engineers, linguists, ecologists, artists, performers, and community organizers to transform the world. With the revenues of the global commercial transactions fee that my brother and I propose, we can catalyze sustained, yet flexible NGO-community partnerships to mobilize a generation's growth into adulthood through community service worldwide.

What is common to all of today's living generations—today's Millennials, GenXers, Boomers, and even the elder Silents—is their lifelong exposure to the impact of global telecommunications. All over the world, television has educated these generations to understand that humanity shares a common fate. Leaving aside the inevitable reactionary fringe in each, these generations know that our futures and that of the entire world are mutually interdependent. We know this intuitively. When we embrace it consciously, the global cultural revolution will unfold, and the new social contract will be written.

Let's get it on!

Chapter 5 Response

Avoiding Visions of Armageddon

Charles:

I first read the *Mass Psychology of Fascism* as part of a college political philosophy class taught by the late Herbert Marcuse in 1972. Marcuse, a charismatic white-haired social theoretician at the time, would guide himself down the overflowing aisles crowded with the hungry ears of New Left students to the auditorium's podium. There, in a deep, warm, expressive voice accentuated by a thick German accent, he extolled the virtues of a Marxist political-economic analysis and the need for a cultural revolution against the stale mass culture of Western capitalism. Building his lecture without notes, he poetically and emphatically constructed a near unassailable web of arguments that crushed the over-consumptive lifestyles and depersonalization so characteristic of modern society, and he critiqued the excesses of authoritarian regimes too often aligned with Western democracies. Armed with social theory, he obliterated the one-dimensional mass culture of the 50s and 60s that led to passive social conformity, and he railed against the lack of alternatives to Western reduction of everything in life to an economic value. Then-Governor Reagan hated Marcuse. We students, of course, idolized him.

The Specter of Practical Skepticism Is Seen Again

Those were the glory days of the New Left and popular activism, a period my brother and I dedicated many years to support. The "Movement," as we all called it, represented that part of the Marxist-socialist debate that chose cultural protest and mass demonstrations to resist the further penetration of capitalist ethics into our lives and which fought to extend democratic rights to the world's dispossessed peoples. We thought we'd win. Marcuse always knew, however, that winning required the right material conditions. He loved our spirit and urged us forward, but he knew what we didn't know as rebellious youth: The time was not ripe. Capitalism was still ascendant and we could not win.

Marcuse always remained true to the class analysis Marx set out for us so long ago—that revolution was a matter for the industrial working class to take up, and until they did, cultural reformulations were just that, holding actions to keep resistance alive until material conditions changed. For our part today, my brother and I are less enamored with classic Marxism. Instead of conditions ripening for a labor-led revolution, what really has happened is that the whole dichotomous capitalist-worker (industrial) system has grown less relevant for future decision-making.

But we still think that cultural revolution is needed to supply the alternatives so desperately needed for problem-solving in this world. What makes Marcuse so important to our book is that he believed that the culture of resistance held *the* machine in check, putting brakes on bureaucracy and the authoritarian hand of conformity. The counterculture has and continues to provide evidence that alternative practices such as cooperatives, renewable energy, and NGOs can and do work better than established social relationships for problem-solving. But by itself, cultural resistance is not enough to overcome real-world conditions, so, like Marcuse, we wait for conditions to ripen. For forty years we have asked ourselves whether material conditions are propelling revolutionary change. We now answer in the affirmative. Material conditions are nearing the tipping point, but the tip will be towards a service economy rather than an industrial one run by workers.

Oh sure, I have continuing skepticism whether the time is really ripe, whether the moment is at hand for a great social turning. But I want to believe because I see signs all around that only a new cultural vision can save us from ourselves. Democrats, with characteristic lack of vision, hold to the same Axis of Evil as George Bush, a list that includes all the progressive

Latin American socialist leaders who have ascended to power in Brazil, Venezuela, Chile, and Bolivia in recent years. These nations should be our allies. Liberals time after time vote for the Great American Taxpayer Rip-Off that steals taxpayer savings to bail out rich speculators, just like the Republicans do. Both parties demand more troops for Afghanistan and see continued warfare as the root of American foreign diplomacy.

On the other hand, my skepticism of impending change has not been assuaged. In the wake of American political capitulation to a speculative war-based economy, there has been no youthful revolt against years of continuous warfare, no popular disgust against the environmental travesties of our age, not a single word of concern during the Presidential campaign about the deteriorated urban centers whose blight traps millions of Americans, mostly Black and Latino, in poverty and hopelessness. The middle class, we hear, needs its already elevated status over other workers protected. The last generation's advantages, we hear, must be protected for the next forty years or else… Or else what? That's what I want to hear. What are our options? What are our alternatives? Why do politicians demand that we follow the same old paths that brought us to the edge of global economic ruin in the first place? I want to see what a non-investor-dominated economy would look like, what an economic system based in problem-solving would be. I'm tired of one without alternatives and diversity.

Mass psychology and ideology are real, and they exert real social force in the political and cultural worlds. But something is missing from the generational account my brother gives. Mass psychology doesn't always work in our favor; it doesn't always lead to alternatives that pull us out of our complacent doldrums. Sometimes it chains us to a dead past. Mass psychology too often contributes to the power of those already holding the throne of society. Fear and symbols, as Reich pointed out, reinforce the grip of powerbrokers over our lives, making us passive when we should be strong, leading us to believe in the false ideology. Images of grandeur and illusionary past glory entice us to sleep-walk toward our own Soylent Green future. Mass psychology commonly offers a single ideological framework and nothing else. Capitalism and the God of Money. Too frequently, it is inherently authoritarian and distrusts change. I learned that from Marcuse.

My brother's hopeful view of a generational change in mass psychology and an impending global cultural transformation forces me to reconcile my distaste for state-managed mass psychology with prognostications that a new constellation favoring a revised social contract is at hand. How, I ask, can psychology be both authoritarian and freeing at the same time?

Generations *are* different. I lived through one of the most liberating periods of American history, traversing the time from Rosa Parks to Watergate. We did transform American culture, and neoconservative rewrites of history cannot take that away from us. But the 60s wasn't the only period of American generational awakening, as my brother calls it. The Roaring Twenties came on the heels of the suffragette movement, the emancipation of slaves offered to free the rest of us from the evils of racism, the American liberation from English colonization birthed de Toquevillian individual liberty. And even before that, Native American social democracy showed the way forward toward our system of representative democracy. But in between, generations of dogmatic pragmatists, oppressive bureaucratic bunglers, and die-hard fear mongerers strangled human rights and unleashed caustic warfare on poor, unsuspecting victims.

A second problem I have, besides mass psychological untrustworthiness, is that the parameters I would use to divide generations are not the same as those used by my brother or Strauss and Howe. My parameters would begin with generations that live liberation rather than with those that fight the crisis of foreign wars. If we start with those that ignite the spark for social justice, peace, and environmental sensitivity with their idealism, we can feel more hope that tomorrow is our day. We don't have to wait for material conditions to ripen before we act.

For my brother, crisis provides the opportunity for change and revised ways to rethink problems because crisis forces new ideas to the surface irrespective of human will. His is a carefully measured Marcusian voice. For me, a crisis may well be a prelude to reactionary oppression, followed by a boring litany of generations that accept social conformity. Mine is the voice of a skeptic who has lost hope waiting too long for liberation to cut the tentacles of capitalist rigidity and its monetary barrage against social diversity. We just can't find the same generational measuring stick for both of us. The problem with social cycles, like any circle, is that there is no beginning or end. How one interprets events still rests with the eyes of the beholder.

We also disagree on when the dying days of industrialism will happen. He sees it as past, superseded entirely by the global service economy. Certainly industrialism has entered decadency in America. But I am less sure about the rest of the world, particularly the underdeveloped areas. This isn't an argument between us, just signs of a nagging uncertainty about when material conditions for the transformation will occur. Now or fifty long years into the future? For Mother Earth's sake, I hope my brother's vision is the one we make happen.

Finally, I do not believe that 9/11 was the opening salvo of crisis for our times. That is too American-centric for my tastes. A response to 9/11, as protracted as American warfare against Muslim states is, will ultimately prove not to be significant enough to hold the world's political configuration together long enough to solve global problems. Anti-terrorism is a front for reactionaries to reassert their power in a dying industrial world; it is not a strategy for global mobilization or global liberation. Global reconstruction requires a positive ideology, one that demands social justice and ecological justice be forever linked together.

A Rosier Glimpse of Things to Come

Changing the social contract commits us to change that must last far longer than the psyche of any one generation. So I think when my brother talks about an opportune constellation of generational psychology, he really suggests that when we address crisis during opportune periods, we have a chance to set the course of history in a new direction. We still have to create the social institutions that will maintain that momentum. But changing the social contract between a people and their institutions guarantees that efforts taken now will carry into the long passage of future history. That is what we need, to preserve cultural transformation as the guiding feature of future society by building it into the structure of social relations. Patchwork solutions no longer suffice.

Global problem-solving requires the means to do it as much as the will to do it. Money and technology. Capital and investment. A social philosophy emboldened by economic justice and social restructuring. New organization, new ways of conceiving and imaging our collective tasks in front of us. New forms of collaboration. Embedding a new social contract in social relations requires that each of these be re-envisioned and redesigned with new purpose.

But I do not live in a goody-two-shoes world. Maintaining resolve to confront global problems over generations will take a helluva lot of angry, open resistance. Refusing to join the armies of repression and the organizations of the self-proclaimed protectorates of the status quo. Organizing to stop the cyclical turnings, be they industrialist ones or generational ones, so progress out of them is possible.

I believe this and only this: *Only through resistance can alternatives appear.* I'm glad the generational constellation is aligned for change, but the hard work is still to be done. We still must mobilize to establish an uncompromising voice of criticism against the status quo.

The paradigm shift I look forward to is not the one that leads to greater regulation of modern financial markets. They need to be completely restructured to represent the interests of different people than investors. I think I could have done more with five billion dollars than the whole financial bailout will do to bring about substantial change to meet our socioecological crisis. Money needs to go to where it makes a difference, not to where it returns profits to those already possessing more than they can reasonably spend. Many poorer Americans could make better investment decisions than our portfolio experts and national financiers. The trillions of dollars invested in speculative markets, in the wars in Iraq and Afghanistan, in the expansion of the world's global armies, in the expansion of long-distance trade networks, in debt, debt, debt—these are not real investments, and they demonstrate the bankruptcy of what we now consider real. The image of realness is only a smokescreen. The lesson we must learn is simple. We have been living a lie.

The generation that finally recognizes this fact and then develops the tools to do something different about it will be the one that actually opens the door to change. My Boomer generation certainly didn't do that. We ushered in possibility, not change. We learned to organize to protect small areas of naturalism and cultural creativity, but we never really succeeded in turning idealism into a socially progressive force. I hanker back to the cautions of Marcuse. The time may not yet be ripe. Wishing it were so does not make it so.

The current young adult generation is truly one of hope, but potential energy is not mechanical energy. Many of the young lack the racial biases that inhibited progressive action in the past. They have been raised on the values of opportunity, self-regulation, and collaborative team spirit that underlie the service culture. In these, we await their leadership. But they also reject theory and history to a large degree, being the ultimate self-absorbed and ahistoric generation. They lack the perspective that demonstrates that the here and now is, in fact, a product of the then and there. Without that fundamental materialism, I find it difficult to assume that their functional practicality will result in substantial change.

The experiences of the Boomer generation could provide a leadership critique to guide younger generations. After all, we fought the cultural war bitterly and with prolonged resolve. But overall, the signs are not positive. Too many of us became speculators ourselves, too many sought rewards in the good life and forgot and discarded those billions who can never even dream of its rewards. Too many fell victims to the simulacra of life, the false, profane images of money madness that prove almost too strong to be ignored by the human social psyche. The mass psychology of consumption and the mass psychology of national arrogance are powerful forces, even for progressive Boomers.

Marcuse's shadowy image haunts me still. Western social surplus is not imaginary, but it is a product of all the hard work and knowledge that people today and in the past expended, often under poor working conditions and underpaid wages. Capitalists do not own our social achievements. Social surplus exists because common folk suffered, scrimped, and saved whatever savings they could muster. Not because they traded and speculated on other people's debt. A progressive mode of production allows us to increase our savings rate, to invest wisely in intergenerational stability and hope. As we now know, the promise of industrialism could reach only so far in this direction before it began to drag down hope for human development. Now, it survives off the lives of those yet to come, and it is unsustainable because it does so.

Generational theory cannot just be built on models of past cycles and crises but must be made to account for future potential and opportunities. It must look forward as well as backward. But to overcome our growing global crisis, the mass psychology of hope must be built on critiques of the present, not its reproduction and protection. The ecological footprint of the middle class lifestyle must be altered to be sustainable, and sustainable must mean that it can share its resources with others. The task for the generation of global youth looms very large, indeed. It will be complicated, and it will demand sacrifice. The generation arising to adulthood now must burst the surreal bubble of nonreality characteristic of the lives of their elders and find the courage to build opportunity for future generations. Their sacrifice is to want the future so bad they commit to changing the present. Boomers, for their part, should be ashamed of wasting so much accumulated wealth and leaving so few treasures to pass on.

Chapter 6

Opening the Door for Future Diversity

Charles:

A number of years ago I assigned a short article to an introductory sociology class on what its author called the "McDonaldization of America" (Ritzer 2002). You know, the standardized set-ups and selling practices that make every McDonalds seem the same, every Wal-Mart identical, every Chiles or Taco Bell or what-have-you the same. Consumerization gone boring. I figured the discussion would be a great way to begin a discussion of alternatives about the future as we opened the final class section on strategies for change.

But before I could even get the concept explained for discussion, I was interrupted by a man who always sat in the back row. An African-American student from poor urban roots, he often provided our discussions with one of the more unique perspectives on social issues for this largely white, middle-class group.

"I don't see what's so wrong with McDonalds," he argued unapologetically. "They were the only ones to provide jobs in the 'hood. Everyone I know got their first job with McDonalds. I love their food, man. I grew up on it. We couldn't afford nothin' else."

Looking back on his comment, I remember an old lesson from my teaching days that came with a series of hard knocks that contested how I then imagined the educational realm should work. When participating in classes open to an honest diversity of perspectives, students often didn't go where I wanted to lead them. That's, of course, what makes diversity so uncomfortable because our own experiences, what we *know* to be true, just doesn't jive with someone else's truth. I hate that! We all do, whenever the changes that others want have little to do with what our experiences have prepared us to accept.

Yet, at a moment when the world's economic meltdown is demonstrating so emphatically the need for major systemic changes, it irks me to think that just a few years ago college students balked at the idea of promoting change, favoring instead to prepare for roles in the status quo. My student's rejoinder backing the rationality of poorly paid entry jobs at McDonalds illustrates how complex future social change will be, precisely because the present is complex too.

I also learned that students inevitably viewed me and my long hair as a symbol of social discontent, and this young generation finds discontent an impractical way to live. I always found resistance a necessity for life. Unprovoked by social realities and uninterested in social change, they saw little value in social theory and my assertion that theory should guide analysis and group practices for change. They didn't like the imposition of theory on free roaming discussions, and most fought against theoretical authority instead of learning to use theory to their (and I should say social) advantage.

But then, they were young students. At their age, I doubt that I was any more ready for a theoretical thorn in the side! In the case of McDonalds, I gave up on theory and let the battle over corporate responsibility reflect the counter ideas of my student. He won that debate with the view that mass production did more for social equality than all the environmental NGOs in the U.S. ever did. It gave goods and jobs to the people who needed them.

Albeit poorly paid ones, and ones without any real associated training or skills. Entry level jobs we call them, service jobs with no personal empowerment at all. One may wonder just how liberating the first job at minimum wage really is, and we now know that McDonalds' high calorie food product hasn't upheld any high standard of nutrition and health. In fact, my student had it wrong. Mass consumption produces problems, it does not eliminate them. It dehumanizes us, takes away our initiative, and makes us all the same, homogenizing the cultural diversity that is so essential to healthy social life.

But his vision—goods and jobs for people that need them—was not wrong. He expressed what we social scientists call a subaltern perspective, a view from people marginalized way too long from the dominant cultural and political forums. Marginalized people see the world and life differently. Their viewpoints deserve not only our respect but ultimately the right to share in leading society forward. Right now, we need subaltern perspectives in the forefront. We need jobs in poor neighborhoods as a primary response to global warming and economic upheaval. Doing the right thing means we must revamp our degenerated and hypocritical sense of moral righteousness and get back to the task of promoting diversity and social justice. We need a cultural transformation, a cultural revival to meet the demands of all these problems we have failed to fix. Upscale jobs on the wealthy side of town won't solve anything.

Bottom-line Socioecological Theory for the Service Age

In an earlier chapter we stated unequivocally that our current lifeways threaten global ecology because they lack social justice. Too many of our actions fail the Simultaneity Principle that requires, in a contracting, transforming world, that every action both lessen social inequality and restore ecological balance. That means that both the neutrality found in scientific objectiveness and the dominant trend toward political centrism just won't suffice to bring about the changes we now need so badly. We grant that relative to established norms, necessary social vision *does* appear radical. But radical vision accompanied with determined global action will chart a new course for global problem-solving.

For middle class consumers and service providers in highly developed countries, the daily insulation of their lives from poverty, crime, neighborhood degradation, and social disintegration obscures the relationship between profiteering capitalism and social deprivation. That obscurity and its resulting social ignorance have become a major obstacle to environmental protection around the world. The assumption that a lifestyle filled with environmental amenities and high tech inventions is somehow "green" and politically justifiable is part and parcel of the myth of the middle class. Rather, the very real manifestations of the techno-green justification have proven disastrous to the world's storehouse of cultural diversity and our sense of social fairness, and they weaken ecosystem resilience whenever they surface unopposed. High consumptive lifestyles in developed nations eat the resources needed by poorer ones to develop. Period. The existence of the middle class provokes worldwide poverty. We have to stop protecting middle class lifestyles and begin changing them so that what is good for some is not disaster for others. And we all know that under unfettered industrialism, global and local logics both trend toward the unsustainable overconsumption of environmental resources.

No theoretical alternative exists to resolve current resource degradation.

Lacking an adequate theory or model of natural resource depletion and degradation, we are unable to effectively tackle the questions of crisis management and the development of a social and environmental strategy for the future. We hang on to hopes of profit maximization at every level yet turn a blind eye toward the poverty under our noses that such a policy has fostered—bankrupt rural and ghetto communities, disintegrating infrastructure, a global health crisis, economic instability, credit debt, mortgage debt, national debt—all at record high levels. The ecological side of the equation is no better off. Species extinctions are at an all-time high, climate changes produce ever greater and costlier tragedies each year, rainforests continue to disappear at alarming rates, and soil organics are depleted and destroyed by chemicals and drought well beyond Mother Nature's ability to repair them. These are serious problems, both the social ones and the environmental ones. They need to be addressed in short order with massive funding, global in scope, carried out in local programs that are sustained to make a difference in real people's lives.

To that end, we must advance new theories about social organization and practice, something that dares make a difference in global lives. The goal cannot be to protect the wealth of the today's middle class citizens who have thus far failed to mobilize in the name of global equality. In fact, as we have already seen, the middle class cannot be mobilized because it does not really exist as a class, being based in income similarity and not in a shared social position in the relations of production. But we recognize that many middle income families share unity through their participation in service production, and hence we developed our theory of the service class to offer a way to better conceptualize organizing the middle strata of people toward global action.

Now we must add to that theory. Here we introduce the theory of socioecology as a new standard for praxis to be built on the experience of citizen scientists, organized around the Simultaneity Principle, and carried out through an expanded role for civil society. The service class needs an outlook, an ideology that separates it from the old and, dare we say, arcane industrial worldview of private profiteerism. Socioecology is that new standard.

Socioecology arises each day out of the work people do to repair this damaged global ecosystem and encourage greater and open economic opportunity for diverse cultures and peoples. It is the advocacy science of global citizens, and it demands that each and every political and economic action be subjected to criticism based in a single criteria: *Does this action reduce both environmental degradation and social inequality at the same time?* This Simultaneity Principle must guide all our future work.

Listen to me. I've been at this issue for over forty years, and I am worried that despite winning so many battles along the way, we are losing the war. The war I am talking about is the one for environmental justice, for a cultural value system that demands that the steps we take today, politically, economically, and socially, be designed so that they lead us to a better actual future, not a pretend "American dream" of more little boxes for the working poor and greater mansions for the nouveau riche, not longer lines at Wal-Mart with its cheap goods that drive quality products off the shelves, not the mass advertising for things we hardly want and certainly do not need. Need is real in the world, but most of the developed world doesn't need more things. We gotta get real. The people who need help are the ones who cannot afford it. What the developed world needs is to lose its fear of losing what it has and to begin sharing what it has before there is no future left for any of us to fear.

When we use the criterion of the simultaneity of socioecological necessity, many current programs and policies fail miserably. What seemed to be progressive, environmentally-sensitive programs prove unable to meet the mettle of our criterion. Giving hybrid car buyers large tax credits for purchasing fuel efficient automobiles fails, not only in that the tax credits cannot increase what is already in undersupply (they only extend the demand and waiting time for hybrid vehicles) but they transfer middle class welfare onto the backs of taxpayers unable to afford a new car purchase in the first place. Middle class tax credits increase the financial burden on the working poor but do not transfer the ability to enjoy the fruits of environmental greening downward.

Congressional support of ethanol production likewise fails the simultaneity test. Farmers continue to lap up enormous subsidies as they take land out of food production and turn it into an arm of the oil industry. While it spreads the massive oil subsidies to a new breed of "farm-based oil producer," it simultaneously expands the Gulf of Mexico dead zone caused by fertilizer pollution. It also reduces the supply of food corn in the world and increases the cost of a basic food staple beyond the means of the world's poor. Corn ethanol is a socioecological dead end. It makes matters worse for all but a few farmers, and in reality most of the recipients of farm aid are corporations, not small farmers.

Most global warming responses to date also fail the test. At this point, the vast majority of the market-oriented proposals to deal with global warming guarantee that the same people, the same companies, the same nations that got this planet into trouble in the first place are going to be the ones who control our destiny in getting us out of our problem. Social inequality will not be confronted. There will be no social restructuring, no new value system to replace mass production profiteering and private gain, no political movement toward greater social responsibility and greater representation of the world's majority in major economic decision-making. Climate change advocates don't question the "realness" of investment decisions, or the lack of savings initiatives, or the necessity of military expenditures that "protect" vested interests in world development.

The general knee-jerk reactions to early signs of global warming express humanity's more general tendency towards irrationality whenever possible. Both the doomsday soothsayers of global warming destruction and the naysayers who discount global warming science as a hoax perpetrated by environmental radicals to disband economic solvency have it wrong. Most environmental problems, and we have many across the globe, are not direct products of climate change but of three major social forces: (a) capitalist exploitation of natural resources, (b) the heavy toll of rising populations and their consumptive resource needs, and (c) the ecological degradation needed to sustain our increasingly urbanized lifestyles. These are unsustainable processes. We do ourselves a disservice by being so faddish over global warming. Planetary climate change is not a fad but an established trend that humans have accelerated with our energy-based, industrial mode of production. Concentration on global warming alone makes the restoration of global ecosystems untenable because, while global warming can only be resolved through long-run lifestyle changes in developed countries, many more environmental and social problems can be solved much quicker with adequate social resolve to do so. In fact, it is in the resolution of these more local issues that we will develop the means and skills to overcome the broader questions of adaptations to global climate change.

It seems to me that the roots to an adequate response to climate change have already been established by civil society groups, citizen scientists, academics, and even some companies and government agencies in their attempts to deal with international political and economic issues over the last few decades. These measures were taken in response to a number of social and ecological crises, but they predated global warming science in general. Their contribution to climate change social action has been to establish how scientific analysis of conditions can be activated as social change in local development strategies. Science becomes a real motivator for action when local problem-solving is empowered, when cultural diversity is respected, when scientists facilitate local processes rather than direct them. We must learn, in retrospect, to make global warming initiatives local ones that bring people together to solve their own issues.

Just as the service-led economy was born as experiments and rationalities within industrialism, so has socioecology found life among the myriad of responses to ethnic genocide, environmental degradation, and economic catastrophes exasperated by Mother Nature and global militarism. While we need to take global warming issues seriously and respond collectively to them, many of the tools and lessons we need lie buried in already on-going human practices. We don't have time to reinvent the wheel.

As an advocacy science, socioecology has two fronts. The first has to do with its particular objectives to reduce ecological degradation and social inequality and the second with the forms of mobilization that might bring it to fruition in human lives. The notion that a science can or should have an advocacy/mobilization component is new to most people. We are used to thinking of science as neutral in human affairs, though it does not take much effort to find examples where implementing scientific findings through applied science changed lives and communities. Sometimes, that's beneficial, such as with cell phones and computers; sometimes, implementing technology throws people out of work and sends jobs overseas, brings scary health risks and diseases, or demolishes ecological niches in a flash. In times when social action is demanded by deteriorating conditions, knowledge without the effort to embrace change isn't knowledge at all. It's collective, irresponsible cowardice. We make no claims to neutrality here. Socioecology is advocacy science.

As a foundation, socioecology promotes decreasing social inequality while increasing ecological protection across the globe. We need to end the dichotomy between human rights and environmental ones, and we need to guarantee that human rights include the right to an improvement in family economic, health, and food security. Constructing the infrastructure to provide social services is a central objective of socioecology—the roads, sanitation systems, potable water, hospitals, housing, and the like that we all need. Thus, socioecology is advocacy science that demands praxis, that is, putting theory into practice and learning from social experiments and experience. We all must become socioecological entrepreneurs.

To reach that end, civil society will have to expand its role in political and economic decision-making, placing both states and corporations under its growing scrutiny. As part of the service-led mode of production, elements in civil society must learn to oppose private profiteering values and to support collaboration and co-management of resources so that benefits pass on to marginalized people.

Effective public scrutiny over corporate and government decision-making involves the serial processes of critical thinking about current relationships, the design of alternative proposals for change, and the demonstration of field projects to prove the practicality of proposed service-led models. Only with persistent citizen oversight can we issue critiques of past failures and problems, prepare summations of lessons learned, and then propagate and replicate successes in the future. We must quit believing that profit-making businesses are the only ones with the skills, knowledge, and understanding capable of producing results. Civil society's NGOs are already replete with the knowledge and experience that we need.

Because the service-led mode of production will necessarily develop its own cultural norms and values to sustain its reproduction, the need for critical perspectives on our current modes of thoughts and social organizations must be fine tuned and expanded. People in industrialized, developed nations must learn to become self-critical, to examine the reasons why their lifestyles are threatening earth ecology and why, through nearly a hundred years of persistent capitalist-based economic competition and warfare, we have failed to raise the standards of living of most of the world's citizens. Overconsumption and militarization by the already wealthy of the world are solutions to nothing. Broad-based social and economic opportunity can be the only root of a sustainable global society. Global solutions lie in servicing and transferring knowledge so that people in underdeveloped areas can learn to be self-reliant as well as self-conscious.

Finding effective alternative social theories to guide future society is no little task. Capitalist nations have already spent a century of military and political might combating socialist claims that wealth must be more fairly distributed in the world system. Now, under global capitalist hegemony, our new social theories must demonstrate their power by leading to alternatives. These need to be practical and to prove they can alter our current social structure and the political economy toward ones that guide our global relationships under the Simultaneity Principle. Piece by piece, the old theories must be dismantled and replaced.

The major change suggested in this book is that civil society be guaranteed adequate funding and independence to transfer wealth, knowledge, skills, and networking tools to marginalized people. NGOs are already testing the waters of such an agenda in international development programs throughout the world, but the insufficiency of the effort is clear. OXFAM has invested capital in thousands of neighborhood development programs the world over. Food First has rethought and re-theorized the relationship between population growth and food security and reorganized environmental crisis management around social redevelopment and local economic expansion.

The Rainforest Action Network has re-envisioned environmental protection as strengthening indigenous rights to community-based natural resource management. There are too many others who have stepped forward to initiate innovative social experiment to name here. But their work is not unimportant, as industrial theory suggests. Rather, they are essential to an adequate vision of the future. Less and less we should discuss change in terms of a greening of the economy while leaving power and money in the same hands as in the industrial era. Increasingly, under the service-led mode of production, power is transferred to the public sphere—not government, per se, but transparent, accountable, mission-driven organizations that have a public purpose—where economic and political decisions will be made by civil society rather than by nation-states and corporations.

In the demonstration of the utility of the alternatives we propose, NGOs prove the inevitability of people as masters of our own fate. People can change the future, and, if action is taken on a global scale, the coming *dark age* of industrialism can be avoided. In many cases, the utility of this alternative vision has already been shown as NGOs have created small bank, microlending institutions among women's groups and communities, nurtured food security through agricultural programs geared toward sustainability, and enhanced local empowerment through control of forests and other natural resources. Many private people have purchased solar equipment and demonstrated the utility of small-scale power production and net metering. But so far, the effort by the developed world and its NGOs to be ecologically friendly and climate change sensitive has been woefully inadequate, horribly underfunded, and too often carried out as the aftermath of military intervention rather than as an alternative to it. An honest effort at global reform must become effective at not only slowing the degradation of nature by advanced capitalist nations, but also at learning to transfer to the underdeveloped world the technology, knowledge, and collaborative lessons of developed countries without legal and profit strings attached. Since private, profit-oriented corporations refuse to do so, civil society must learn to compete with corporations for technology and the rights to transfer information to others.

Ultimately, the solution to the world's environmental and social dilemmas lies in decentralization of the benefits of modern production to the entire world, not hoarding them in wealthy nations.

Ultimately, the solution to the world's environmental and social dilemmas lies in the decentralization of the power of modern production decision-making in favor of global civil society assessments conducted in local contexts.

Ultimately, we must reorganize ourselves to permit future social alternatives to thrive.

Personal Notes on Alternatives

For myself, I came to these "ultimate" appreciations through experience on two fronts: experiments in alternative agriculture that were part of the environmental and social critique of the Sixties counterculture movement in the U.S. and exposure to "liberation sociology" and its practice in Latin America during my research and travel in the region in the 1980s and 90s.

In the early 1970s I began an organic farm in southern California believing that what was missing from American politics were real examples of successful alternatives to profit-driven agro-capitalism. I was concerned about the growing international infatuation with chemical farming, and my plan was to grow local organic vegetables for the People's Food cooperative across the highway as a way to both protest the status quo and to present an alternative. I proved a horrible farmer, a prime example of suburban ignorance of material realities, and my small farm proved remarkably unsuccessful even as a commune. In early summer, the ocean fog would roll in at 10 a.m. and roll out at 2 p.m., stunting early growth of corn, beans, and many root crops. Tomatoes developed rapidly after the fog season, but inevitably caught a fungus that my primitive organic methods could not overcome. Only broccoli thrived during the cooler winter months, though by the time it formed heads in spring, sunnier organic gardens further up the coast had beaten me to the punch and driven the price down to less than a third of early spring. Ecology imposed its limits. Ultimately I must take much of the blame—my lack of experience and available funds doomed my enterprise. But I learned many lessons, improved greenhouse designs, and, most importantly, never grew discouraged about organic alternatives.

While my efforts failed in terms of their primary objective of growing organic produce profitably, they proved to be one of thousands of such experiments that changed American health practices and eating habits after the mid-1970s. We lost many battles, but time suggests we won that war. What began as a surfer subculture—vegetarianism, religious holism, environmental recreation as central to lifestyle—slowly edged its way into the mainstream culture of the country. We created an effective critique of pesticide farming and federal farm subsidies, of a medical industry addicted to drug treatments, of fast food marketing and consumption. We demonstrated what used to be known by our grandparents and their forbearers as true—that organic food tastes better and is more nutritious than commercial products, that herbal remedies suffice well as preventative health procedures, that cooking and eating whole grains really is not that time-consuming and is extremely beneficial—is still the truth. We presented the world with an alternative conception concerning health in general and demonstrated it with practice. One need not look too far to see the signs of survival of that movement for alternative health practices—chain organic food stores like Wild Oats, small rural food cooperatives now central to their community's eating habits, farmers' markets, herbal treatment centers at drug stores, an exercised-crazed society with escalating life expectancy and quality of life improvements well into old age.

We didn't win the health war by making everyone quit their white bread and tobacco addictions. We didn't win the knowledge war by ignoring science or turning our back on medical technology and science when it was useful. We didn't win the cultural war by making everyone abandon Christianity in favor of global holism and respect for other religions. We moved forward in all three by changing our culture, by building examples of how a world based in our values could fare better than a world without them, by networking and working with others to make eating and health alternatives both viable and reproducible. We sought alternatives in Chinese acupuncture and Japanese shiatsu, Native American herbal folklore, and Rodale organic farm experiments. We changed a counterculture set in confrontation with capitalist exploitation into a subculture of hope, raising critique first and then making it work as a social experiment within our own social milieu.

Not everyone followed our lead, but even in centers of anti-environmentalism, signs of greening are apparent. In the Western farm belt, billboards at farms and county fairgrounds declare farmers as the true endangered species while marking disappearing salmon as interlopers. But lately these farmers have supported organic solutions to soil pest control, accepted large subsidies for integrating water conservation into their farming practices, and initiated experiments with local marketing and solar power as means to overcome the rising costs of energy for irrigation. Cultural materialism explains that opposition to change is overcome only when conditions are ripe. Ripe conditions, however, don't evolve spontaneously but appear as the direct result of actions by activists who demonstrated the practicality of alternatives decades ago. I admit I take the current environmental alacrity with a sense of bitter irony. It hasn't been easy living a life as a social and environmental entrepreneur trying to open new and greener ground in the American psyche. Unlike capitalist counterparts who make rapid riches off inventiveness, social entrepreneurs are frequently saddled with cultural epithets mocking their achievements even as those ideas are adopted into the social mainstream.

Defenders of the old industrial system of mass production on farms, in the woods, and in the factories are losing the larger struggle to control future global events. They are out of touch with the people's movement toward alternative strategies for social change that include such elements as less costly health treatments, local renewable energy development, and more effective natural resource management.

Listen, I understand. People will defend their turf. The vested interests of corporations, the state, and entrenched political and economic constituencies will continue to demand their unfair share of tomorrow's profits and socioecological amenities. That's why socioecology is a program of advocacy and, thus, significantly different than the "neutral" science of environmental sociology that is taught in colleges across the country. Socioecological advocates cannot rest on their laurels and hope that individuals will change personal attitudes and beliefs. Time is too short. Socioecology needs the assistance of propaganda campaigns, political lobbyists, economic supporters, and social reformers to mobilize a countermovement to unchanging social inertia. Too many people think that because they are doing well, the world is doing well. They are wrong.

Making change won't be easy because vested interests work selfishly to restrict alternate options, while our own past experiences limit our insights about what actually can be done. Self-liberation strategies among disempowered groups become a necessity in overcoming interests and experiences that prevent people from taking action.

Liberation sociology is the study of how marginalized people empower themselves to change the world. Less you think self-liberation is a lark, I should tell you that it's no lark that Brazil, Venezuela, Ecuador, Bolivia, and Chile all voted for socialist governments over the past decade after years of American military intervention to prevent that from happening. Those election results favoring democratic socialism are a product of forty years of community organizing by liberation educators and religious leaders who joined with peasant-based and indigenous revolutionaries in Latin America to bring about social change. By developing social critiques and raising them in their communities, people learn to understand the disadvantages they face in the social system in which they live, and in Latin America disempowered people have come to command enough power to force open the opportunity structure of society. People can make a difference when they act in concert with others with similar problems, when they take the time to learn the lessons of other people's struggles, when they take both social theory and spiritualism and lend them to a political focus. Liberation sociology studies the struggles of marginalized people and explores their successes and failures in attempts to restructure society toward a more open and inclusive opportunity structure. Since an open opportunity structure is a necessary basis of service-led political economy, socioecological science must account for the experiences of people throughout the world who have resisted imperialist efforts to exploit their natural resources, religious sites, and labor power.

Subaltern strategies are going to be important for our global future. That they have a socialist perspective in general is not surprising. Unless the wealthy learn to share their wealth with the poor, not through consumerism but through empowerment in the economic system, there can be no adequate response to global crises in the future. Under status quo capitalism, one crisis can only be traded for another. But what distinguishes the service-led mode of production from its previous industrial counterpart is that now the emphasis of aiding the poor—of reversing the world's economic and social polarization—becomes a central strategy in repairing the global economic and ecological systems. We serve those in need rather than exploit them. We earn sustenance by empowering others in their lives and work.

Profiteering and speculative investing are relatively easy pursuits under industrialism. Changing people's lives so they can do for themselves what they see fit is quite another process. Individualization and invention become much less valuable as social tools while networking, education, and servicing problem-solving become so much more important. These are skills for tomorrow. They also are skills that marginalized people everywhere already possess or can develop out of necessity. In Chapter 4 we expressed the view that women have traditionally possessed the social and communicative skills needed for tomorrow's daily transactions and that the patriarchy of surplus extraction and inheritance no longer suffices to solve modern socioecological problems. In Chapter 5 we demonstrated that the current youth generation has adapted a popular culture grounded in networking and social inclusion without discrimination toward race, gender, or ethnicity. Now, we make the case that socioecological action demands not only feminine communicative skills and youthful inclusionary networking but also subaltern critiques of past practices in order to construct alternative strategies for collective action in the future.

Socioecological necessity requires that the service class make a self-conscious effort to assert its open opportunity structure at center stage of world events. Technology and networking communications have rapidly transformed knowledge, skills, and service production into global commodities. However, the assumed equal access to information and know-how that will establish the basis for a truly reformed world economy has not come with the information transition. It is not that communication technologies have not reached all parts of the world—they have and they are transforming it. But communication and knowledge will remain selective until the opportunity structure of economic and political systems are opened to those of all classes with talent and capability. Yet the world lacks a systematic effort to train and empower people who do not already have ample access to the benefits of capitalist accumulation. Service values and work have yet to prove the power of their materialism as forces that can radically alter our culture and make us account for a diversity of opinions and strategies beyond our past experience. Crisis management within the service-led mode of production, however, could institute global change at a pace which other material forces favoring globalization—imperialism and finance capitalism—cannot. Humans can combine skill and experience with conscious decision-making. We can use our new class and cultural basis to change the world if we so choose.

The importance of the subaltern perspective comes as the apogee of American leadership of the global economic and political world passes. For most Americans, declining centrality to the global network is an improbable and seemingly bitter pill to swallow, but social progressiveness and morality no longer flow spontaneously from the American way of life. Unable to constrain its massive consumption of global resources, instability in the American economy has destabilized the rest of the world time after time. Since the 1980s, international NGOs have taken up the moral banner that should fly over social processes in the future. Working to meet the enormous need for social opportunity and to oppose environmental degradation, NGOs have paraded human rights along with economic development and the protection of ecological diversity. Human rights, economic development for the marginalized, and ensuring ecological diversity—these are the fundamental principles of the service-led mode of production. Put another way, servicing the future requires investment in human capital, global infrastructure, and ecological restoration.

How or whether Americans change cultural perspectives that now hold the line against global wealth redistribution will be central to the speed of world response to global warming and other massive global inequities. But few in the world believe that the United States will ever use its democratic principles to lead us to restore humanity to fair and equitable social and environmental relationships. Too many times over the past half a century, the United States has led with military might rather than technological egalitarianism, it has supported alliances with dictatorships rather than mass movements for democratic socialism, and it has negotiated with fear and rejection rather than an honest international collaborative effort. Today, the United States prefers to use unskilled military troops to rebuild broken economies rather than organize sociologists and social workers as a skilled workforce in international development. NGOs who follow the American military lead into nation-building walk a slippery path. How can they provide critical social assistance to people in need while supporting the very forces of power that continue to make violent resistance to imperialism so necessary for the world's poor?

The resurgence of democratic socialism in Latin America provides a lesson to us all. Unlike dogmatic Marxism that plagued the world's revolutionary movements in the 60s and 70s, socialism in Latin America has always had to confront the reality of subaltern realities. Indigenous rights counter-balanced traditional class analysis from the beginning, demanding respect for indigenous cultural practices even within modern capitalist life and class conflict. Peasants suffered from proletarian propaganda that dismissed small farmers as "backward" and "outmoded." Yet, it was peasants that carried out the successful socialist revolutions of twentieth century. Furthermore, Latin American countries survived first European imperialism and then North American imperialism, and people in Latin America have had to find ways to combat the repressive nature of U.S.-backed dictatorships for the last 130 years. Latin Americans discovered ways to get their voices heard and their lives organized for dealing with the problems their governments and the capitalist economy refused to handle.

They found answers through the movement of liberation pedagogy and liberation theology that took root in Brazil in the early 1960s and spread widely through support from Catholic clergy in the following decade. Liberation pedagogy, pedagogy being the science of teaching, asserted that illiterate adults could rapidly learn to read and develop communicative skills if the subject of their education was their own lives. The key was to teach people to use critical thinking in collective contexts under the guide of a facilitator, a person who's knowledge, training, and experience was more "worldly" than those of local people and whose goal was to introduce theory that clarified how social conditions might limit the choices of marginalized people. By working on their own problems, people could educate themselves and learn the skills to deal with their problems. Liberation education became the working model for liberation theology, a Catholic program of community development that encouraged lay church members to study and discuss the Bible on their own, but to discuss it in terms of their own problems of poverty, landlessness, and powerlessness. Receiving Vatican support in 1968 but approbation in later years, liberation praxis that combined critical class analysis with spiritual communitarianism became the working model for community organizing throughout Latin America. Not surprisingly, efforts by the U.S. to derail democratic socialism in Latin America through support of repressive regimes in Brazil, Nicaragua, Guatemala, Colombia, Chile, and Peru proved fruitless as the people of these nations continued to demand that social equality be part and parcel of any system that considers itself democratic.

The lessons of the persistence of social democracy in Latin America for the service-led mode of production are clear.

First, as radical environmentalists have demonstrated through forty years of campaigns against corporate profiteering and ecological destruction, by arming themselves with knowledge and attending to local problems with the spirit of learning and fostering greater local unity, a movement cannot be derailed by big money, big government, or big guns. Thus, to maintain that civil society groups such as NGOs and volunteer organizations will be the basis of a new global alignment between people of the developed and underdeveloped worlds is not the least bit impractical. Global unity comes through local practice.

Second, local practice is based in collaborative exercises in which diverse groups negotiate and work out their corresponding roles in ensuring better social and economic outcomes. Collaboration requires time, science, criticism, and a willingness to learn by both leading and following others. These are not characteristics usually associated with speculative capital or western capitalist imperialism.

Third, when people decide to negotiate issues, they need a basis for unifying their objectives. Patriotism, religion, and race have all had their failures, and while capitalism has integrated the world's economy, it too lacks redistributive justice. Some form of scientific advocacy is necessary to link diverse interests, and we have learned through decades of Marxist revolt and environmental controversy that the answer lies in the simultaneity of socioecology—social equality and environmental protection as the only form of justice.

Fourth, a central state or global big brother is unnecessary for the development of knowledge and social organization as long as issues are addressed locally through critical thinking. In realizing that people everywhere have the ability to learn about socioecology and to change their circumstances if given assistance, we find no need of an outside entity to tell us what and how to do things. The service of facilitation becomes the world's major mode of survival.

We need to provide knowledge, training, financing, and assistance in organizing subaltern realities. But that cannot happen if one arm threatens with a big stick, one steals resources with impunity, one erects tariffs against foreign products and demands free trade access for its own, and one engages in providing counter-productive intelligence and assistance for repressive police forces. Americans must restructure both their culture and economic system so the rest of the world has a chance to do it for themselves. Socioecology must become the science of developed countries so it can, in turn, become the world's science.

Socioecology begins in communities, yet it relies on global financing. In this unequal world, communities can hardly expect to be self-sufficient any time soon. This contradiction re-emphasizes the importance of service class leadership and the need for a service class that is self-aware and able to pursue its own interests. Service providers the world over must come to see their roles as central to the future. They must quit relying on others to lead, must abandon their slavish pursuits of fast profits and their acceptance of corporate management over human affairs. Service class duty has a much higher calling. Two are most important: (1) preventing us from destroying ourselves by degrading our global environment and (2) reversing population growth by advancing social equity and opportunity. These two objectives are keys to a new service value system, but there are many others as well. We must protect and expand cultural diversity, restore biological diversity, ensure public health, and provide liberating education for girls and women the world over. We must kick the "good ol' boys" out of political offices and grant power to the voices of displaced factory workers, small business owners, farm workers, indigenous peoples, ghetto residents, minorities, and women. We must gather together to promote social reinvestment in broken neighborhoods, guarantee rights to everyone to have both homes and home security, and fight against forced migration by rebuilding communities from which people must migrate. We need to encourage citizen science and grant it the right to guide our lives as much as technologists working for industry and medical corporations do to our lives now. Only a self-conscious service community can do all these things together.

Citizen science—and I mention this, in particular, as important—is usually based in the knowledge systems of local people. While we must not fantasize about the harmony or unity of local communities, we can at least respect the value of a sense of place, of homeland, of linkages to other people who share the same land and often significant parts of the same culture. When local people become scientists, both social scientists and ecologists, they empower themselves, because they use modern knowledge as tools and modern ways of thinking to strengthen local visions and local histories. With the rise of socioecological science and the service class comes a vision that once and for all grants respect to ethnic history and customs, even within the context of the global responsibilities we all must shoulder in coming decades.

By finding ways to tax the global financial transactions of the service class we can find ways to finance social experiments on the local level. Self-conscious social experimentation takes time, sometimes years. It needs to mature and ripen. Years of participatory research have shown the value of bringing diverse interests into projects that require the input and work of each in the co-management of resources and the development of locally based economic and ecological restoration projects. People can learn to deal with their own problems if given assistance and the means to do so. The overriding goal of service must be to make this decentralized process happen by finding a way to support its continuance, its expansion, and its empowerment.

How can this be done?

By limiting state power and nationalist culture and giving voice and authority to the local-global nexus. We must take power over our local lives and take it away from corporations and financial investors who declare we are here only to service their greed. By accepting face-to-face diversity, negotiating with other special interests over our common goals, and not rejecting global ties, we assert our right to do what we feel is best. We can bring the service economy into our communities, embrace its power and potential, and raise our status and consciousness to that of service providers. We can play our role in the cultural revolution that will avert the *dark age* and open the road to a just, sustainable, global future.

Chapter 6 Response

The Middle Class—Love 'Em or Leave 'Em?

Steve:

"The existence of the middle class," my brother writes, "provokes worldwide poverty."

That's a strong statement, and I think it deserves further elaboration.

My brother's point is that the lifestyle now common throughout Europe and North America is only sustainable if ways can be found to make sure that the rest of the world never comes to enjoy the same thing. If it did, we'd rapidly deplete the remaining fossil fuel while irrevocably polluting all the earth's air and water, and no one could enjoy a middle class lifestyle.

Yet, given the state of global communications and commercial integration, the rest of the world inevitably strives for the luxury that is commonplace in Europe and America. They'll insist on getting it, too. We already see that in the swelling migrations of industrious poor people into not only Europe and North America, but also into urban centers all over the world.

Of course, the striving for the "good life" is probably less a motive than escaping the bad, but the effect is the same. The present system wasn't set up to satisfy this craving for everyone on earth.

On the other hand, the failure to ensure stability for everyone on earth is already producing social rebellion and other dislocations—terrorism, genocide, starvation, disease, sexual slavery, the aforementioned migrations—so global stability must be addressed, lest the world's economy be undermined "from below" as surely as it has been undermined "from above" by the meltdown of global financial institutions and mechanisms.

If only the number of poor families were much smaller, perhaps our task would be more manageable. Yet, the irony is that the only proven way to reduce human population is to raise people's standards of living. In other words, if we hope to reduce the *number* of people, including the number of poor people, to make achieving social stability more realistic, we have to first raise the overall quality of life for the world's masses.

With that in mind, you can see clearly why my brother says the existence of the middle class provokes worldwide poverty. We can't have a large and expanding middle class in Europe, America, China, India, Dubai, Cape Town, Caracas, and elsewhere *and* a successful fight against poverty. And without a successful fight against poverty, we can't have global stability and an accompanying reduction in human population, resource depletion, and pollution.

We're in a squeeze. That's why we're on the brink of a global *dark age*.

My brother's style is to throw it in your middle class face. I understand. Long ago, despite his own middle class upbringing, he rejected middle class life and its consumptive lifestyle. Cantankerous as he is, he deserves credit, not only for seeing the writing on the wall, but having the courage to actually risk living outside middle class boundaries. After college, he "dropped out," moved to Idaho, met his future wife, and, to meet the reality of survival, took work together with her picking fruit in Washington and Montana. They learned rudimentary Spanish, and for a few years, adopted the migratory lifestyle of their co-workers, wintering in Mexico where they could live off their less-than-middle-class savings. This choice in life put him off the career track that most of us middle class Americans inexorably adopt, and, decades into it, he's not going back. Yet his chosen rural poverty did not end his alternatives. Indeed, in his forties, he tapped his savings to get his Ph.D. in Latin American environmental sociology, as much to gain skills to better to fight for environmental and social justice as to establish a stable career. He earned a Fulbright and headed straight back to Latin America to re-explore as an intellectual the world he first came to know as a sojourner. Afterwards, he taught at a few American colleges, occasionally travelling south to lecture (in Spanish) to development audiences.

Now, when he writes—as you can see—he pulls no punches when it comes to America's middle class. His voice has become one of America's subaltern voices. I, on the other hand, am still a member of that amorphous middle class and want his perspective to go "easier" on us. Let me make a few points about the middle class.

First, "middle class" isn't a scientific formulation. It's just descriptive. As we noted in Chapter 2, back in the early days of industrialism two new classes formed: the mill owners and the millworkers, later known as capitalists and proletarians. Much later, around the turn of the twentieth century, a distinct, intermediate stratum emerged that provided the increasingly complex services necessary for industrialism's expansive commodity production and distribution. This stratum was the early basis for what has developed, in the last fifty years, into the service class.

If "middle class" only described this stratum, we could accept it as a scientific category, but it was muddled by an important social development that occurred through the middle part of the twentieth century: the maturation of the industrial and craft union movement.

In the 1930s—as western industrialism endured the crisis of the Great Depression at the same time that the Soviet Union offered the western working class a plausible, revolutionary, socialist alternative—the industrialists entered into the New Deal, a revised social contract in which they and the government accepted the labor movement as an equal partner. That alliance assisted the U.S. and Western Europe through the Depression and the war against fascism, but the price was a broader sharing of industrial profit with the working class, particularly its union sector. Though the 1930s and 40s, empowered by New Deal legislation, the unions gained respectability and strength. In the post-war era of the 50s, they garnered increased wages and compensation, including (in the U.S.) employer-paid health care and retirement (these were state-financed in Europe).

The relative prosperity of western industrial production in the post-war era brought industrial compensation into the range of the still nascent, intermediate service stratum. In the absence of any clear tradition of class concepts in western social analysis, the gathering wealth of factory workers in combination with the rising compensation of service providers created the impression of a broad layer of simply "middle class" employees. The leaders of unions—who, themselves, were and are service providers, not industrial workers—capitalized on the era's unique characteristics, including the lack of a place in the social contract for service providers, to position themselves as the champions of the "middle class." As a result, middle class values became synonymous with industrial and craft union themes of consumption and job protection, of keeping up as much as possible with the opulence and private security of the capitalist way of life.

Today, the New Deal social contract, as well as the post-war compensation package, is failing fast, and industrial workers are a small and shrinking portion of the western workforce. Union workers now represent only seven percent of the private sector (though, as the economy has transitioned, they have come to represent about a third of all public sector employees, the vast majority of whom are service providers). Though the 2008 American Presidential election was fought largely over hollow claims of who would fight better for the middle class—mostly, in terms of tax policy—there is, in fact, no such thing as a middle class. While reasons exist to support each other, the industrial working class and the service class must each find ways to fight for itself and its own interests.

Diverging interests between the industrial working class and service workers have caused the breakdown of the accumulation- and consumption-oriented program of personal, private security that was created by finance capital and endorsed by its union intermediaries during the social crisis of the 30s. In the Service Age, a new system of collective security must develop, one that constrains consumption and allows a steady contraction in mass production, the sale of "things," and private hoarding. While commodity exchange shrinks, service exchange expands. Instead of hoarding cash and commodities "to keep up with the Joneses"—or more the rub in today's economy, to protect one's own little nest egg in the face of a roaring, global depression—we need to develop a worldwide system of mutual service in which everyone has a role and place and through which we keep ourselves alive and well.

After the Bush Administration's neoconservative policies, it is reasonable to examine the failure of ideology, but we should be precise about the ideology we eviscerate. The Bush Administration's ideology was the combined outlook of oil industry dinosaurs and the greedy financial capitalists, albeit covered in a thin veneer of patriotic idealism. The mature service class of the future will have an outlook all its own, distinct from the speculative financiers and the oil industrialists, and different from the industrial working class as well. But the dividing lines remain muddled in the current crisis, as if society awaits the service class to gather, clarify, and articulate its particular outlook as the basis to lead the whole world forward.

What are the key elements of a service class perspective? I say: The Local-Global Nexus. Collaboration. We're all in this together with science as our guide.

By the nature of their work, servers must know and appreciate their customers. So, servers are oriented to appreciate their customers' diversity and their specificity. Customers can be anywhere in the world, yet, for the most part, they are rooted in localities and communities with definite histories and well-established cultures. Knowing this, the service class cares less about national interests, borders, and international conflict and more about dynamics along the local-global nexus.

Servers also know that we're all in this together. Neither bullying nor hustlerism is a viable option. Oh sure, in the commodity exchange that is characteristic of the passé industrial age, where achieving and maintaining hegemony was the rule of the day, such tactics were often profitable for the big boys and emulated by the most desperate. But in the constantly evolving markets of service exchange, there is not possibility of significant or sustained hegemony. The best hope of long-term stability rests in good and respectful, collaborative relations with everyone. And bringing the world's masses into the service economy just expands the potential of service exchange, providing more security and more options for everyone's future. The service economy really is win-win. You pursue your own interests but only in the context of advancing the whole. Holism is the philosophy of the service class.

Finally, service providers know their personal limitations and, therefore, respect the insights of scientific endeavors of all sorts—market research, physical science, and social science. Because nothing in service provision inherently requires the broad destruction of nature and because human life, itself, requires a healthy global ecosystem, service providers respect ecology and seek to embrace environmental insights. Similarly, given that social dislocation and rebellion are destabilizing factors in the local-global marketplace, service providers embrace sociological study to uncover and attack the causes of polarization.

Indeed, it is hard to imagine a person who makes a living by serving others that does not appreciate the value of a scientific orientation. However, as my brother asserts, something is still lacking in the scientific outlooks common in today's society: *advocacy*. Like journalism, science still strives for a neutrality or objectivity that is, nevertheless, an impossible goal. Even science cannot escape the bias of its researchers and analysts. That is why scientific thought should never be considered settled; it must always be subject to new facts, new perspective, and new debate. Embracing the fundamental role of science in guiding social choices does not mean pretending that its practitioners have no grist—intended or not—to grind. In fact, they all do. Though the empty-headed, backward, anti-science sentiments of the Bush Administration gained credence among fundamentalists by attacking the alleged certainty of science, real scientists know science is never certain.

With this knowledge firmly in mind, we ask readers to embrace the socioecological science that is the foundation of this book. It is science in the people's interest, citizen science, taking a stand with the vast majority of the world's people. We know science can be manipulated to advance almost any interest, so we don't ask you to accept all scientific assertion as truth. Rather, we ask you to become a citizen scientist so that you can make your own assessments about what really serves our needs on this earth. Join in a new process of global problem-solving. Let's debate what works best for the vast majority of people and ecosystems. Let's make collective decisions based on that debate. Let's put those decisions into practice and assess how well they work. We can then adjust our actions accordingly.

That is science with advocacy, science with a stand, socioecology, science for the people. That is the world scientific outlook, a key ideological component for the service class.

Summing up, the ideological outlook of the service class is:

- Global in scope
- Local in particulars
- Appreciative of diversity
- Holistic in philosophy

- Scientific in approach
- Firmly committed to advancing the interests of the world's people through advocacy

The service class is done with pandering to "middle class" values taken from an old era, and it refutes the notion that people can buy their way to security and prosperity. My brother is right, "The existence of the middle class provokes worldwide poverty."

Yet, if we're going to avert industrialism's *dark age*, we must re-establish and greatly broaden the economic and social stability that is so rapidly slipping from our grip. Using service class theory as a framework, the outlines of an alternative to industrialism's failed matrix become clear.

Instead of a private, consumptive, competitive, inherently polarizing, and illusory model for achieving stability, we need a collaborative, public, investment model that provides overall security by fortifying the local-global nexus of service exchange. It needs to greatly strengthen civil society and bolster it with mass participation. It needs to construct global infrastructure—electrification, sanitation, transportation, communications, health facilities, and schools—while investing heavily in human capital—health, literacy, education, and conflict resolution. As these investments come online, the need to hoard for one's personal wealth for the future will diminish, and we can bring consumption, population, and pollution under control.

Is the post-industrial economy a contracting one, as my brother suggests? Yes, it is, in at least two ways. First, for those of us adapted to "middle class" life, we must learn to do with fewer "things," with less individual excess. To some extent, our constraint will be offset by the benefits of a more broadly secured social existence. Second, we must all join in reducing human population and, thus, its resource consumption and waste production. Unfortunately, this cannot happen quickly. It will take the sacrifice of the next several generations. In the meantime, the only way to launch broad endeavors to reduce population is to stabilize and secure the lives of all the world's poor and historically oppressed people. Thus, the contraction must begin with significant consumptive constraint in Europe, America, and the other concentrations of current global wealth combined with steady investment in locally-oriented, service-based, economic expansion in other areas of the world.

Subaltern voices already speak to this necessity. Some are reasonable, even scientific. Others, such as al Qaeda, speak harshly and act destructively. Whichever, they should not be dismissed. Finding ways to provide for the collective security of the people of our diverse world requires listening to their complaints, to their demands, to their ideas, and to their suggestions. Service isn't one size fits all. It's no size fits many. To provide the service that will marshal participation worldwide and eventually forge a new epoch of human social and ecological security means abandoning the consumptive formulation of the "middle class" that the banks and energy monopolies promote and embracing the self-reliant diversity of local people and cultures too long suppressed and trampled by industrial era conformity. If it's not rooted in the voices of the global grassroots, it's not service at all, and it won't solve our problems.

Chapter 7

Why Do We Keep Following the Pied Piper When We Already Know the Story?

Charles:

Capitalism and democracy, the industrial dynamic duo of the world's economic and political system, promised to liberate individuals everywhere, to raise their standard of living and freedom of expression simultaneously. For many, particularly in Europe and North America, the Industrial Age fostered a period of previously unheard of free speech, wealth, right of association, and freedom to pursue independent action and organization.

Set in the Napoleonic Code that dedicated rights to the common man in contrast to the aristocracy, industrialism grew large by advancing in two political directions—toward individual rights for citizens and toward corporate rights as individuals. Both built upon the Hegelian right to private property as the ultimate expression of human will—ownership as next to godliness. The state was the ultimate arbiter between the interests of the two, the force in society that regulated and guaranteed private property rights. Later, as the devastation of economic cycles and competitive warfare between capitalist states became apparent, the state extended its regulation to include tariff and trade issues, citizenship guarantees, democracy, and ultimately human rights. It is important to realize that private property rights, democracy, and human rights were not established simultaneously— these were benefits restricted to landed and corporate elites—and only with public resistance were they spread to wider society. Only through continued public scrutiny are they maintained. Around the world, people continue to struggle against state repression, trying to link economic, political, and human rights together despite state efforts to apply these rights selectively and only in particular situations. For the near future, popular resistance to state policies will remain central to changing global political agendas because states continue to protect vested and national interests even if they harm the civil rights of ordinary people.

In spite of its great ideological promises for social egalitarianism, industrialism failed utterly to live up to its promises at the global level. Much of the world remains impoverished, and the rules of trade worked out after WWII and revamped significantly in the late 1980s seem to guarantee that only the nations that adopted Western capitalism a century ago, or the recent few which successfully instituted some form of socialism, have any real chance of economic success. The rest of the world faces many more generations of lost lives, or at least lost opportunities, to the voracious appetite of the middle and upper classes of developed countries. Much of the world is being robbed of local resources that should be spent providing a better standard of living for local residents.

And, of course, that's the rub. Mass production industrialism was based in social inequality, the guarantee of wealth and power for the few at the expense of the many. It never really intended to share them across national or class boundaries. Workers were not given the opportunity to advance; in fact, they were denied it to the brink of revolution, and only when unions and socialist organizations encroached into the workplace did industrial "democracy" grant higher wages, workplace safety, voting rights, and property protection to the working underclasses and minority populations of nations (for a discussion of the working underclass of the U.S., see Perrucci and Wysong 2003). Even in doing so, industrial democracies tied themselves to imperial international politics and to accommodation with dictatorial rulers outside their own borders, too often basing their prosperity on repression and the genocide of indigenous groups, peasants, and proletarians elsewhere. Even today, the voices from within that cry out against injustice are thwarted and denied access to media to espouse their critiques. How can a global system based in such flaws be expected to carry the world forward toward resolution of the problems of the twenty-first century? Well, in truth, it can't.

Already, civil society and its numerous organizations are taking control of world development and environmental protection. They are replacing states as the moral authority among peoples.

Inside the Workings of Civil Society

In the United States, civil society is little understood, a sad state of affairs given civil society's role as the center of political and judicial conscience within the service economy. "Civil," of course, describes the social arena that is neither governmental nor corporate in nature, and "society" refers to the fact that what comes out of civil society, that is, its production of particular types of service, involves collective effort by persons holding shared beliefs and concerns. Civil society is a society of people who have chosen consciously to apply their training and experience to resolving social problems in ways governments and corporations have refused to do. They address the roots of social problems even if to do so means to organize and operate outside of the profit streams of big business and commerce and the stale bureaucracy of the welfare state.

Civil society is composed of different forms of social organizations— nongovernmental organizations (NGOs), private volunteer organizations (PVOs), and citizen advocacy groups (CAGs). In Western democracies, where state bureaucracies and formal laws are well established, civil society organizations tend to concentrate on either servicing the welfare of the poor or advocating for some form of social or environmental justice, though many just represent particular interest groups such as religious and ethnic organizations or gender-based rights activists. The latter groups are frequently called "identity groups" in that their members are people who share a chosen or acknowledged identity—gay, environmentalist, Baptist, feminist—and, because their membership is cross-class, cross-racial, and often cross-political, they no longer represent a particular structural position in the economy such as farmer, worker, or manager. In lesser developed countries, where governments are often financially strapped and organizationally underdeveloped, civil society groups frequently fill roles that are more normally filled by government in developed nations such as managing national forests and wildlife areas, dispensing public health information, and organizing farmer cooperatives. Americans in particular should be careful in assuming that how things are done in the U.S. is necessarily how things are done elsewhere.

The significance of the enormous expansion of civil society organizations over the past three decades defies explanation unless another concept, the public sphere, is also understood. Ask yourself this: What does it really mean to have a system "of, by, and for the people" in a world in which power is largely concentrated in the hands of enormously wealthy individuals, industrial corporate interests, and big government? As early as the sixteenth century, the power of the press, the free printed word, had begun to transform the nature of state and corporate power through its ability to offer criticisms of the dominant system of politics and economics. Known as the "fourth estate" (i.e., other than the landed gentry, the capitalist bourgeoisie, and the government), the press initiated the democratic era by challenging the status quo whenever public policies and private interests threatened the general welfare. The second aspect of the modern public sphere involves the spread of science and scientific thought and their underlying premise that, through study and training, virtually anyone is capable of learning skills and assuming control over technical and social processes. Together, public criticism and citizen science have become the cornerstones of civil ethics exerted through the public sphere of human relations by civil society organizations.

The social transformation ushered in by the new mode of service-led production may be unheralded, but it is also unprecedented. Today, virtually anyone with opportunity and dedication can become a player in public affairs, working to alter social relations for the better. But the last thirty years have aptly demonstrated that it is not individuals that are playing the most significant roles in this regard but, rather, civil society organizations. They combine the talents of multi-disciplined personnel to address issues ignored by capitalist investment and state policies. They go where no one dared go before. And civil society goes there because service-led ethics have spread widely among the public, because of gains in public education, because a widening opportunity structure opens to minorities and the poor, and because science makes ignorance and prejudice openly contestable (and contemptible) social practices. These gains were products that originated in mass industrialism, but civil-scientific ethics can no longer survive within the industrial framework. They need to be released, to lead us forward out of the growing number of problems that industrialism has created.

NGOs, PVOs and CAGs respond to real world needs. They marshal knowledge, funds, and experiences to meet problems created by concentrated industrial capital—that list of social and environmental ills we have mentioned so often already. The myth that these problems are being adequately addressed by industrial capitalism must be overthrown. Industrialism survives by continuing these inequalities, by moving jobs to areas of cheap labor, by ignoring the plight of millions so that others can live with ease. Capitalist ethics survive because of social inequality, not to remedy it.

Civil society represents new hope to human communities. Around the world, skilled service personnel are studying problems, applying scientific analysis in developing solutions, and bringing local people into negotiations to learn self-sufficiency in dealing with their problems. Horribly underfunded, these groups have but one measure to mark their daily work—make the lives of the people they work with better at the end of each day, each week, each month, project by project, program by program. They do restorative work among human communities and the environment we all depend upon. Civil society groups employ socioecology, advocating praxis that combines ecological science with social science in ways that empower user groups and communities.

Socioecology is not something that can be learned individually. Because it develops over time and through negotiated practice in real social contexts (Habermas called this communicative action), it demands that knowledge, information, theory, and experiential history be taught to people through the resolution of problems that people face in their daily lives. Socioecological science is never neutral. It is always a form of political advocacy. And political advocacy always must be open to public critiques and negotiated outcomes. Because no one outcome is possible, no individual has the answer for the twenty-first century and its myriad of problems. We all must play a part.

The Transformation of Relations of Production in Service-led Production

Entrepreneurial niches and the marketing of specialized products and services are replacing mass production as humanity's central form of economic exchange. This is not accidental. For decades mass industrialism has survived only because it granted the service sector increasing space in its operations and because opportunities opened by the 60s social awakening were accompanied by a major technical revolution in communication and Internet transactions. That transformation initially permitted industrial franchises to move operations offshore to free enterprise zones in areas with cheap labor, thus never losing effective control over operations. Early on, it also allowed media moguls to manipulate and consolidate control over mass media, thereby controlling the information and options available to the public. But in time, technological change released innovative challenges to the hegemony of the industrial system itself. The new mode of production now demands transformed values, communications, and social relations.

As history shows, social transformations do not come rapidly, nor do they proceed easily. The New Left of the 1960s unleashed critiques of social inequality inherent to mass production when civil rights protesters and students filled the streets. Revolution was in the air in American ghettos, Africa and Latin America, Cuba, the Philippines, and Indonesia. The 1970s pried open labor markets, colleges, and training programs for the truly qualified regardless of race, ethnicity, or gender, forcing Affirmative Action down the throats of white, male-dominated corporations and state agencies. The 70s also revamped the ineffective Peace Corps into a useful international workforce as civil society volunteers and specialists began practicing alternative development policies. The 1980s revolutionized the financial and currency markets, heaping great poverty on the backs of poorer nations but freeing finance capital from its industrial bondage. Environmentalists grabbed center stage and forced the public's right to participate in management decisions out into the open. The 1990s followed with resurgent entrepreneurial spirit that drove niche markets to new heights and brought computers into homes and businesses throughout the world—technology at everyone's finger tips. But the 90s also opened the door on a new round of international competition, ending Western dominance in mass production and shifting it to Brazil, China, India, and other Asian nations. The Internet became a political tool as people across the world organized support for the Zapatista Liberation Army in Chiapas, Mexico, and environmentalists like Greenpeace crusaded against state-assisted ecological degradation through international campaigns organized with networked computers. Since the turn of the century, we have watched collaboration become the operating mantra of civil society work. On the Dark Side of modern coalition building, however, oil wars and economic competition eventually built international coalitions around fear as developed countries did whatever was necessary to avoid global economic restructuring. Change is all about us, yet the static and stale relations of industrialism remain powerful as they dominate our outmoded cultural values.

True, mass production is not disappearing. It continues to expand, as it must, as the world's rapid population growth creates ever more need for commodities. Americans recoil at the growing Chinese giant that, like Brazil, India, and a world raised on exported images of American wealth, increasingly demands a part in the global economy, a share in the wealth, a piece of the action. But one can also wonder about a future filled with underpaid, overworked, and under-protected workers and wonder what stability might mean when foreign producers face the anger of their own workforce. Instability, now so characteristic of financial speculation markets, may soon become a by-product of the organizing drives of disenchanted factory workers throughout the world.

The most significant change for the global service-led economy has come through niche marketing that produces specialized products and services and delivers them to particular, *predesignated* consumers. Service provides for needs that customers have already identified. Identification with production, as sociologists explain, is both material, in that we all need goods to live successful lives, and cultural, in that we expect our desires, our wishes for happiness, to be fulfilled as well. Mass production can only go so far in meeting identified needs. It fails when asked to respond to diversity, to imagination, to cultural sensitivity, to popular interest—unless, of course, it can first manufacture those needs through advertisements and image management media. Those days are passing. We are all growing too smart for such inelastic, plastic culture.

Niche marketing recognizes diversity of interests in terms of customers and works to provide specialization and quality in terms of products and services. If niche production and marketing could exist without resource constraints, we would all enjoy a much livelier and diverse world where we could buy only what we wanted. But niche marketing, as part of the service-led mode of production, arose as a step-child of industrialism, not free from it. In a world of scarce resources, both natural and economic, niche production still falls within limits or economies to scale. Provided products and services still must balance quality with efficiency in production, use technological innovation but not exclude repetitive reproduction, and seek an expanding niche to make the provider more profits. Niche production is not now—and probably will not be for a very long time—completely free of industrialism's ever-existing need to expand. The issue of profitability will continue as a source of contradiction in service-led ethics for years to come, for as a step-child of industrialism, niche production and service provision will find it difficult to rein in industrial extravagance and lead us to a global contraction in natural resource use.

Niche marketing requires expertise, salesmanship, efficient management, and service quality. Many of these are determined not by the producer but by the customer, at least to the level of the customer's understanding of the specialty for which he or she contracts. There has been a great democratization of global relations over the past forty years, but democracy has taken root less in the actions of governments around the world than in the gains of the niche service field. In a growing proportion of situations, production decisions have switched from owners to consumers with specific needs whose satisfaction must be fulfilled to insure future relations. Customers now demand products and services that facilitate their operations, and niche marketers and service providers must find ways to meet those needs given their own ability to access science, technology, and resources. To succeed, they must mobilize a highly differentiated and specialized workforce.

Thus, successful global marketing relations require things that industrial production did not—intelligence concerning customer's location, probable needs, and development strategies; knowledge of production techniques and suppliers; ability to match a wide array of skills and experiences with new problems in new conditions; and the ability to attract a labor force that complements and expands the flexibility of niche production in general. Unlike industrial production that required mass-based advertising campaigns to create a market for products, mass media advertising is not critical to finding customers with specific needs in the service economy.

As already noted, all of these niche factors favor the creation of networks with other niche marketers who possess different intelligence, skills, and production abilities. They also favor the growth of an independent and relatively powerful service workforce in which individuals, by the nature of their specialized knowledge, gain significantly more control over the sale and use of their labor power than industrial workers. Furthermore, with modern communications technology and the ease of international shipping, niche marketers and service providers are partnering with providers anywhere in the world that are capable of meeting the requirements of the customers. Unless one is overly patriotic or nationalistic, finding a foreign partner to meet economic obligations is usually much less expensive and often without serious negative considerations. The global workforce in the niche service economy has essentially the same qualifications as any national workforce today.

Because the global economy is so large and so diverse, successful niche marketers must design organization around flexibility and periodic expansion and contraction of employees and operations. While America lags behind, Europe has already revamped workplace conditions and contracts, allowing skilled workers to take more time off with shorter work weeks and longer vacations. Many European companies encourage employees to travel extensively, knowing full well that economic success ultimately depends on finding new niches and establishing new global relationships. It is hard to find a successful business anymore that does not have global relations and sales as a significant part of its operations. Thus, a growing requirement for any national workforce is, in fact, global experience.

Without trying to detail the exact nature of niche marketing and service providers, a task better left to sociologists and economists who study such things in detail, we want to stress here the more than obvious connections between the economic character of the emerging service-led mode of production and the civil society superstructure. These connections are the reasons why our theory of an emerging service class encompasses both. In these developments—civil society organizations, service providers, and niche production and marketing—we see the positive elements of the service-led mode of production that will eventually restructure the global order. Unfortunately, we find much less hope that the speculative capital of major financial markets is so progressive. Indeed, speculation, even under state regulation in the current industrial mode of production, appears harmful to the future of human life on the planet.

A Changed Social Structure Emerges with a Global Culture

The key to handling the contradiction between speculative investment and the needs presented by changing social institutions involves cultural transformation. As the innate social relations that combine service provision, niche production, and civil society administration of development evolve, it becomes ever more apparent that a cultural shift from nationalism to globalism is occurring. Nearly every aspect of human culture has demonstrated this shift—business relations, travel and leisure, scientific research and educational exchange, migration patterns, media and entertainment, and trade and investment decisions. Beach and boardroom life alike transport people, who once built lives on local and regional relationships, around the globe to meet, experience, and remodel the lives of people from other cultures. In the process of movement and cultural exchange, we are transformed and so are the people we meet. We need not fool ourselves that this is necessarily good, nor necessarily necessary. But as Joe Kane (1995) reports in his book *Savages* about the modern changes to Huaorani culture in Ecuador's rainforests, even the most remote civilizations, if they hope to survive in coming years, must learn to cope with global issues and the political and cultural complexities introduced by globalization.

Again, it is the developed nations that may well face the greatest need for cultural transformation in future decades. After all, their inventions and lifestyles are ultimately responsible for the greatest portion of environmental injustice and ecological degradation. Their human rights record abroad provides a long litany of compromises with dictatorships, colonial exploitation, imperialist economics, and outright shameful conduct in business and political affairs. Just the suggestion, in 2010, by South American leaders that an economic alliance with the European Union was in the offing led thousands of people to protest in the streets of Lima, Peru. The Peruvian indigenous culture had already suffered the consequences of European colonialism, and citizens refused to step in any direction that might reassert foreign dominance over the continent. The division of Africa by European leaders in the late 1800s led to decades of revolutionary activity in Africa and continues to plague social relationships throughout that continent, as did the division of the Middle East and the artificial unification of divided peoples in Afghanistan in the 1900s. While it may not be vogue to use the word imperialism anymore, the effects of its global reach still interfere with the resolution of social and environmental problems worldwide. Its heritage prevents us from honestly addressing global warming and global poverty.

Thus, the great need for the twenty-first century is a restructuring of the cultural practices and perceptions of developed nations so that the underdeveloped areas of the world can establish global perspectives through positive rather than negative international social relationships. Many educators, politicians, and development practitioners around the world recoil at the thought of restructuration, not because it is unnecessary, but because the last effort at global restructuring occurred in the 1980s under the name of stabilization and structural adjustment policy promoted by the International Monetary Fund and supported by the World Bank, the Food and Agriculture Organization, the International Fund for Agricultural Development, the Inter-American Development Bank, the World Trade Organization, and others. That neoconservative restructuration produced such tragic poverty in poorer nations that even some of its own administrators, in following years, rebuked the programs of currency stabilization and destruction of national tariff barriers as unfair and regressive.

Of interest to note was the difference between the European and American response to globalization. The former countries reduced nationalism from patriotic fervor to sublime culture, taking profound restructuring steps to prevent any one nation's dominance over regional political economics and, at the same time, striking a balance between regional development and international aid. In spite of severe tests from the current global recession, European nations stepped toward recognizing the local-global nexus in place of patriotic nationalism. In the United States, on the other hand, the Bush Administration invoked anti-terrorism and national security to force a general redefinition of human rights both internally and in the occupied and militarized colonies of Iraq and Afghanistan. At the same time, the U.S. administration avoided steps to stop capital flight or the destruction of the American industrial base, and it allowed deregulated speculative investments to run markets. It constructed a culture of fear based on national isolation while opening the economy to the worst trends of corporate flight and predation abroad. Unprepared for the global transition that is occurring, American culture continues to fall back on reactionary isolationism and American exceptionalism in defense of its unsustainable lifestyle and militaristic proclivities. The cultural transformation that is needed is quite the opposite. The service-led mode of production demands relationships built around respect for global interests, not their diminution. Nationalist fervor must be replaced with concern over restructuring rural economies and building a base for a more stable tomorrow through local development. As social scientists have noted, citizens and vested interest groups develop structured patterns of thoughts and perceptions known as "logics." These have deep psychological and social roots and often are not readily evident even to people who espouse them. Patriotism, male chauvinism, racism, and classism are all forms of logics that give structure and meaning to our lives but which also serve to justify the oppression and disrespect of human diversity. Business leaders think they are the only ones who should run the economy because their logic of profiteering implies that non-entrepreneurs know nothing of economic matters. Politicians assume, because they were elected, that they should run the government, not the people who put them in office. Military logics suggest that democracy survives because of war and not despite it. National logics get in the way of global perspectives, leading us to ignore critical information and to refuse to partner with people who are unlike ourselves. The service-based cultural transformation will reject such logics and replace them, slowly through acculturation and socialization, with new ones for the new age.

Niche marketing, service provision, and civil society organization all target local development, all proceed through the extension of social networks and the exchange of information, all respond to needs generated on an non-nationalistic basis. Tomorrow's world and culture is necessarily in opposition to that of today. In spite of conservative and fundamentalist attempts to go back to what is imagined as having been so, what really is needed is a new way of envisioning global citizenship and global responsibility. And from that perspective, we must seek out and learn how to implement globalism. Globalism transforms local culture, leading locals to accept the science necessary to development without demanding assimilation, yet strengthening local areas against dominance by outside forces. This is a daunting task but not an impossible one, as NGOs have demonstrated. There are ways to empower local communities and to encourage nations and institutions to side with local development options that improve local economies. But these usually demand restructuring national priorities and even global responsibilities. They demand new visions of democratic decision-making, property rights, conservation ethics, and development priorities.

A Personal Account of Globalism

In the summer of 1998, I received a $1,600 travel grant from the University of New Mexico's Latin American Institute for summer research in the country of Belize in Central America. The grant was a lifesaver. Earlier that spring, the World Bank had reneged on promised support for my study of cultural-environmental linkages along the Belize-Guatemala border. The World Bank had already accepted my personal documentation for a World Bank ID card to use that summer when raging fires broke out in the region, started from campesinos clearing their fields across Belize, Guatemala, and southern Mexico. The regional director of the World Bank later said she forgot to process my grant in the rush to divert so much funding toward established NGOs and governments to fight the disastrous fires. A friend's comment seemed apropos. "You screwed up. You only asked for $2,000 a month and no extra travel and luxury costs. The going rate for international consultation and research is $6,000 a month plus expenses! She never took you seriously."

I can't explain the World Bank's failure to meet what I took as obligations. I'd already made flight plans and reservations, contacted people in Central America for accommodations, and received letters of support from a number of collaborating institutions. When I left Albuquerque, the drifting smoke from the fires (the worst, I learned several years later, started by Zapatista enthusiasts burning down the cabin of a government informant in Chiapas) had obscured the Sandia Mountain range above the city and was putting emphysema patients in Houston in the hospital. I did my three months of research on a Latin American Institute travel grant of just $1,600, including covering my wife's in-country expenses for a few weeks. I traveled up and down Belize and into the back-country of Guatemala on dust-filled buses and by foot, not exactly a World Bank researcher's fare! We'd traversed Central America that way for years, and bootstrap science proved my lifeblood throughout my two-and-a half years of college field research. It's always been a cornerstone of citizen science, but I'd hoped for a little more as I worked my through the academic realm.

Anyway, the point I want to get to is how, under the new globalist regime, niche production, targeted services, and NGO experiences seem to intertwine in spite of their obvious differences.

Belize made ecotourism its national priority during its independence movement from Great Britain in 1981. A long-standing commitment to natural resource protection (42 percent of its land is under resource protection laws) and social justice comes out in its commitment to ecotourism development. Aided by development and environmental NGOs, the country has sponsored a huge national program to encourage and create ecotourism at multiple levels—large commercial enterprises on offshore islands and reefs, wealthy tropical hideaways owned by national elites and foreign interests, and community ecotourism projects to highlight community development, ethnic strengthening, and local ecology. My study of property rights conflicts at the edges of protected areas involved a number of Maya communities in the north, west, and south of Belize and across extensive areas of the Petén in northern Guatemala. In my last year, I extended the study to Chiapas, Mexico, as well.

As part of my research, I interviewed the regional director of Belize's Development Finance Corporation office in Punta Gorda and learned that over 50 percent of the International Fund for Agricultural Development's (IFAD) loans to small farmers in the area were in default. The origins of these loans were situated in OPEC success in the 1970s that raised the price of oil so much that Arab bank accounts were swollen and underinvested. The modern capitalist underinvestment crisis that is consuming the mortgage finance industry today had begun. Unable to find markets for its rapidly accumulating wealth, the Arabs sought ways to invest it. One of the more interesting means of investing their sums was in world agricultural development projects under the UN-associated IFAD. Essentially, IFAD loaned money to lesser developed countries for agricultural training, seed purchase, crop diversification, and the global marketing of products. A lot of government agencies, multilateral development banks, NGOs, and communities participated in IFAD programs throughout the world, working in five- and ten-year programs. When I heard that so many small farmers in southern Belize had gone into land default through the program and were nearing foreclosure on their lands (shades of mortgage foreclosures today), I checked out the leads. I began by interviewing a leader of an ecotourist association that had facilities near the village around which many of the rumors of default were centered, then followed the murky path of research toward the village itself.

Ecotourism is a specialized subset of the global explosion of international recreational travel. There was time when international travel was the reserved right of corporate executives, the military, and wealthy vacationers seeking decadent playgrounds for short periods of vacation. *Au contraire* today, streams of travelers move about the globe learning about environmental issues by visiting remote sites that combine recreational tours with environmental lessons. These usually involve ethnic minorities as well, and cultural tourism is linked with ecotourism in many countries. The goal is—in a world where borders have largely disappeared in the wake of major recreation-, labor-, and environmentally-driven migrations—to make boundaries between people also more invisible. Cultural interchange today is much different from the one I experienced as a backpacker in Central America decades ago. Those travels were best deemed experimental cultural exchanges, taken to share understanding between people of significantly different class and national perspectives rather than as recreation itself. They were difficult, uncomfortable trips requiring humility on the part of my wife and me and hospitality on the part of the villages we visited. The trips taken today by the younger generation seem like pre-economic training to me, based in inter-cultural networks whose global skills will play out in civil society in the coming decades. While ethnic and cultural diversity are recognized and respected by modern travelers, both the traveler and the native are likely to use cell phones and the Internet, speak multiple languages, and have the ability to discuss environmental science on a relatively sophisticated level. Tourism has changed.

Anyway, I set out one morning for the village of Aguacate in a packed, dusty bus, the morning 105°F heat promising to reach near 130°F by late afternoon. A broken axle led to an unscheduled five-hour stop at a mechanic's house, and I reached Blue Creek, the village before Aguacate, so late in the afternoon that the local ecotourist facility seemed like the best bet for the night's accommodation. I would traverse the five miles to Aguacate in the morning. I didn't expect that the local servicing of this research tourist's needs would be so hard.

Servicing foreign travelers has become the world's largest industry, and not surprisingly, in accordance with the times, tourism has undergone its own specialization—ecotourism, cultural tourism, research tourism, sun and beach tourism, gambling tourism. Large cruise ships course the seas carrying tourists in and out of ports in Latin America, Africa, Asia, even China. But smaller tour lines run intelligence tours—they actually teach history, science, environmental issues, and political ones—as tourists travel about. They, too, are in the business of reproducing global culture. As all these tourists move about, NGOs busily organize ecocultural sites. These are places that tourists can pay to experience local culture and learn about local environmental problems. You might call them laboratories for budding socioecologists. Each tourist location has to be trained and taught how to respond to the needs of tourists. In Blue Creek, I had to knock on several doors before I found anyone in the village that had ever heard of the ecotourist program. They had all heard of the fancier lodge up the creek that sported student tours from American colleges on tropical research jaunts, but none had heard of the ecotourist association's services. Finally, I found a man who apologetically opened the door to a small building, letting me into a room of bunk beds that had never been slept in, the mattresses still in plastic wrap. "Sorry," he said. "We've never had a visitor. The man in charge is out in his fields and won't be back until later. Make yourself comfortable."

The vagaries of ethnographic field research. Ethnography studies issues through the eyes and lives of the people who are afflicted with problems, at least in sociology where the researcher usually is looking for trouble to investigate. With land conflicts, that's not hard to find. I like ethnography— everything has meaning and significance, unlike "straight" science where the researcher chooses what he/she is to study beforehand and then ignores most of the evidence except what has direct bearing on the self-chosen problem. I guess I'm a scientific holist!

About five-thirty in the evening I heard a small knock on the door, one almost too quiet to believe it was there (the tourist house, unlike many local houses, actually had a door). I opened the door to see the large dark eyes of a little girl, no more than four years old, standing just taller than my knees. "L'es go!" she commanded in her best Belizean accent, and she wheeled and headed down the path without another word or even a glance back at me. I followed.

At the gate to a small hut with a pole fence around the yard she stepped through the poles of the fence without slowing, then turned and opened the gate for me. She led the way to the door where I was met by her young mother who ushered me in to a small dark room with a table pushed against the wall in the back. She sat me at the table's lone chair facing the mud-covered wall, so that I had to struggle to see behind me to look about the room. It was a typical rural Mayan house—clothes hung on nails on the walls, a few hammocks slung about or folded against the wall to make more room, an open pit fireplace with two small shelves of kitchenware, and just one large chest made of rough wood for personal effects, pushed against the daub and waddle wall. Nothing else. Both openings used as windows in the room were closed with plank shutters, so the only light came from a small oil lamp and the doorway. She asked me if I wanted to eat chicken or beans.

Ecotourism, and global travel and relations in general, raise all sorts of unexpected quandaries and value conflicts. I'd been in that situation before and once made the mistake of saying, "Chicken." Moments later I had heard the last futile squawk of one of the family's three chickens. This time I knew better. I said, "Beans."

When the man, Ronaldo, returned, he joined me eating at the table while his children and wife waited patiently for us to finish. There might not be enough for them if I ate too much. I professed not to be that hungry. Ronaldo directed his wife to do something in a Maya dialect I did not understand,

and soon a she had retrieved a plastic bag from the large chest. She emptied its contents into some water in a pot and placed it over the wood fire to boil. A short while later she served me, and me alone, a cup of hot cacao, a drink somewhat like hot chocolate but much more bitter with a thick layer of oily gruel on the surface. I drank with relish. This may have been an ecotourist flourish, but I knew it was also an honor among some Maya groups, a drink shared in ceremony rather than drunk as daily fare.

I rose early in the morning, promising to return for the night, and I trekked out to the road to Aguacate to wait for a ride. An hour later, the sun rising all too fast, I started out for the village in the distant hills on foot, the road deserted. "Not much traffic these days," I murmured to myself. Four hours later I reached the village without ever seeing a vehicle, the road lengthening with each degree of sunrise until its end seemed lost in the glaring heat behind the profuse sweat that soaked me through and through. I finally met a young boy leading four horses out to pasture. When I told him I was researching land problems, he told me to talk with his father, a Guatemalan refugee living in this Belizean village. As he continued on, I walked up a large hill that overlooked the village just below. I didn't see anyone or any movement in the village. I didn't know anyone in the village, didn't have the name of anyone in the village. I stood there a long time wondering what to do.

Above me to my left, I could just barely make out two women in a doorway talking intently inside the shadows of a hut. Finally a woman exited, headed my way, wearing a wrap-around skirt of typical K'ekchí cloth but bare-breasted and barefoot. She walked right up to me and stood in front of me, her vision cutting deep into my eyes from two feet away. "H-a-r-r-u-m-p-h!" was all she said. She walked away. I didn't need an interpretation. I had been cut down to the size of a very conspicuous and generally unwanted foreigner in her village.

Once in the center of village, I found the reason for the lack of activity. All the men had gathered for a work party to build some newly-weds a house, and they were feverishly tying palm frond thatch to the roof. One man finally separated from the party and asked what I was doing in the village. Researching land problems. Looking for a Guatemalan. His H-a-r-r-u-m-p-h! wasn't so loud or decisive, and he sent me down a side street to another house.

Strangely, almost miraculously, throughout that afternoon I was directed, in part by residents and in part by my own curiosity, to four different houses to hear four different stories of land issues, each perspective entirely different than the others. As if just having the courage to come here, on foot, without pretense, was enough for villagers and fate to direct me to all four corners of the local universe in which land played a significant part. Late in the day, on the way out of town, the village chairman met me in front of the only store in the village, the only one with a telephone. We discussed the politics of land, of development, of communal and private ownership, of agricultural loans for a long time before he abruptly turned to other issues and left me alone on the street again.

At the edge of town I met a young man who owned the only pick-up in town. No wonder the road was so deserted. He blamed the problem of bank loan default on lazy villagers who didn't want to get ahead. Others had blamed it on lies told to them when the bankers came offering loans, some on internecine squabbles between members over land rights, a third on the failure of government to provide harvesting equipment in a timely manner, allowing their investments in rice to rot in subsequent rains. The village chairman blamed it on lost ethnic values and young men who had become selfish, forcing the community to give up communal rights to land so they could enter private loan agreements with the Development Finance Bank. "They don't care about the old ways any more. So now we are going to lose our land that used to belong to all of us because of growing individualism in the community."

I left Belize two days later, reluctantly telling my story to an established environmental sociologist from the University of Wisconsin who was vacationing in Belize and had been offered a job helping the government design an environmental analysis for development in southern Belize. He published my research as his own and was given credit in official Belizean accounts for discovering the problem of loan defaults. I'm sure he drove to the village in air conditioned rental cars paid for with World Bank money. He also was well paid for his work. I walked the five miles back to my ecotourist bed in torching sunlight because I didn't want to get caught out on the road after nightfall praying that I wouldn't step on a poisonous snake. My subsequent efforts to publish my research findings were scorned, and my version of events, focused on the diversity of property relations within Maya culture induced by modernization, was called too "biased" to be printed in American journals. You won't find it there.

I guess every story has a moral. All I can say is that tourism, whether it is ecotourism, recreation tourism, or research tourism, is harmful if it doesn't empower the communities it involves. My work made a difference—the prospective foreclosures were still in abeyance five years later when I returned for my final visit before writing my dissertation. And this wasn't the only time in my research career that my findings made it back to the villagers in reformed political policies. The local-global nexus, in servicing the needs of the global traveler, must also produce products and services that make a difference in local people's lives. But when civil society NGOs go off to the other worlds of this planet, they soon find that simple formulations of problems are not easily satisfied. Priorities on one side of the globe aren't necessarily the same as those on the other. Truth varies by perspective, too. A fair system of development cannot require that people put up homes and land for collateral just to have a chance at economic opportunity that most of us in the developed world take for granted. If only the American mortgage bank bailout was helping poor people get homes and better opportunities. It isn't.

I included this story so that when I talk about real investment rather than speculative investment in this book you might begin to understand what I mean. The lesson certainly isn't that people in rural Belize need cement homes and metal roofs, or doors and glass windows, either. These creations actually are often less than useful—they attract mosquitoes into the interior of buildings and superheat them during the day. Modernity is not always the answer, and poverty is not always bad. But what they may need most is the machinery to guarantee that their meager harvests at least get to market— harvesting machines delivered on time, trucks to transport products, price protections by the government, and banks to reliably hold saved earnings. They need networks that link farmers together so they can produce with sufficient economic scale; they need transportation centers close enough to home so their delivery costs are not too high. They need lawyers to protect their rights, and government lobbyists to press their causes. They need schools and training. IFAD tried to do all that in Belize, but it will succeed only if the experiments are tried again and improved with greater cultural sensitivity and more appropriate technology. It is not acceptable to make communal land a form of privatized loan collateral. Land is a means to guarantee a community's survival and cannot be compromised by bankers. Poor people in general cannot control all the variables that affect their work. This world has to learn to service their needs, just like academics need to support advocacy science rather than impartial, value-free science.

The most important lesson I learned during my many research trips to Latin America was that people everywhere can learn what they need to in order to survive in the modern world. I used to get so tired of American responses to my stories. "Aren't you glad you're back in the best country in the world?"! They just didn't get it. I never missed that American world because what mattered to me was understanding the foundations of other cultures and getting a chance to practice a more global vision. So what if the beans were cooked on an open fire, if water was drawn from an open stream, if floors were earthen and walls of poles and roofs of thatch? Who cared if roads were dusty or coffee watered down? The key was sharing, sharing sweat and seething heat, sharing stories while swatting black flies and digging chiggers out from behind one's knees, of carrying bundles long distances through mud and pastures for an old grandmother and her tiny granddaughter.

What we lack today is a vision of development, of the developed world, that includes the vision of the world's lesser developed communities. Don't be mistaken. They are not lesser communities. When we network with them, when we learn to turn our service brawn toward their needs, when we create more appropriately designed goods instead of the throwaway plastic bottles and tooth-rotting soft drinks, we will have found ways to make the whole globe more compatible with itself and with its environment. I think we can do that if we want to do it. That's why I think NGOs are the world's new moral authority. We should listen to them and give them the power and money they need to change our world for the better.

Chapter 7 Response

Global Problem-Solving Just Isn't Business as Usual

Steve:

Unlike my brother, I've had few opportunities to travel internationally, much less to conduct research or do actual work in other countries, but I have had extensive experience working with non-profit, mission-driven organizations in the U.S.

At one—the Godman Guild in Columbus, Ohio, where I worked for several years in the mid 1980s—I learned a little about the history of service organizations in America. The Guild was (is) a settlement house, the third oldest in the U.S., founded in 1898, just a few years after Jane Addams' famous Hull House in Chicago.

Non-Profit History in America

Churches and private colleges were the first non-profit organizations in America, the former serving like-minded spiritual groups and the latter rather small batches of mostly male off-spring of elite families. Anti-slavery and women's rights advocacy groups appeared before the Civil War, along with temperance organizations. Volunteer fire departments also got their start in the early 1800s. During the war, the Red Cross came into existence, and, afterwards, as medical science developed, community and church-related hospitals multiplied. Also after the war, as industrial forces gained increasing influence in Washington, the Grange and other farm-oriented advocacy groups formed in response. Freedmen societies pursued opportunity for former slaves. Among workers, unions—generally illegal and suppressed by industrialists—proliferated. Fraternal societies, such as the Elks Club, served as social centers for local small businessmen. In the late 1800s, Andrew Carnegie's private donations established the first libraries in many American towns and cities.

Even this cursory review of late nineteenth century non-profits shows the broad range of service organizations that took shape as accumulating and broadening wealth opened the possibility of private action to address diverse, mounting social concerns that were beyond the domain of government.

While many of these were self-interested, self-serving organizations, settlement houses reached deeper, taking up the plight of the poor, immigrant families that were flooding American cities at the turn of the century. By the 1920s, private charity, known as the Community Chest, was in vogue, emulating Carnegie's philanthropic example and riding the economic surge that followed World War I.

But, being private, charity had its limits, and these were brutally exposed in 1929 when the Great Depression struck. When that bubble burst and economic contraction set in, donors disappeared, and charity faded to a tightening trickle just as the need for it exploded.

Meanwhile, in Russia, the socialist revolution was just a dozen years old, and many American union leaders—long labeled "subversive" by industrial elites and the U.S. government—suggested that socialism might be the only answer for struggling American workers. Intent on undermining the possibility of a revolutionary movement in the U.S., the nation's ruling elites switched gears. Offering the New Deal, they recommended a new social contract, one in which organized labor could join the industrialists and a greatly expanded government in managing society and the economy. Supplanting private charity, collective bargaining and the welfare state came into existence.

I was working at the Godman Guild in the early 1980s when that New Deal social contract began unraveling. Actually, conditions for its decline had been set a decade earlier when, after launching the Great Society—the greatest expansion of public welfare programs since the Depression—the

Johnson Administration got itself bogged down in an unwinnable war in Viet Nam. The country couldn't afford both, and the resulting inflation undermined confidence in government social leadership. When the war was ultimately lost and the first serious post-WWII economic contraction took hold, something had to give. The "Reagan Revolution" prevailed.

Reagan vowed to unravel the Great Society, and throughout the 80s, it became increasingly clear that the U.S. government was never again going to fund social welfare like it had under the New Deal social contract. Instead, non-governmental organizations acquired a fresh imperative. At the Godman Guild—and at private non-profit social service agencies across the nation—we began searching for new, non-government funding streams.

It wasn't easy then and it's still not now. If the government doesn't fund, the only alternative is the private sector. Social responsibility became, once more, a matter of private charity. However, due to the emergence of service-led production and the efforts of long-established industrial corporations to reposition themselves in that emerging economy, tax laws were rewritten to allow and encourage corporate giving in lieu of the higher corporate taxes that would have been required to sustain the welfare state. The state's role in planning, overseeing, and evaluating social service was privatized, handed over to corporations and their associated foundations.

Corporate "Giving" and Cause Marketing

This new funding stream is well-illustrated by the National SAFE Kids Campaign, a public health campaign on which I did a little work in 1989. A project of the non-profit Children's Hospital in Washington, D.C.—itself, part of a network of independent children's hospitals nationwide—and the Johnson & Johnson Company, the campaign was designed to advance the cause of childhood safety while providing its corporate funder, J&J, with both an enhanced reputation for public service and a vehicle alongside which it could more readily market its home safety products. A huge success, the campaign still operates today.

Although seldom as successful as SAFE Kids, similar "cause-marketing" programs developed in service to other issues of social problem-solving. When the government was also involved—usually as a convener, not as a funder—they were called "public-private partnerships." For instance, in the late 1980s, writing about what amounted to a domestic ecotourism program, I reported for the Ohio governor on the state's success in revitalizing the decaying industrial towns along Lake Erie as recreational destinations.

In the 1990s, I wrote ad copy for Greenpeace, a famous non-profit advocacy group that was then swimming in contributions from private donors. I also wrote brochures for a pharmaceutical company that, reacting to the flu epidemic of the time, was promoting vaccination as a public health initiative—which also enabled it to sell more vaccines. For a while, I also had a job with a non-profit that promoted highway safety legislation—motorcycle helmets, safety belt use—and it was funded by an array of American insurance companies.

Today, the Bill and Melinda Gates Foundation is the largest private donor organization in the world. Its annual giving program—required by law to be at least 5 percent of its investment income—is about $1.5 billion or so (estimated before the 2008 market dive). Along with an ever-growing array of corporate-related foundations, the Gates Foundation and its peers have become vital funders of the world's steadily expanding civil society. By way of comparison, USAID—the government's program of foreign aid—gives about $15 billion annually in foreign assistance, sometimes to governments, sometimes to NGOs. While total government aid exceeds private aid, the gap is narrowing. Moreover, government aid is contingent on national interest and the political priorities of ruling administrations. It is not mission-driven.

In pointing out the narrowing gap between state and private aid to civil society, I do not mean to laud either party. Governments can certainly do better, but so long as military spending and warfare remain so prominent in state affairs, no substantial improvement is likely. Private philanthropy, of course, is wonderful, but it would not be so great were it not for support through tax code benefits for corporations, and, in any case, private sponsorship of social development is never going to produce the resources necessary to make an appreciable dent in our world's problems.

If we're really going to avert the *dark age*, we have to qualitatively upgrade our response to its developing devastation. If civil society is the answer, it must get more funding, vastly more funding. Inevitably, that funding must come from the service economy.

A Service Economy Finances Social Problem-Solving

Centuries ago, when the bourgeoisie was rising in resistance against the feudal aristocracy, it didn't count on the lords and vassals to pay for its revolution. The bourgeoisie raised money among its own. Later, after it got state power, it augmented traditional, aristocratic, land-based tithes to the state, that is, property taxes, with taxes on income and sales.

Similarly, now, as the service class struggles for power and authority in our world's emerging global economy, it cannot rely on the elites of the industrial era to fund its cause. Land, income, and sales taxes are controlled by national interests, mainly for national purposes. It is illusory to expect much digression from that deeply-rooted model. The global revolution, if it is going to empower civil society problem-solving, must tap its own class and social forces, that is, commerce along the local-global nexus of human exchange. Hence, my brother and I advocate a universal commercial transactions fee, to be collected by the world's banking industry and channeled to civil society through a new global problem-solving authority. This is not, in our contemplation, a state-imposed tax. Indeed, no state has the authority to tax the global banking system. Nor is it a state-authorized collection of some federated body of states, such as the UN. Rather, we see this fee as a self-imposed obligation of the world's service-oriented commercial operations to finance socioecological problem-solving in their collective, common interest. It is a voluntary effort to save our world, not one imposed by state authority.

Is there another way to adequately fund socioecological problem-solving by civil society? We've racked out brains and don't have another proposal. However, we're all ears. Right before our very eyes, we can see the limits of private charity, the welfare state, and socialism. Whatever the plan, it needs to take a giant step beyond where we've been before.

One of the great advantages of civil society, relative to the welfare state or socialism, is its character as a vast, evolving array of independent entities, each with a unique mission, a professional staff, a public board of oversight, and a transparent record of action that is subject to scrutiny by competitors, clients, communities, states, the media, and funders, alike. Also, because it is not a monolith like the state, civil society is a flexible, fluid operation that does not ossify but, rather, continually evolves with the marketplace of ideas as real world problems are tackled. Moreover, virtually any kind of collaboration can occur within its own organizations and between civil society and the corporations and communities that are also part of the local-global nexus. As we already know from international development programs in existence today, civil society often forms collaborations with nation-states and their federated associations. An expanded civil society will not exclude current relations but greatly add to them.

Thus, civil society is not some kind of new, global bureaucracy—a remote and impersonal, uncaring and self-serving jobs program for careerist professionals. Sadly but inevitably, this is what the UN—its best efforts to the contrary—has become. Rather, civil society is a market-based (non-profit competition) collection of front-edge service providers, each trying to perfect its capacity to solve problems along the local-global nexus.

As such, civil society also is not subservient to national interests or national whims as are, for instance, U.S. contributions to the UN. Thus, while it must operate in an international framework of self-governing states, civil society is not beholden to any particular state or any particular amalgamation of states. Unless states block its efforts, civil society can sustain its popular, science-based, mission-driven agendas across borders, worldwide, for as long as it takes to make them work.

Civil society is a new kind of human response to our common, collective problems, but it is not, itself, government. Rather, at this stage and for the foreseeable future at least, civil society must operate as a service-oriented mechanism of social problem-solving that is driven not by desires for profit maximization for shareholders but by the needs satisfaction of stakeholders—communities (its client base), staff, directors, corporate partners, and government allies. NGOs that do not do a good job falter and lose funding. Their staff is often recruited by others or reforms to serve a different, newly evolving niche. NGOs that succeed win greater and more sustained funding, but funding is still program-based and subject to evolving expectations of progress and success. No NGO can be static, rigid, or hegemonic because the supply and demand of the problem-solving marketplace never stops changing.

The governing structure and mechanisms for popular administration of civil society's problem-solving efforts have yet to be devised. Since we are calling for a massive expansion of human commitment to civil society—in effect, for a new social contract among global commerce, local communities, and civil society—we also are calling for a new system to effectively manage the NGO-corporate-community problem-solving process. In proposing the formation of a new global problem-solving authority, we recognize that the transition to such an authority will require a social struggle over investment patterns and needs in the global economy and how changes in that system must build new forms of global management. We also know that struggle will never occur unless the theory of that possibility is iterated and its potential structure illuminated. But, if it's not going to be some huge, international bureaucracy like the UN and if it is to exist alongside our established national governments, what is it and how will it work? Good questions. We'll try to answer those questions in the pages ahead.

Chapter 8

A Social Bulimic's Dream—Disgorging the State

Charles:

Revisioning the Current Crisis

In the last chapter we mentioned that a 1973 jump in the price of oil following the creation of OPEC produced significant ramifications for the world's economy. For the first time in its history, capitalism faced an underinvestment crisis. So much money flowed into the coiffeurs of the oil-producing states that they couldn't find financial markets large enough to invest it.

In retrospect, the oil-boom initiated the end of state regulation of banking procedures, demanding in its place the opening of global markets to free-flowing transnational finance capital. Protectionist measures such as tariffs, currency controls (such as the American gold standard), and national investment markets became dinosaurs overnight, fetters, as Marx would say, on global "development." The domino effect brought the rapid fall of state-regulated capitalism in favor of deregulation, global flexibility, capital flight into high risk but lucrative international stocks, and the creation of a slew of innovative speculative investment markets. Once these speculative opportunities were unleashed, their quick, steep earnings potential relative to the slow growth potentials of most global development projects sucked the air out of real investment. Without knowing or understanding what we were a part of, we all became speculators—however late we arrived—

seeking future wealth by throwing our money into money markets and CDs, not comprehending that the heyday of industrial capitalism was passing. Capitalism had, with its demanding growth policies, reached the point where there was just too much money in speculative circulation and not enough flowing into real problem-solving. The underinvestment crisis was upon us in full force.

But problems associated with the under-utilization of developed-world capital became apparent almost immediately. When Mexico defaulted on its loans in 1982, with Brazil, Peru and many other nations not far behind, the writing was on the wall. Speculative borrowing did not produce equal results among all borrowers. Capital markets allowed nations to acquire easy loans for infrastructure projects and centralized services regardless of their credit worthiness, and bankruptcy would be the inevitable end. The fact that the oil-producing state of Mexico defaulted was in itself reason to fear global collapse, but international currency regulators at the International Monetary Fund (IMF) chose to approach the finance crisis as a state-created, nationally specific problem. Mexico was forced to renegotiate its loans and, in the process, meet IMF requirements that it accept currency stabilization and austerity measures as well. Perfected by the IMF throughout the 1980s and early 1990s, these policies forced nation after nation to accept currency stabilization and structural adjustment that linked other currencies to the value of the American dollar while enforcing deep cuts for social programs and infrastructure development. The IMF dictated that nation after nation achieve solvency by selling off whatever dollars a nation had managed to save and then selling off nationally-owned enterprises to the private sector, thus tying its development to free trade policies and global financial speculation in its currency. These policies were designed to right a sinking ship, usually one that had borrowed too many cheap oil dollars at low rates. While Brazil ultimately made headway under left-leaning management over austerity measures, by the end of the Clinton Administration most of the world was deeply in debt and clearly beyond hope when it came to paying off national debts. The American economic recovery was fueled by the failing economies of desperate nations.

Looking back at the origins of earlier global financial crises, we shouldn't be so surprised that the subprime mortgage crisis started in the U.S. and rapidly expanded across the globe. Home loans for over-priced properties (they had spiraled upward under pressure from investment speculators) were proffered to financially unstable households under promises of cheap refinancing once the variable rate mortgages kicked in two years down the road. But economic managers should have known that interest rates never fall in a bullish economy. Furthermore, the same crisis had already hit a hundred nations around the world. People, businesses, and governments with too much free cash available could only invest it if they could get people, families, municipalities, retirement funds, and even countries to gamble on the future. Credit lines skyrocketed and debt became the wonder strategy to get ahead. That strategy hasn't worked out at all. Even Joseph Stiglitz, who presided over the IMF's loan and economic restructuring program in the 90s, later reneged on his support of structural adjustment and stabilization programs. In a world where banks always make money (the World Bank has never had a losing year), someone has to pay. The plan was always that the guy on the bottom—that is, many guys on the bottom—would be the sinkers while the Wall Street brokerage houses and the Citi-Banks of the world would be the swimmers. We call that a ponzi scheme, finance capital with an industrial value system. Screw the poor and redecorate the new addition to the villa on the hill.

When Paolo Freire initiated experiments with liberation pedagogy in Brazil in the early 1960s, before the military dictatorship supported by the United States overthrew Brazilian democracy in 1964, his program presented adults who were learning to read with pictures of their neighborhood, mostly cardboard and scrap metal barrios. The pictures were accompanied with words printed on them—"house," "street," "store," "table," and the like. The objects were familiar things, much like the ones in their daily experiences. Then, a second set of pictures with the same names were presented. These, however, held pictures of the other side of town, the wealthy neighborhoods and their accoutrements. House, street, store, and table quickly took on different form and meanings, and soon facilitators turned the lessons to discussions of conditions and the differences between their class and the one on the other side of the tracks. Guess what? Adults learned to read fast. They also learned to talk to their neighbors and organize.

In the fall of 2007, as the American subprime mortgage lending crisis surfaced, I was a steady listener of National Public Radio (NPR) reports. For the first three months, report after report blamed the growing crisis on irresponsible borrowers who had simply and illogically borrowed beyond their means. Sure, due to rising interest rates, the fine print was proving particularly harsh and difficult to meet, but the fault of the crisis was laid squarely on the shoulders of the working poor. I called it the "Poor Dumb Bastards" analysis, the "How dare they take us all down with them" mode of incrimination. I already knew better. We'd been trying to buy a house in town that summer and prices kept jumping $20,000 every time we hesitated on a deal. I'm a builder, and I know when property just isn't worth its mettle. We quickly found that most cheaper houses were not being bought by working class people but by speculators who, in hundreds of houses in the area, slapped on a new coat of paint, swapped out the old kitchen for a cheap Home Depot replacement, mowed the lawn and planted a few flowers, and placed flowers in a glass on a prominent end table in the living room. *Voilá*, a rotting, energy inefficient, ramshackle dwelling from the logging legacy of the West was back on the market, now worth $70,000 to $100,000 more than a month before, or supposedly so. I just grew madder and madder listening to NPR bemoan the plight of our "wonderful" investor class.

Four months into the housing crisis, NPR began to air reports that criticized lending policies, not many but a few. Every once in awhile, a university professor would debunk the Poor Dumb Bastards analysis for what really was going on, a financial scam that had finally caught up with itself. But then, the next week NPR would be back blaming the working poor who couldn't even afford to own a home after years of working for the American dream. A dream that has now become a global nightmare.

George Soros, himself a well-known speculator of the highest sorts in currency markets and hedge funds, believes the crisis of 2008 is on a different level than other ones—the IMF loan defaults by poor countries in the 1980s, the silver speculation crisis, the small bank crisis of the 1990s, the Millikan junk bond crisis, the Asian money market collapse of 1997. If Soros is right, the subprime crisis will likely alter our global investment processes and may even debunk the dollar as the basis of the global economy. But, listen, Soros is also wrong. This is not a problem of poor regulation, as he maintains, but rather a major crisis in the investment strategies of capitalism. Properly called an underinvestment crisis, it is built around:

- Wild financial speculation in international money markets and stock markets with excess capital rather than investments in real production and social change

- Market guarantees taken from the life savings of the service and working classes to back up high-risk gambling by financial houses and banks (taken by means of tax shifts downward, inflation, and government deficit spending that will be paid from future taxes)

- Risk-taking in secondary loan and insurance markets which sold debt liability like a commodity to speculators (Soros reports 50 percent of current investment is in such imaginary goods)

- Mortgage guaranteed-loan sharking such that only 10 percent of the subprime loans even went to primary housing

- A failed regulatory system whereby both private banks and government agencies enjoyed the flight of financial fantasy until it ran out of gas, never reading the obvious signs that the economy was in trouble

This latest crisis was no accident. It resulted from the standardized daily operations of capitalism and the propensities of individuals and groups to gamble *rather than invest* savings. These are the people who say we still must trust them to lead our economy. You gotta be kidding me...

The Real Crisis Is the Underinvestment Crisis

This is an underinvestment crisis to be sure, one characterized by the naked failure of people with capital and savings to invest their money in real investment—infrastructure, urban renewal, factory renovation and modernization, jobs, education, health, international development, and environmental protection. Finance capital has lost its bid to be the moral center of the service-led mode of production in just twenty-five years of unrestricted dominance. They had the chance to take their earnings and spend it wisely. Instead their greedy addiction to gambling has led us into global economic despair for workers and the poor, lost service class savings, and net zero public social investment. But clearly finance capital couldn't have done this without our tacit support, so it is only fair to also blame the service class for letting their retirement funds speculate in stocks, bonds, and property markets as well. We didn't demand that our savings be used wisely to improve social conditions. We didn't pay attention to what was happening with our future.

The global economic system is bankrupt, even if we are afraid to admit that it's beyond repair. What was will never be again. Investment in a service-led mode of production will look nothing like investment under industrial priorities or its deregulated and irresponsible financial transition. *When service values lead investment decisions, the goal of investment becomes the development and assistance of those who receive investments, not the lives of those who make them.* The measure of success of service-led investment will be its ability to direct excess, free-floating capital toward real outcome changes in society, be those changes material products, better services, or more refined social organization. Investment strategies need social underpinnings that accept responsibility for ecological restoration and social equity improvements under the tutelage of civil society organizations freed of national and corporate dependence.

Service-led investment alters the quality and utility of industrial products toward ecological sensitivity, encouraging the mass production of alternative renewable energy, super-insulated homes, bioregional-based agriculture, and recycle-ability—production-to-consumption, resource-to-grave utilization of commercial products. Service-led mass production sounds like an enigma, but our point is that mass production is redirected and reorganized to fit service goals—ecofriendly action adopted as national character, critical analysis with tough love in commodity production. Service-led mass production introduces standardization and interchangeability in many products, invests in both private and business decisions to incorporate green technologies in daily practices, and extends, as a matter of principle, environmental amenities to those who lack them. American examples of such investment might include putting solar panels on every house in the sunbelt, building solar water heaters to supplement home and domestic water heating, encouraging (as Finland does) masonry stoves in the North, or requiring all new construction to use ground source heat pumps. The cheap and flimsy, anti-ecological construction characteristic of American building would be outlawed through building codes changes and investment would be forced into construction that is long-lasting and energy efficient.

The second part of the service-led production revolution will come through an expansion of niche marketing that increases investments in research, design, product flexibility, and component design. In the future economy, we can imagine a scenario where public investment in private enterprise expands, but not along the bulk rate theory of massive government subsidies for big corporations as in the past. Instead, subsidies for business development make economic investments transparent and revolve around fair assessments of ecological and social externalities. The intransigence of state-supported big business, such as American Congressional pork barrel projects that too often defy rational economic logic, is finally overcome by new economic structures that encourage innovative programs to improve bioregional development. Those investments renovate transportation systems, highlight natural resource management and utilization efficiency, and support the continued expansion of small scale production facilities over large ones. "Economies of scale" reverses its meaning. Restructured accomplishments come not through backroom decisions by corporate boards but by collaborative networking in communities and among communities, NGOs, and companies.

Economic theory is turned on its head in the service economy. Investment in better services challenges the old habits of industrial nation-states, no better represented than by renewed investment in a universal health care program, urban renewal programs, rural development, and focused foreign aid. Because the service sector of the economy, not mass production, is expanding, it advances education, training, and skill development among citizens of all nations as central to economic growth. Protection of proprietary knowledge is seen in its true form as a privilege that diminishes economic vitality. In turn, service demands what the world needs most—more teachers and trainers, better global access to opportunity programs, an expansion of social science and surveys in decision-making, improved service facilities in rural communities, and redistribution of urban services toward those communities lacking them.

The expansion of ecologically based production, niche marketing, and service provision demands investment in social organization and social restructuring. Years ago, during timber debates in the Northwest, the Clinton Administration promised rural redevelopment funds and training to small communities affected by timber cut-backs. While the heart was in the right place, redevelopment programs never materialized. Instead, the Rural Self-Sufficiency Act led the feds to merely make yearly payments to rural counties in lieu of its "moral responsibility" to replace lost tax revenue with other funding. Business as usual. Rural counties in the West never invested the funds in effective redevelopment but, for the most part, used the funds to support traditional operations. Rural counties became even more dependent on the public dole than ever before because redevelopment, whether rural or urban (are you old enough to remember our forgotten and failed urban renewal projects?), requires far more investment than expenditures of huge sums of money thrown at problems from afar. Development requires revamped social organization, long term commitment to local negotiations over redevelopment planning, and implementation through newly conceived marketing strategies and organizational niches. The point of this scenario is that these will surface only after immense investments of time and money are consciously made by the service-led economy.

Service, Economic Contraction, and the State

The problem for America and other developed countries is that the world is entering a period of economic contraction. At no time in human history have the stakes been so obvious—if we do not contract our economic impacts on the environment, our global ecosystem will collapse. Social contraction in the past proved cataclysmic as Harris, Chew, and Diamond have more than adequately demonstrated. How can we guide ourselves around the obstacles before us? Fortunately, the cultural revolution inherent in modern communications, globalization, educational advancement, and scientific exposure of wrong-doing brings us to the brink of a major opportunity to consciously revamp our socioecological relations. For the first time in history, we can, as collective humanity, approach a scientific remedy to prevent future devastation and collapse before it happens. We can address economic contraction through social expansion. The stage is set for the conscious development of service-led investment strategies that will avoid collapse, avert ecological destruction, and sidestep the social chaos that springs from rapidly collapsing economies. Service strategies bring renewed hope, hope that the massification strategies of dying industrialism and the whimsical finance wizardry of deregulated finance capital could never promise.

For now we set ourselves to the task of learning how to rein in industrialism in order to efficiently manage a contracting global economy. A contracting population and economy create the material conditions for social restructuring on a grand scale. Innovative cultural logics promoted growth coalitions in developed nations in the past. Now these old forms from industrial society, such as philanthropy and centralized stock exchanges, will find that their social utility is fading and that alternative social organization necessarily will take social precedence. When we look at the current power brokers in capitalist nations, we can identify those interests which, themselves, will contract with economy—industrial and speculative capital, centralized government, mass media advertising, and the military-industrial complex. These have been openly complicit in the degradation of the environment and the maintenance of social inequality among human societies, and each has passed by ample opportunities to alleviate the situation. What else could they do? Their very survival, the very logic of their existence, has been to withdraw social surplus and use it for private investment. Whenever the public outcry grew loud enough, some of that surplus was shifted by government and corporate foundations into the public sphere, but never a very large portion of it. Over recent decades, these growth coalitions worked to guide patriotic fervor, election results, business acumen, scientific research, and media attention toward supporting their growth politics and their self-interests. We all fell victim to the view that there was only one path forward—more and better. Less and better received very little fanfare. Furthermore, our passivity in the face of the power of vested interests made us grant them special favors such as tax breaks, tariffs, subsidies, and deregulation. Yet, the current economic crisis provides ample evidence that past leadership is bankrupt and inadequate to meet the goals they set for themselves, and we for ourselves, under Industrial Age ideology.

Of course, the necessary mantra for the twenty-first century must be less and better, with definitive redistribution of wealth, power, knowledge, and opportunity to a more diverse public. Many of the proposed solutions to world problems—renewable energy, community development, bioregional economics, collaborative resource management, citizen science, and wealth redistribution through targeted public sphere expenditures—require decentralization of the centralized processes operating under state-supported industrialism. While some decentralized processes flourish in spaces left open by the current system of corporate hegemony, such as niche markets and public service, others with less fundamental economic rationality flounder. They will require substantial investment to develop the complex social organization needed to sustain them. Once the illusion that growth solves all problems is dropped, then the emphasis of crisis management falls on other criteria such as scientific investigation, personnel training, cultural interchange, social networking, and subaltern perspectives expressed through innovative local leadership. These forces direct decision-making toward values that are less economic and more political, environmental, and culturally diverse.

Not surprisingly, as the financial capital markets of U.S. and other nations fail, a scramble is occurring among the established power brokers to right the ship, to return to the old order, to maintain their hierarchical social positions even as events dislodge their prerogatives. Being the masters of surplus extraction under the old order, large mega-corporations and the industrial states of the world have stepped forward to proclaim themselves the world's saviors. Exxon-Mobil advertises its central role in exterminating malaria by providing funding for mosquito nets throughout Africa; the Gates Foundation proclaims its importance in the resolution of the world's health crisis; Texaco and Monsanto become green to the bone in their TV and magazine ads while, behind the scenes, USAID pushes its image as the big brother of problem-solving for poor people the world over.

Yet, concurrent with this joint, global propaganda campaign of self-proclaimed greenness and social responsibility, other arms of these entities manipulate financial markets, tax structures, and resource ownership to reap record profit margins in the sale of oil, foodstuffs, energy, computer technology, potable water, and minerals. They take, and take, and take for themselves while they pollute and discard their refuse with impunity.

Furthermore, they stand together in opposition to universal health care, urban renewal, preferences for small business expansion, and public entitlement programs. This is a dangerous period for world democracy and social equity because the powers that be are attempting to transfer their traditional, industrial era dominance to control over service-led values and social reconstruction. We can't let that happen because democracy cannot survive another corporate onslaught. New leadership from different centers of knowledge and social strength is essential to global survival.

Under both Republican and Democrat American administrations—and one could add nearly every state government in the world to this list—the role of government since 1980 has been to encourage and allow corporate diversification and the expansion of global financial speculation. Under deregulation mantras, industrial corporations were released from national obligations to working class communities. From government politicians, large companies received free license to participate in speculative investments while they outsourced their production to other countries. Companies and stock and bond gamblers consolidated their global position and power, but laborers faced a lower standard of living (real income for workers in the U.S. has declined every year since 1972). In coordination with corporate irresponsibility, governments abandoned public investment associated with the New Deal social contract in favor of debt utilization as the basis for commodity exchange. Rather than demand investment integrity, governments chose to back credit institutions that promote citizen and global debt. Not surprisingly, national, consumer, and small business defaults reached historically high levels. We should be greatly concerned about these events for a number of reasons.

First, warfare artificially expands the nonproductive apparatuses of the state and economy. We expect that current financial stabilization schemes will be undermined if soldiers are returned to the workforce in large numbers at a time when Congress busily works to curtail efforts to spend the economy out of its recession. Not surprisingly, neither conservatives nor liberals are in any hurry to end the war. Meanwhile, governments across the globe support the reestablishment of credit transactions as the basis for future economic stability, but in doing so they discourage higher savings rates and improved investment strategies by companies and individuals. We must stop this insane love affair with debt financing and make real dollar investments in innovative service-oriented social organization instead.

Second, class divisions increase as a result of speculative inflation. We have seen the disastrous effects of speculative inflation in the housing, corn, and oil sectors in recent years, each leaving the working poor and middle classes in a weaker economic position. Yet, pundits and reactionaries rail against "class warfare" whenever widening socioeconomic gaps mobilize public reaction against wealth accumulation and worsening economic conditions for workers and the poor. Not surprisingly, mobilization favoring social equity is too often met with state repression and a media response all too close to cultural fascism.

We are not surprised that deteriorating economic conditions encourage resistance to the failing condition of human affairs, or that rising resistance leads to reconsolidation of wealth and power as a priority of capital. Entrenched interests marshal all facets of society to support the politics of fear—fear of class, fear of terrorism, fear of immigrants, fear of unions, fear of the truth. Fear in this period of mass media hegemony becomes fear against science and Mother Nature herself, and it operates as the means to the end, the way that passivity among citizens can be guaranteed. Be concerned that democratic and human rights are being infringed upon these days. They are.

Third, capitalist reconsolidation threatens our ability to invoke the Simultaneity Principle to deal with environmental and social injustice. Since the maintenance of class privileges during crisis periods further divides classes, opportunities for cross-class negotiations over needed change is blocked. Instead of discussions about fairer wealth redistribution and investment, economic decision-making becomes less transparent and less democratic, guaranteeing that adequate responses to crisis will not be found. Instead of emphasizing the protection of ecological diversity, big businesses and special interests lobby governments for tax credits, support endeavors to overthrow environmental legislation, and seek effective control over just what a "greener" economy means. On the other hand, the service-led economy and its innovative experiments in social organization and ecological protection is in need of a giant infusion of capital to finance global redevelopment. We believe that the civil society sector of the global economy deserves the right, and must learn to use it, to openly counteract the hegemony of corporations, the mass media, and the state when necessary.

We suggest that the first role of the state during the upcoming period should be largely to get out of the way. It is odd to find that we have something in common with both Marx and the Reagan Revolution—we want an end to big government. The role of government is to contract, to withdraw from its centralized regulatory mission, to renegotiate its social contract with its people. We suggest that citizens are capable of governing themselves and resolving their issues without state remediation, both here and abroad. The implication is quite obvious. The state must promote the localization of solution-making power. The state must become a social organization entrepreneur, not the where-withal, all-knowing, all-powerful governing body.

States already are service-based, and the bulk of their workers are, as recent Wisconsin public employee union struggles make clear, service workers. But a service-led state now must promote economic contraction with research, training programs, and social organizational facilitation on the one hand, while using its regulatory power to rein in speculation and white collar crime on the other. Ultimately, the state must coordinate, where possible, national interests with the expansion of the local-global problem-solving nexus.

But real solutions under the new service-led mode of production will be supra-national, beyond simple reformation of the nation-state by its particular citizens. Reformation of the state is complimentary to but distinct from the global strategy of funding an independent, innovative, and effective civil society to address global problems. With luck, the state's future role will be to foster a period of redevelopment and empowerment of marginalized people and end the special interest programs that now subsidize poor economic and environmental decision-making. Two areas of state expansion will come in controlling white collar crime and enforcing stringent environmental regulations. The ecopolice may be coming, but they will be much more tolerant and conscientious than the industrial-military complex has been, and they will come by employing reconstruction and redevelopment strategies worked out by collaborative communities and global professional development organizations made up of social scientists and skilled technicians. We must end this enthralling and highly imaginary dependence on "intelligence," secret police, coercive integration, and top-down militarism and envision, once and for all, bottom-up control over economic and political spheres of life.

Global social reorganization will be accomplished through the construction of new social forums for global decision-making outside of corporate and state influence. To that end, we must imagine a future in which civil society is supported by global income and left independent enough to follow its own leading civic theories and values. When we talk about the consolidation of a Global Consciousness Movement, we imagine the institutionalization of processes already begun with the World Social Forums wherein representatives of NGOs, PVOs, and CAGs from around the world meet, share information and mobilization strategies, and commit to working together on problem-solving in the future. We want to see that organizational expansion funded by a global tax on electronic commercial transactions because we are tired of watching an underfunded civil society beg industrial foundations for support. Once an independent global movement is granted guaranteed income to organize its service projects as it sees fit, and as benefits are distributed among a growing number of NGOs and development projects, we anticipate a second stage in which states align with the political agenda of the new global regime. States will be called upon to limit national financial speculation and encourage increased, not diminished, social investment. We hold no illusions. State action will not precede civil society strengthening, and it will be vociferously opposed by economic pundits and politicians alike. States, even democratic ones, are hopelessly tied to elite money streams, and politicians are aggressively attacked by media and social opposition groups if they veer from support of elite and big corporation interests. Only when civil society demonstrates the way forward, based in bioregional and local characteristics, will states themselves contribute to wide-scale funding of civil society projects.

A universal commercial transaction fee will provide the on-going funding for international redevelopment, education, ecological restoration, health care, and human and political rights advocacy in developing areas. As project after project gains footing through documented successes, demands for servicing needs instead of self-interest will grow among other disadvantaged communities. Overwhelming demand for development work will pressure more and more national governments to conform to global expectations. Our plan would be to adjust the commercial transaction fee upwards as increasing social demands are registered. Special oversight will impose higher transaction fees on speculative transactions than on general commercial transactions. A universal transaction fee discourages debt incursion by the poor and speculation by the rich, thus forcing the overall savings rate to grow. With time, however, more progressive fee nuances can be instituted to reduce fees paid by means-tested (lower income) transactors, but the first step must be universal to stop debt speculation by rich and poor alike. In any case, of course, those who participate only in cash exchange will not be subject to the fee.

In accordance with presumed needs for greater development funding, we anticipate that both mass production industrialism and commercial sales eventually will be taxed to fund an expansion of the global service industry. Since taxes are nationally specific and global taxation highly unlikely in any near future, we would expect that such revenues would support bioregional development in host countries, contributing in a more local manner to expanding service provision and niche markets. The goal of the overall process is to drive human society toward economic contraction and socioecological justice as fast as possible.

The sovereign states of the world will not be needed to implement the proposed funding scheme, as transaction fees will automatically be collected by banks and transferred to global accounts used by civil society for projects. But the endorsement of the plan by states would certainly ease its adoption and implementation. States under the service social contract will continue to play a role in national economics, particularly in establishing fair doctrines for investment, redirecting funding toward infrastructure development, supporting scientific research, and regulating environmental controls.

For its part, civil society takes responsibility to identify opportunities to employ the Simultaneity Principle, examining and studying local contexts and working with local collaborations and co-management groups to develop sustainability programs. Civil society, as an independent social actor, develops rights now accorded to corporations and individuals. We expect that the heart of the service sector of civil society's daily organization will include:

- Multidisciplinary scientific teams of social and technical scientists
- Facilitators for negotiated social collaboration
- Educators and trainers for local human capital development
- Business and accounting representatives to assist bioregional economic acumen
- Organizational professionals

These personnel will administer tasks using collaborative teams that include community, state agency, and business representatives. The co-management experiments around the world, that already involve hundreds of thousands of people in watershed and forest resource management, provide one potential avenue of expansion, as do collective local work associations such as irrigation management groups, agricultural cooperatives, and communal indigenous associations. The forms of civil society organization cannot be predetermined since they arise among local contexts and needs, but we can say that the organization to which civil society aspires must include global political leadership, regional administration, multilateral negotiated settlements, and the co-management of local resources through collaborative efforts.

Besides supporting civil society development, the state alone can dismantle the production of weapons of mass destruction, and it must develop sensitive measures capable of assisting means-tested investment with public savings. We believe these two are dialectically related—that the defense departments of the world need to be replaced with an expansion of investment in poorer neighborhoods, job creation, environmental amelioration, and social justice. We have grown tired of populist complaints about tax burdens, though certainly we share concerns about tax breaks for the wealthy and corporations that push the tax burden downwards and produce pronounced constraints on social development. But socioecological analysis is clear on the point that the average Western family consumes four to five times the world's resources than do poorer families, communities, and nations. The issue is not that the working and service class families pay too much in taxes, but that the wealthy, speculators, banks, oil companies, and others pay too little. Even the working and service classes of developed nations must learn to contract their impacts on global resources and to shift resources from private consumption to social spending. And they need to reduce their nearly overwhelming support for war and their love of military heroism. Patriotic fervor has become a dead end for human civilization.

That is hard talk for people who already are worried about their family's future and who have struggled to defend their hard-won privileges against modern economic deterioration. They have the right to feel their position is precarious. In particular, the middle class has been a near-majority in Western industrial nations for only fifty years, and already material changes in the world economy are weakening its position. Unlikely to survive the coming industrial era crisis, the middle class is consumption-oriented and politically weak. It is held together more by a combination of income-based amenities and rights than distinct, common relations to production or tangible needs. Middle class characteristics such as high voting levels, property ownership, educational or training achievement, relatively steady levels of personal savings, neighborhood amenities, and household stability established a shared middle class lifestyle, but they offer no way to organize people for social betterment. It is also the middle class nature to oppose extension of social benefits to those who lack them whenever that extension of benefits suggests economic contraction. Too many values associated with middle class existence—patriotism, the priority of lifestyle amenities, independence from social responsibility—allow the continuance of social inequalities and socioecological injustices. A greater valuation of peace and stable human relations, built around respect for cultural diversity, freedom of expression, and social science, is a preferable objective. These values stem directly from the roles the service class plays in the economic system, not just their level of income, and thus the service class provides the basis for an opportunity to mobilize for wider social reorganization.

The militarization of the global political economy is one of the greatest fetters on world redevelopment and peace. Not only does it promote the false illusion that weapons development is real development, but it siphons large sums of investment money into questionable causes. Every decade, billions of dollars of potential redevelopment funds are literally blown up, while between wars billions more pay armies to do nothing of social value while waiting for the next war to break out. Furthermore, enormous budgets must be spent in the reconstruction of nations destroyed in war. Developed nations have transferred responsibility for infrastructure construction and international development—sometimes called "nation building"—to the military itself. You should be worried about this trend, too.

The military is untrained, hierarchical, uncritical, and grossly expensive in carrying out its social operations. Soldiers are not developers; soldiers are not human rights activists; soldiers are not environmentally sensitive; soldiers are not highly specialized, niche providers in the service-led economy. The military remains a regressive throwback to the era of warring industrial competition, imperialism, and state-controlled power and might. We refuse to believe that collaboration and social negotiation are better left in the hands of military officers and professional war managers than in the hands of trained social scientists, community leaders, resource-dependent workers, and the like. People can solve their own problems without warfare and the unimpeded direction of officers who establish a career wielding weapons and managing wars.

Instead of war expenditures, we need means-tested investment— investment made with the concerted purpose of improving the opportunity structures of the poorer peoples and regions of the globe. We are not paying lip service to trickle down policies here. We demand a contracting economy that is reorganized with different purposes and power structures, where opportunity comes from re-envisioned social concerns and a change in the human heart away from evaluating everything real in terms of money security. Value comes in freedom and opportunity, in broad social and community stability, in habitat protection and biodiversity, in landscape imagery and cultural expression. These do not all carry monetary equivalents that can be translated into economic time lines and progressions.

There already are too many monuments to the veterans of foreign wars. We need monuments to the veterans of internal struggles, to the people who stand up and speak their minds and demand changed politics, changed economics, changed lifestyles. We need monuments to the critics of mass consumerism, to those that fight against ecologically degrading industrialism, to the men and women who organize against unfair labor practices, and to everyone who is disgusted with global exploitation of one people by another. We need new types of heroes that exalt people who stand up and say, "No more." When you think about it, there are a lot of "no mores" that we need, but we can start by declaring that military justice is not social justice. As we have demonstrated throughout this discussion, negotiation is the foundation of the new order. The global economy must be restructured to fund an expansion of projects under the Simultaneity Principle. We should do that by expanding service and by being critical of what is not service. We should empower people, helping them to collaborate with scientists, specialists, facilitators, and each other as they seek solutions to the problems they face every day. Not the fears they face every day. An economy of fear plays back into military options or state repression. The world needs real investment in solutions that are on the ground. Change that really counts.

Chapter 8 Response

Visions of a Global Social Contract

Steve:

Speaking as citizen scientists, my brother and I can unequivocally say that the world is now in need of a new social contract, one that empowers the potent, rising forces of the world's global economy and organizes humanity to address its looming socioecological crisis. The good news is that all the forces necessary to create this social contract exist and are in political agitation. Further advance, however, requires specific demands and a plan of action from the forces favoring a new social contract. We need a political struggle and resolution.

Although generally codified in the political terms, social contracts are broad cultural formations that are redefined every eighty years or so as a new constellation of generations—ones not even alive when the last contract was drawn up—faces another round of crisis with society's evolving problems (see Chapter 5). Sometimes, the formation of a new contract is a revolutionary process and dramatically restructures human relations; sometimes, it does not.

In the cases of the American Revolution and the Civil War, violence was necessary to boot out entrenched, reactionary class forces: the British and Tory colonial elites, in the first case, and the South's slave-owning plantation aristocracy, in the second. In contrast, the New Deal social contract, forged from 1932 to 1944, thrust no class forces out of the compact. Rather, the ruling elites of that era—the industrial and finance capitalists—made room for organized labor. This accommodation avoided the possibility of a more radical and possibly violent resolution. While programmatically addressing labor's key social security concerns, the New Deal left the form of the state intact and in the hands of capitalist elites.

Another generational cycle has passed since then, and over the last few years, Boomers have moved into position as society's elders. Not only in the U.S. but throughout the world, an urgent mood is now forming, demanding that we address the accelerating insecurity of social affairs. Political crisis encroaches and invites redesign of the outdated social contract of the welfare state.

Next Contract Will Set the Stage for Generations to Come

My brother and I find it particularly fortuitous that the generational tide now seeking a new social contract arises at the very moment that humanity also must address its global socioecological crisis.

While we realize that averting a *dark age* will require many generations of sustained effort to adopt and implement alternative lifestyles, *the particularities of what we choose to do at this critical juncture in human affairs will define the parameters of many future social contracts.* This is our chance to revolutionize society, to restructure its basic social and political systems to fit the needs of future generations. If we fail to grasp this moment in history when the social mood demands decisive change, another eighty years will likely pass before the mood again turns to serious social transformation. Yet, scientific evidence is unequivocal. Eighty more years without a progressive system to address global problems will impose immense hardship on humanity and push us four generations further down the slide into the *dark age* abyss.

We have described the array of social forces now on the rise. Chief among these is the service class whose skills and networks are vital to the emerging mode of production. Advancing the interest of this class (in serving others) is humanity's most vital necessity. As the embodiment of the service class' desire to solve human problems, civil society must be empowered and unleashed by any genuinely forward-looking social contract. As women constitute the bulk of the world's present and potential service providers and because their full-scale cooperation is required to reduce global population, women also must gain power and influence through the new arrangement. Indeed, the bulk of the world's people—whether peasants, proletarians, or servers—must gain a decisive voice in the direction of human affairs.

In contrast, the ruling elites of the Industrial Age must accept subordinate status if a long-successful, reoriented social contract is to be forged. We don't mean to belittle the significance or difficulty of "accepting subordinate status." That is a revolutionary proposition.

The giants of the Industrial Age were its huge, multinational corporations and the energy monopolies that supplied the power for mass production and international distribution. The need of these companies to capture and control markets propelled the enormous expansion of defense industries, military might, and warfare through the nineteenth and twentieth centuries. But today, the hegemonic agenda of these corporations is out of step with the world's need to collaborate in the face of its global crisis. While the forces of mass production will be with us for a long time to come, they no longer can be allowed predominate influence in the social contract. Like all real forces and interests in society, their input remains relevant and important, but only in a way that is subordinate to the rising interests of service production.

Cutting out the multinational, corporate energy industry is a revolutionary proposition, one difficult to imagine, given its deeply-rooted power in Western states such as the U.S. Fortunately, the advent of the global age makes this proposition more amenable. On the one hand, the extreme schism that industrialism, in its dying decades, has imposed on the world— that is, the production of the bulk of the world's commodities in a just a few concentrations of cheap labor and, then, the shipment of these commodities all over the world for sale—is fiscally unsustainable due to the already high and escalating cost of energy for transportation. On the other hand, further expansion of the budding economy in service—the one option with the potential to employ the world's people while we solve our problems—requires opening service to those presently underserved, that is, the vast majority of the world's people, people situated in the underdeveloped regions of the world. As a way to sustain human life on earth, energy-dependent mass production has reached its limit while the nearly limitless opportunities to expand service provision lead in an entirely new direction. Strategically, the nexus of power has shifted away from Big Oil.

This strategic shift means that the next social contract can cut the energy giants out simply by enshrining a new system of local-global problem solving, one that is both transnational (global) and subnational (local). While Big Oil, defense industries, and their warring politics may continue to dominate nation-states and their policies, the world can move on to a new, global formation to deploy service in the interest of human survival.

While industrial era energy corporations must cede authority, the financial sector—which shared in industrial era rule—necessarily will remain a key player in the post-industrial social contract. The service economy needs a banking system, and it needs productive investment. Because they fill as vital a niche in the service economy as in the industrial economy, financial corporations will get a seat at the table. Yet, it must be clearly said that their place at the table must be constrained by new, strengthened Service Age ethics that curtail speculation and hoarding while exalting investment in social and ecological problem-solving.

So, the next social contract—the one that will use the Simultaneity Principle to guide humanity into its generations-long struggle to forge and manage a shrinking global economy—will marshal and embody these key forces of the Service Age:

- The worldwide service class in all its diversity
- Women
- Civil society
- Local communities
- Bioregional small businesses
- The financial elite

But, practically, how would such a social contract operate? Politically, how will these forces rule?

Politics in the Global Era

My brother and I have already discounted the feasibility of overthrowing— by violence or other means—the industrial era states, like the U.S., that currently dominate world affairs. They will continue to do their thing, including, unfortunately, conducting wars against other states, nations, and rebellious antagonists. While people will continue to lament such destructive endeavors, until the potential of a new, Service Age problem-solving system is demonstrated, no entity will have the moral authority necessary to constrain states and put an end to war.

While overthrowing states is not a reasonable way to envision instituting a new social contract, some readers may think these states can be "reformed." We favor efforts to reform states—and, in particular, to win their support of the global initiatives we propose—but we adamantly assert that, because our problems are now global in nature, we must pursue a global solution. States can and should be part of that, but we'd be foolish to confine our battle for a global social contract to the various realms of national politics.

We hope states will back our agenda and become willing partners in its implementation, but the real focus of struggle must now be to gain social control over our world's financial elites. Roughly speaking, these are the big banks, insurance companies, and national treasuries that currently decide the rules and mechanisms of financial investment and commercial exchange. These powerful forces must be compelled to accept the new partnership of the Service Age social contract.

Charles and I racked our brains to uncover some kind of specific, practical demand that would hold the world's financial elites socially accountable while simultaneously empowering the rest of the service class, civil society, and women. Turns out, it was sitting there all along: a modified Tobin Tax—a fee on every electronic commercial transaction.

As we know, few modern transactions are cash. Nowadays, the vast majority of transactions are electronic. The banks keep records of them all. They are known, finite, and specific. If the banks collected a commercial transactions fee (CTF) on each one and made those revenues available to a new, popularly-managed, Global Problem-Solving Authority (GPSA), we could empower and institutionalize the social contract we need to launch our defense against the *dark age* of industrialism.

No single state, of course, has the authority to tax the world's commercial exchange, and the notion that all states would get together and agree to do so seems farfetched at best. But, neither has any single state the authority to block the banking system from collecting a CTF to fund global problem-solving. Moreover, acknowledging human need as well as their own interests in the epoch ahead, the world's financial elites—intelligent people, we presume—can be won to this program (particularly, given the alternative of mounting social unrest and economic disintegration). My brother and I wish to encourage the formation of a Global Consciousness Movement to pressure financial elites to embrace their duty and to create the structures through which the funds to restore the environment and abate our social polarization can be applied.

Some people may want to call these proposed structures a new form of governance, but we appreciate the horror with which people may rightly view Global Government. It can conjure images of a massive, worldwide regime—you know, the worst features of today's states magnified by a global amalgamation. We don't call for a Global Government. We prefer to call these necessary, innovative processes a Global Problem-Solving Authority, and we believe the GPSA will form the practical foundation of the global era's social contract.

Global Problem-Solving

It is one thing to define a workable mechanism—the CTF—to congregate adequate funds to address the world's problems, but it is a big next step to define the scope of the GPSA's work and its means of decision-making and operations. While it might go without saying that the shape of global problem-solving will evolve with time and practice, it is a political reality that finding the common ground on which to build a Global Consciousness Movement requires some effort to sketch a GPSA's general plan of action.

The GPSA will guide the restructuration of the global economy toward social problem-solving. For that, citizen science and popular participation are fundamental necessities.

First, while collaborating with states, the GPSA must work primarily along the *local-global nexus* of emergent human commerce and social exchange, thus involving the global grassroots—citizens and communities—in direct problem-solving and avoiding the trap of bureaucratization. Local empowerment is a more promising and practical means than state bureaucracy to getting plans implemented where they do the most good.

Second, GPSA programs must be designed to avert the calamities of industrialism by embodying the Simultaneity Principle. Of course, planning and conducting global problem-solving will be an immense and complex undertaking. The Simultaneity Principle provides strategic guidance, a means to define and assess proposed problem-solving initiatives. If they don't promise to restore the environment and reduce polarization, they are non-starters. Beyond that, they must be comprehensive and overarching, global in scope but with local applicability.

We live in one world and exist as one humanity. Yet, we are immensely diverse in our life ways and perspectives. How do we join in a common attack on our problems? How should the GPSA marshal a united response?

The key to forging such a united response is adoption of a GPSA program that reasonably purports to address humanity's *comprehensive dilemma* through diverse, intensive, sustained, globally-coordinated, local action. Though it risks oversimplification, the content of a comprehensive, global program can be boiled down to five realms.

1) *Popular Empowerment and Human Rights*

The first realm is popular empowerment and human rights. Social problems cannot be solved without community participation in programs that resolve local socioecological issues. The means to insure participation for every person in development and decision-making is a fundamental necessity. This means everyone must have a discreet identity in his or her community, be identifiable within the global system, and have opportunities to participate in problem-solving both locally and globally. To empower people, the GPSA will endow community involvement, individual liberty, healthy lifestyles, education, and food security wherever it works, promoting universal access to the global communications grid and encouraging everyone to be bi-literate, capable of reading and writing in their native language as well as the evolving language of global commerce. *We have to forge a culture of active participation in scientific problem-solving, beginning with individuals, their families, and their communities and ranging into bioregional, national, and global levels as well.*

2) *Ecological Restoration*

A second realm operates through ecological restoration. We must achieve universal food security without further destruction of wild habitat. Exchange relations related to food security and basic living conditions will be separated from global financial markets so they reflect need rather than private profit-taking. Controls of climate change and ozone depletion will expand with massive GPSA reinvestments in energy efficiency and high-tech knowledge transfers across borders. *Intergenerational sustainability must guide resource consumption, air and water quality regulation, and biodiversity protections.* Waste recycling and management, along with population control, also fit in this realm of GPSA activity.

3) *Human Capital*

A third realm for GPSA attention is human capital development and the reduction of global social inequity. *All people now alive or yet to be born must have opportunities to fully develop themselves as a participating members of global society.* The GPSA will work to:

- Guarantee sanitation and health care as universal rights
- Provide young people with ways to earn a living serving their families and communities
- Offer every responsible person access to a line of credit in the global marketplace through a community-based banking system that functions as a public utility

4) *Global Infrastructure*

In a fourth realm, GPSA programs will organize and invest in the development of a global infrastructure that prioritizes alternative renewable energy development and energy efficiency at all levels of society, not for private interests alone, but as a public good for the wellbeing and future of global society. GPSA-guided infrastructure projects will include:

- Hydraulic systems to ensure worldwide access to clean water, sanitation, and irrigation

- A global electrical grid, powered by renewable energy

- Communications access for every interested individual

- Public health and educational facilities for every community

The capitalist underinvestment crisis must be countered with profound investment in public infrastructure and expanded social service organization the world over to reverse the economic and social polarization that is the root of today's antagonism and violence.

5) Conflict Management

A final realm of social problem-solving involves grounded collaboration and conflict management among nations and ethnic groups through communicative action projects at local levels. Collaborative processes must be systemically strengthened to enhance peaceful conflict resolution and avoid state violence, armed resistance, terrorism, and vigilante justice. A heightened moral stance against the unilateral use of force by states and private groups is essential. In many regions of our world—Jerusalem, Pristina, Kashmir, and Sarajevo come to mind—centuries of conquest have created sites of diverse ethnic heritage which must be managed for common usage. Humanity has the capacity to manage these places, as well as the multitude of other conflicts that threaten peace, but a fundamental shift from force applications to social interventions is required. *In the context of a conscientious global program to attack problems through local initiative, we can turn people from violence and toward collaboration.* Forging multinational administrations of regions of diverse heritage remains essential to peace efforts. Moreover, an ethic of sharing local knowledge as well as technical insight will advance problem-solving across the globe. Scientific and technical knowledge should not be hoarded by corporations or wealthy nations for private gain; instead, it should be propagated to reduce local tensions by helping people and communities save energy and expand local services.

Each of these realms is essential to future strategies for global development and can be usefully applied to a vast array of site-specific programs. When each realm is addressed as part of an integrated, holistic, local-global endeavor, the overall quality of life on earth can only improve. In the process, we expect mitigation of social conflict and better managed investments that are focused where they are needed.

Indeed, holism is the underlying philosophy of the global age and its service-based economy. Holism accepts that people inevitably pursue their own self-interest as they best understand it, but holism alters the context of such pursuits so that self-interest is best achieved within advancing the whole. As the global age develops, people and communities, not to mention nations and the world as a whole, will discover ways to inure society against hegemonic and "me first" logic and enforce holistic outlooks throughout.

Commercial Enterprise

We have already said that the world's financial elites will be part of the Service Age social contract, but what of the world's commercial enterprises more generally? They produce our food, raw materials, energy, commodities, and services. These take a variety of forms, some as rudimentary as self-employment, most are small businesses, and others as complex as multinational corporations.

The Industrial Age was marked by the increasing concentration of production facilities in the hands of fewer and fewer, ever larger corporations, but the advent of service production has spawned a systemic reversal. Today, small business is growing by leaps and bounds. Moreover, despite inevitable efforts by corporate giants to take over or control small enterprise, the very nature of prospering by providing service to others ensures that small, flexible, fluid business operations are the wave of the future.

A GPSA that embraces the mission of solving problems through expanded service cannot fail to boost the development of local- and bioregional-based businesses of all sorts. Business will thrive in a global economy in which trillions of dollars are annually invested to reduce conflict, develop infrastructure, strengthen human capital, restore ecology, and empower people to get involved and solve problems. As service-oriented businesses embrace the opportunity to prosper by advancing the good of the whole community and whole earth, profit will be constrained, but ingenuity and hard work will find reward and satisfaction, nevertheless.

Corporations, in particular, need a fresh reconceptualization so that they can share greater accountability for the public welfare in the global era. Today, they are seen as private, self-interested operations, accountable only to their shareholders. They have no duty in their operational accounting to include the costs of either social and environmental externalities or intergenerational sustainability. They do not operate within a socially-accountable, holistic framework.

Corporate entities are one of the storehouses—along with religions, universities and civil society organizations—of humanity's centuries-long accumulations of real property, scientific knowledge, exchange networks, and fluid assets. Though currently held privately, these corporate accumulations were acquired through generations of effort, not only by owners and investors, but mainly by their employees. As products of humanity's long struggle for survival, corporations are not beyond the criticism that much of their accumulated wealth came through the exploitation of labor, communities, nations, and natural resources that they did not produce but merely co-opted for their private use.

Indeed, when thinking of investors, few of today's corporate shareholders have anything meaningful to do with the actual success of most corporations. Generally, corporations merely provide an investment repository through which people with surplus can deposit their savings to assist economic development while earning a return over time. In fact, with the ascension of finance markets over industrial ones during the past thirty years, the decoupling of corporate investors from the production of real goods and services has produced wild economic swings as investors withdraw and move their savings around in capricious, short-term fashion. In combination with new systems to curtail financial speculation, broader, transparent accountability of corporations to their workers and communities will stabilize investment and return for investors while protecting private savings from periodic ruin.

We need to learn to see corporations and other commercial enterprises as social entities that, while private, must transparently collaborate with the rest of us to serve our common future. Just as every individual must shoulder some responsibility for finding and participating in the solutions to our world's socioecological crisis, so too must every commercial enterprise—and it is the right and duty of society to hold them to it.

Much like corporations, Western nation-states must bend to the new contingencies of service production. The emergence of the global marketplace makes their outdated national regulatory systems impediments to an equitable and efficient global economy. In addition to markets in the acquisition and sale of land, raw materials, energy, agricultural products, manufactured goods, and services, global exchange embraces markets in currency, labor, news (including social oversight and evaluation), knowledge creation and dissemination, arts and culture, creative ideas, and social problem-solving. Rather than the old markets of national exchange, the global marketplace now reflects a nexus of nodes and niches operating within a whirlwind of transnational activity. The regime of national rules and regulations is inadequate for our time. Yet, in the absence of a coherent alternative, the world endures the continuing calamity of nation-state authority.

The political movement to revolutionize global problem-solving by institutionalizing the local-global nexus of civil society and local communities will gel through consistent, targeted appeals to the Service Age constituencies and through actions that demand accountability from the world's financial elites. Since 2008, our world's recession has sharply raised public consciousness of the predatory nature of finance and raised the possibility that a popular global movement can put the financial elites on the defensive, forcing them to accept a new social contract that institutionalizes civil society and the power of the world's people.

Banking as a Public Utility

Given the enormity and complexity of modern exchange, it is no wonder that the world relies so much upon its banking system, despite the disastrous consequences of economic cycles within the system's private, for-profit money management. To be effective and fair, transparency and accountability to the public's interest are essential for a modern banking system. The assumption that merely making profits equates with the public's interest is false and needs contesting.

We think the banking system of the future, including its systems for holding, securing, and investing the savings of people for successful global problem-solving, should be considered a public utility. Banking is no longer sustainable as the private playground of the big nation-states and the world's financial elite, and it cannot be allowed to operate with impunity when it acts as a system for speculation, gambling, and predatory lending. Banks must be restructured as public utilities.

When we say "public utility," we cannot explain exactly how that should be done. Financial market restructuring, like other social changes in the future, will be a socially negotiated outcome, one we cannot predetermine. Instead, here we invoke a concept that people everywhere understand: Some things are so central to survival that they are everyone's responsibility. The public utilities of New Deal era opened the door to serving public interests, operating in areas as diverse as electrical power and public education. Europe, Canada, and China made health care an asset in the public domain. Now, it's time for the banking industry to follow suit. Banking belongs to all of us, and as the current monetary crisis reveals, we all bear its burdens and should have a say in how it functions.

We distinguish banking from "financial services" and we put financial services in quotes because we question the extent of real service provided by that sector once daily banking operations are separated out. There has been something inherently uncomfortable in the way the current crisis has so far been handled under premises that emphasize the stability of speculative investment agencies over the daily lives and shrinking opportunities of most people. The banking system should hold and protect savings, not gambling receipts. Yet, we suspect something real exists in financial services because corporations, corporate stocks, and financial markets are necessary tools in managing modern economic relations. Many people may choose to save within the banking utility, but others will find the greater potential and risk of investment markets enticing. Most people with some income surplus will strike a balance. But the two systems have to be divorced from one another to guarantee protection of working people's savings.

Make no mistake about it. The objectives of transparency, accountability, and a rational investment system are revolutionary ones. They require, not the elimination of nation-state and financial elite power, but its subordination to the holistic interest of the world and its people. That is not a matter of fine words or good intentions. It is a matter of creating a new social contract in which the rising forces of the global service economy have decisive, institutionalized roles. For this, we must create and empower a Global Problem-Solving Authority, and for that, nothing less than a Global Consciousness Movement will do.

Chapter 9

Share the Burden, Change the World

Charles and Steve:

In the introduction, we noted that, for good reason, people all over the world now clamor for change. So far, however, meaningful change has not occurred. Indeed, more lives survive precariously than ever before, while the future for our children has never seemed so dim.

Given our leaders' failure to produce change, we brothers set out to explain why and how real social change occurs and why, at this historic juncture, conditions for vital, revolutionizing change are so ripe. In that, we drew on the most advanced social science available and on our personal experience as social change observers and activists.

Yet, we never intended to stop with an explanation. We said at the outset that this book is a political manifesto. Now, in its concluding chapter, we have the opportunity—and, indeed, the duty—to summarize what theory and practice say about the way forward for humanity, that is, about how we can avert the impending *dark age,* save our planet, and save ourselves.

We see it like this:

1. The industrial mode of production is played out. But as it rushes toward catastrophic collapse, it also creates the seeds of humanity's rescue. The Service Age beckons, a world in which people earn their living by serving others and, in the process, solving the great problems that industrialism has left behind.

2. The last of the Industrial Age's social contracts—the welfare state in the West and socialism in the East—are dissembling. Without safety

nets of any sort, social security has degenerated into a highly uncertain, private affair in which those with the most hoard while those with the least desperately struggle from day to day.

3. Yet, a service class has already come into being, and it struggles to assume management of the global economy. Unfortunately, however, the service class has yet to discard the greedy, hoarding, hustling, war-mongering, me-first ethics it inherited from the Industrial Age, so it is unable to assert the distinct, practical, forward-looking leadership necessary to forge a new social contract.

4. Meanwhile, of necessity people actively work in communities worldwide, addressing diverse aspects of the world's underlying socioecological crisis. Already, humanity has created civil society to guide and fortify local problem-solving with global insight and resources. But piecemeal problem-solving, if not taken to the next level, remains inadequate for the crisis at hand.

5. As the crisis deepens, multinational energy and defense corporations— through their traditional dominance in Western governments—react with unilateralism and war while the financial services industry, essentially ignoring the social crisis, demands cuts in social investment to prop up its sagging profit lines. Speculative bubbles require one publicly-financed bailout after another.

6. With the old social contract shattered, dysfunctional, out-of-date, and irretrievable, it is time to marshal the rising forces of the Service Age and forge a social contract for the global epoch.

7. The financial services industry must be held accountable to Service Age ethics. Civil society and the global grassroots need to be endowed, empowered, and unleashed to attack our world's social and environmental crisis.

8. A Global Consciousness Movement is needed to lead the fight for the collection of a worldwide commercial transaction fee (CTF) and to guide the construction of a popularly-directed Global Problem-Solving Authority (GPSA). The revenues of the CTF will allow the GPSA to pursue effective problem-solving. Its programs will meet the standard of the Simultaneity Principle—advancing ecological restoration and abating social polarization

at the same time—and deploy civil society, service-oriented businesses, and communities in sustained local-global endeavors.

A fine agenda, we brothers assert, and one grounded in the insight of socioecology, the advocacy science for a world in need of change. But we know that a fine agenda is not enough. We know that the decaying, reactionary forces of the industrial order are using fear, inertia, and the narrowly perceived self-interests of "middle class" families to keep people from embracing any cause that supports fundamental change. For the financial, energy, and defense corporations, the old order is their way of life, it benefits them greatly, and they do not want it to change.

And too many of us have become oddly twisted in our values, accepting preservation of the old order at all costs. Increasingly insensitive to the plight of the world under this regime, we fight taxes on our own wages but accept without complaint the trillions of dollars each year spent to "wage war on terrorism" and save banks "too big to fail."

What else can we do, if no alternative is suggested and available?

With *Digging Out,* we brothers make the alternative known. Herein, we've spilled the beans. We've said not only that change is necessary but how it can be achieved. We've offered a practical, yet revolutionary program, one that is comprehensive, non-violent, and constructive. A program that coldly acknowledges the *dark age* at hand while warmly welcoming the rising new forces of the Service Age that are intent upon—and capable of—averting this catastrophe.

What is left is for opinion leaders and activists to embrace and advance this alternative, transforming service ethics into a material force for social change.

We brothers, after four decades of our own advocacy and activism, stand ready to join in this decisive endeavor.

Sources

Chapter 1

Toffler, Alvin and Heidi Toffler. 1980. *The Third Wave*. New York: Bantam Books.

Harris, Marvin. 1977. *Cannibals and Kings*. New York: Vintage Books.

Chew, Sing C. 2007. *The Recurring Dark Ages*. Lanham: AltaMira Press.

Fagan, Brian M. 1990. *The Journey from Eden: The Peopling of Our World*. London: Thames and Hudson.

Sawyer, G.J., Viktor Deak, Esteban Sarmiento, and Richard Miner. 2007. *The Last Human*. New Haven: Yale University Press.

Caird, Rod, and Robert Foley. 1994. *Ape Man, the Story of Human Evolution*. New York: Macmillan.

Harris, Marvin. 1989. *Our Kind: Who We Are, Where We Came From, Where We Are Going*. New York: Harper and Row.

Fisher, Helen. 1992. *Anatomy of Love*. New York: Ballantine Books.

Wolf, Naomi. 1997. *Promiscuities, The Secret Struggle for Womanhood*. New York: Random House.

Diamond, Jared. 1989. *Guns, Germs and Steel*. New York: W.W. Norton & Company.

Engels, Frederick. 1972. *The Origin of the Family, Private Property and the State*. New York: International Publishers.

Boserup, Ester. 1965. *The Conditions of Agricultural Growth*. London: Allen and Unwin.

Chapter 1 Response

Diamond, Jared. 2005. *Collapse: How Societies Choose to Fail or Succeed*. New York: Penguin Books.

Malthus, Thomas Robert. 1798. *An Essay on the Principle of Population*. London: J. Johnson.

Watts, Alan. 1970. *Does it Matter? Essays on Man's Relation to Materiality*. New York: Pantheon Books.

Chapter 2

Marx, Karl, and Frederick Engels. 1964. *The Communist Manifesto*, in *The Communist Manifesto after 100 Years* by Paul M. Sweezy and Leo Huberman. New York: Monthly Review Press.

Dewey, John. 1970 [1945]. "The Need for a Recovery of Philosophy," in *Creative Intelligence: Essays on the pragmatic attitude*. New York: Octagon Books.

Parsons, Talcott. 1977. *Social Systems and the Evolution of Action Theory*. New York: Free Press.

Chapter 2 Response

Jensen, Derrick. 2006. *Endgame*. New York: Seven Stories Press.

Chapter 3

Marx, Karl. 1961. *Economic and Philosophic Manuscripts of 1844*. Moscow: Foreign Language Publishing House.

Tse-Tung, Mao. 1966. *Four Essays on Philosophy*. Peking: Foreign Language Press.

Lenin, V.I. 1966. *Imperialism, The Highest Stage of Capitalism.* New York: International Publishers.

Pielou, E.C. 1991. *After the Ice Age: The Return of Life to Glaciated North America.* Chicago: University of Chicago Press.

Bocking, Stephen. 2004. *Nature's Experts: Science, Politics, and the Environment.* New Brunswick: Rutgers University Press.

Chapter 3 Response

Drucker, Peter. 1992. *The Ecological Vision.* Edison: Transaction Publishers.

Chapter 4 Response

Ehrlich, Paul R., and Anne H. Ehrlich. 1972. *Population, Resources, Environment.* San Francisco: W.H. Freeman and Company.

Hawken, Paul. 2007. *Blessed Unrest: How the Largest Social Movement in History is Restoring Grace, Justice, and Beauty to the World.* London: Penguin Books.

Boucher, Douglas H. (ed.). 1999. *The Paradox of Plenty: Hunger in a Bountiful World.* Oakland: Food First Books.

Chapter 5

Reich, Wilhelm. 1980. *The Mass Psychology of Fascism.* New York: Farrar, Straus and Giroux.

Strauss, William, and Neil Howe. 1997. *The Fourth Turning.* New York: Broadway Books.

Chapter 6

Ritzer, George. 2002. "The McDonaldization of Society," in *Mapping the Social Landscape*, ed. Susan J. Ferguson. Boston: McGraw-Hill.

Freire, Paolo. 1968. *The Pedagogy of the Oppressed.* New York: The Seabury Press.

Chapter 7

Perrucci, Robert and Earl Wysong. 2003. *The New Class Society: Goodbye American Dream?* Boulder: Rowman and Littlefield Publishers, Inc.

Kane, Joe. 1995. *Savages*. New York: Vintage Press.

Chapter 8

Soros, George. 2008. *The New Paradigm for Financial Markets*. New York: Public Affairs.

Chapter 9

Gore, Al. 1992. *Earth in Balance: Ecology and the Human Spirit*. Boston: Houghton Mifflan Company.

Weber, Max. 1993. "Class, Status and Party," in *Social Theory*, ed. C. Lemert. Boulder: Westview Press.

Commoner, Barry. 1990. *Making Peace with the Planet*. New York: Pantheon Press.

Habermas, Jürgen. 1989. *The Structural Transformation of the Public Sphere: An Inquiry into a Category of Bourgeois Society*. Cambridge: The MIT Press.